"You are leaving the American Sector." Along with the nondescript wooden hut, there was only a sign announcing that one was actually about to enter East Berlin—and for anyone lacking English comprehension, the same message was repeated for Soviet, French, and German travelers.

CHECKPOINT CHARLIE

THE COLD WAR, THE BERLIN WALL, AND
THE MOST DANGEROUS PLACE ON EARTH

Iain MacGregor

SCRIBNER

New York   London   Toronto   Sydney   New Delhi

Scribner
An Imprint of Simon & Schuster, Inc.
1230 Avenue of the Americas
New York, NY 10020

First Scribner hardcover edition November 2019

SCRIBNER and design are registered trademarks of The Gale Group, Inc.,
used under license by Simon & Schuster, Inc., the publisher of this work.

For information about special discounts for bulk purchases,
please contact Simon & Schuster Special Sales at 1-866-506-1949
or business@simonandschuster.com.

The Simon & Schuster Speakers Bureau can bring authors to
your live event. For more information or to book an event,
contact the Simon & Schuster Speakers Bureau at 1-866-248-3049
or visit our website at www.simonspeakers.com.

Interior design by Kyle Kabel

Manufactured in the United States of America

1   3   5   7   9   10   8   6   4   2

Library of Congress Cataloging-in-Publication Data is available.

ISBN 978-1-9821-0003-2
ISBN 978-1-9821-0005-6 (ebook)

To the memory of
Gordon Cameron MacGregor and Ivor Robertson,
Scottish soldiers of the Cold War

Contents

"Erich Honecker, ruler of the GDR, watches the sun rise in the East. 'Why are you smiling?' he asks. The sun replies, 'Because I am heading to the West!'"

—East Berlin joke

"Walls in people's heads are sometimes more durable than walls made of concrete blocks."

—Mayor of West Berlin Willy Brandt

October 1961

It would be the first time the young British officer had traveled to West Berlin. Lieutenant Robert Corbett of the Irish Guards looked out the door of the guards' railcar that brought up the rear of the twenty-wagon military supply train. His afternoon had become stressful at the railway loading yard in Hanover as he anxiously watched final preparations being made by West German civilian crews, loading the wagons with essential supplies of fuel oil, ammunition, and foodstuffs, all heading for the British garrison now isolated in West Berlin, though only 177 kilometers (about a hundred miles) away. He knew there would be ample time wasted at the Inner German border crossing at Helmstedt, but he was confident they would still get the train through without a fuss. By October 1961 the East Germans and the Soviets had successfully split the city in two with what would become the Berlin Wall, and the Allies were anxious that the three border crossings into East Germany with access to Berlin should be maintained at all costs. "My orders were very clear," Corbett recalled. "Under no circumstances was I to permit the train's contents to be pilfered, or physically interfered with." Corbett had a small, handpicked reconnaissance platoon—eleven men and his platoon sergeant. With night drawing near, the British troops felt the first sharp bite of an autumn chill as the wind picked up. To keep warm, they quickly withdrew into the central section of the train where the guard stove was situated.

As the train pulled into Helmstedt to cross into the German Democratic Republic at Marienborn, where Checkpoint Alpha was situated,

Corbett adjusted his eyes to the arc lights illuminating the scene. This major crossing point was a set of simple, flimsy huts that marked out the actual border between East and West Germany. The cheery Allied border control officers bade the British troops farewell as they quickly processed the train through their side of the border at Helmstedt. Any feeling of optimism for the journey ended abruptly within a hundred yards, as the train came to a sudden halt, the engine letting out a powerful jet of steam when the brakes were applied. Out of the gloom came at least a dozen East German Transport Police—*Trapos*—to carry out the inspection of the train, check identification of any non-Allied personnel aboard, and search for stowaways. East German border guards—*Grenztruppen*—armed with submachine guns slung loosely across their shoulders maintained a watchful eye as they chatted and smoked cheap cigarettes. As he scanned the borders of the darkness, Corbett could hear dogs barking ferociously in the distance. *The buggers are no doubt sniffing the air for any would-be escapees*, he thought to himself. The border crossing was a shabby, dismal place lit up with the glaring arc lamps, which were placed high above guard towers crisscrossed with barbed wire. Corbett couldn't wait to leave and get going on to Berlin.

Within a few minutes three Soviet border guards joined the *Trapos* and came marching to the rear of the guards' wagon in order to take the British officers' transportation papers back to their commandant's office on the station platform. The driver and train guard from Hanover would depart when the paperwork had been cleared, as East German personnel took the train on from here. For want of anything better to do, the rest of Corbett's platoon quickly disembarked to stretch their legs, have a smoke, and see if they could start a conversation with the Russian conscripts standing near the train's platform. Corbett had been warned that the Communists would stretch out the border checks, and that once in the GDR the train would have to deal with other delays, like the terrible state of the track, which brought speeds down to forty-three miles per hour. When he returned to the guards' wagon, he discovered on his bunk a beautiful Russian leather belt, with a great big brass buckle decorated with the hammer and sickle. Next to it was a red packet of Russian cigarettes with a Soviet design. He turned suspiciously to his men.

"Oh, sir," one of them said, "we thought you'd like it and so we've been doing a bit of swapping."

"What did you swap it for?" He frowned.

"Well, a few half packs of cards!" said another guardsman with a laugh.

Soldiers never change, Corbett thought. *They're all the same*. It broke the tension that had been building inside him, and he leaned out of the guards' wagon window to watch the train crew starting to warm up the engine for travel. He studied the Russian border guards as they went about their business, and he admired their evident discipline. They had offered no opposition or signs of aggression. So long as the paperwork was in order, he had a right to travel to West Berlin, and they efficiently waved him and the train through into East German territory. The young officer had no idea that his problems were about to begin.

"Once we'd got through into East Germany," he later recalled, "our new East German driver was determined that he would cause us as much difficulty as possible. He kept on stopping and starting all the time, and as a result we were up all night long. Going through Magdeburg in the early hours of the morning, we could see the great tank workshops there, the arc welding and engineering going on at that time of day, so this was obviously a twenty-four-hour operation.

"Shortly after first light, east of Magdeburg, the train was stopped, and whenever it stopped, I had been told that I had to patrol it to prevent people perhaps who might want to get on it to get into West Berlin, or who might have been wanting to loot the goods we were transporting.

"The train was halted, and very shortly before that we had gone past a party of about twelve very heavily armed People's Police—*Volkspolizei*—on the railway line, carrying those nasty little Russian submachine guns with vented barrels. It was here that I made a mistake."

As the train's brakes hissed, Corbett took his platoon sergeant up to the front end of the column to see what the issue was—keenly aware he couldn't afford further delays. Almost immediately, the train started off with a mighty hissing of steam, and a loud shunting as the wagons crashed forward. Dancing out of the way of the boiling steam, Corbett anxiously looked back down the train. "I could see one of my guardsmen, a man called Guardsman Kelly—immensely strong but whose intellect did not necessarily match his strength. He was violently grappling with two *Volkspolizisten* who were trying to arrest him, and they were certainly coming off the worse for it as he knocked both to the ground."

Lieutenant Corbett spun around and, hand on his sidearm, sprinted back up the length of the train, bellowing above the noise of the hissing brakes. The train came to an abrupt stop. Someone had pulled the emergency brake cord, thank goodness. Reaching the guards' railcar, lungs bursting, Corbett and his sergeant jumped up onto the platform at the back and barked at the eleven-man platoon to get aboard in short order. They caught sight of a scrum of men double-timing toward them out of the darkness, the sound of boots crunching on gravel growing louder. The East Germans fanned out across the concourse, blocking the railway line. A stern-looking *Volkspolizei* officer stood a few yards away, pointing at Guardsman Kelly, shouting, "This man is trespassing on the sovereign territory of the German Democratic Republic and you will hand this man over to us, now!"

Corbett stood his ground, stared into the face of the *Vopo*, and quickly came to a decision. He wasn't going to back down. "We will not!" he barked back in German, and his sergeant gestured for his men to bring their rifles to bear. Instantly, several Soviet submachine guns were cocked and raised in the British contingent's direction. "In my mind, I could see myself as a young officer sowing the seeds of the Third World War," Corbett recalled. Both sides stood motionless for what seemed like an eternity. Perhaps sensing the futility of escalating the conflict, the men of the *Volkspolizei* slowly lowered their weapons and backed off, cursing the guardsmen as they made their way down the line, their burly shapes melting into the gloom, encouraged along their way by some choice Irish Guards sentiment.

Although relieved, Corbett cursed his luck as the train guard now informed him that pulling the emergency brake had come at a price: They would be delayed a few more precious hours in order for the mechanic to bleed the air out of the train's braking system.

*   *   *

As the dawn broke next morning, the train finally arrived in West Berlin—chugging through the great marshaling yards at Spandau to unload its precious cargo. Corbett dreaded that he was now in trouble—they were very late, and he had caused what he thought was probably close to an international incident.

"Once I had billeted my men, I then went to see the brigade commander in Berlin [Brigadier R. Whitworth] and report myself arrived. I thought I was going to be court-martialed. And I told him exactly what had happened and said, 'I'm very sorry, sir, if I've done the wrong thing here.' He said, 'No, you've done exactly right. Don't worry, Corbett, we're going to look after you.'"

The garrison then arranged for Corbett and his men to see West Berlin and specifically the first preliminary building of the wall on the horseshoe under the Brandenburg Gate. Corbett was keen to see for himself what the world had only begun to see on television or read in the newspapers. He was intrigued by the immensity of the undertaking to sever a whole city through the center with a barrier.

He walked through the Tiergarten, past the Soviet War Memorial and toward the semi-derelict husk that had once been the Reichstag—the grand German center of government. After climbing the vast flights of stairs to the main chamber—up which the Soviet 79th Rifle Corps had famously stormed in May 1945, before planting the Red Flag atop the roof—Corbett managed to find a pathway into the ruins of the Reichstag's upper floors. He marveled at the numerous bullet holes and shrapnel scars in the huge stone columns, symbols of the fierce firefight that had taken place here sixteen years before. Cyrillic graffiti decorated many of the walls—a reminder of who had won. Finally, he neared the highest section made safe by British engineers in the roof of the ruins. Corbett climbed up a long steel ladder to the observation post that had been established by the British Army. A sense of history filled his mind.

Using his binoculars, he took in the broad sweep of the entire center of the city: the stunning monument that was still the Brandenburg Gate, with the beautiful boulevard of *Unter den Linden* ("Under the Lime Trees") stretching off into the distance toward Museum Island

and the tops of grand buildings such as the Berlin Cathedral. Where the beginnings of the Wall now wormed their way around the Gate, he could see trucks, cranes, and dozens of workmen all building the next phase of the barrier, turning barbed-wire fencing into a wall of cement blocks. In the middle distance the boulevard was dotted with people making their way to and from work and the odd vehicle driving toward Friedrichstraße and the crossing point. He spotted *Volkspolizei* on sentry duty along the Wall, stopping every now and then to scan across the no-man's-land to the British Sector. "For the first time," he recalled, "I saw that abomination of a barrier, and how dramatic the impact on the city was."

Lieutenant Robert Corbett of the Irish Guards would leave Berlin in late 1961 and go on to enjoy a brilliant career in the British Army, commanding elite units of the Parachute Brigade and becoming chief of staff of the Falklands garrison and later the commander of the Guards' division. He would rise through the ranks over the next two and a half decades until—as a major general—he was offered the position of commandant of the British Sector, Berlin, in January 1989. Major General Corbett would be the twenty-first, and last, man to hold this pivotal role. Unwittingly, he would find himself at the epicenter of historic events that would bring the Berlin Wall crumbling down, the Cold War to a sudden end, and the divided Germany to reunification. All without a shot being fired.

This narrative is not a grand sweep of historical analysis. Rather, it tells many stories about the Berlin Wall, from a variety of perspectives and voices: of the city's people, of the armies that guarded or imprisoned them—depending on which side you were on—and of the many incidents that shaped the history of the Wall, all enriched by the recollections of a unique group of participants. Be they civilians, journalists, artists, soldiers, spies, politicians, or law enforcement officers, their lives have all been touched by the Wall, and they each have a story to tell—of working near, soldiering by, living close to, spying on, or escaping through Checkpoint Charlie.

PART I

EXODUS

Two East Germans, like hundreds of thousands before them, arriving at what the sign identifies as an "Emergency Reception Camp" at Marienfelde, August 1, 1961.

"If we mean that we are to hold Europe against communism, we must not budge [from Berlin]. I believe the future of democracy requires us to stay here until forced out."

—Lucius D. Clay,
US general, April 1948

East and West Germany,
1949–90

© MDL Design

CHAPTER ONE

Island in the Communist Stream

When the Second World War in Europe ended, with the official surrender of Germany on May 7, 1945, the city Hitler hailed as the beating heart of his "Thousand Year Reich" was left in ruins. RAF and US Air Force bombers had laid waste to more than 70 percent of the housing within a five-mile radius of its center. As they fought street by street to capture the Reichstag, the heart of the Nazi regime, the invading Soviet army had virtually destroyed the rest. The once proud showcase of the finest art and architecture that Prussia could offer was soon a prefabricated shelter to its two million battered and dazed survivors. The city was now divided, as the Potsdam Conference had agreed, into four sectors of occupation, one by each of the four Allied victors. Berlin simply mirrored the sectors of control that Germany herself had been divided into by France, Britain, the USA, and Russia.

Over the next five years the euphoria of victory would give way to paranoia, confrontation, and hostility between the Western powers and Josef Stalin, who schemed to ensure Germany would remain divided as part of an Eastern European buffer to protect Russia from future attacks. The East-West divide hardened into a Cold War, as the democratic governments of Hungary, Czechoslovakia, Poland, Romania, and Bulgaria toppled one by one to Communist-led coups. Under the leadership of Secretary of State George C. Marshall, the United States took on the mantle of protector and benefactor to the Free World, remaining a vigorous presence in Europe and the Pacific, as well as providing the foundation stones of NATO and the UN. Germany was at the heart of this division, and Berlin would become ground zero of the new global conflict to come.

The Allied and Soviet zones stayed in place, as both sides seemed intent on implanting their own visions of what central Europe should be. The Allies' proposal for a new currency to replace the bankrupt Reichsmark in February 1948 led the following month to a dramatic walkout by the Soviet delegation at the Allied Control Council, which had governed Germany since the end of the war. The Russians had intentionally debased and over-circulated the Reichsmark by excessive printing, deliberately reducing the German population to penury, until bartering with cigarettes and the black market underpinned their economy. The introduction by the West of the new Deutschmark in June subsequently brought the hostility of the negotiating table out into the open. On June 16, Colonel Yelizarkov, the deputy to the commander of the Soviet Sector, withdrew from the Four Power *Kommandatura* [the governing body of Berlin]. President Harry Truman would note, "This act merely formalized what had been an obvious fact for some time, namely, that the four-power control machinery had become unworkable. For the city of Berlin, however, this was an indication for a major crisis."

Situated 177 kilometers (approximately 100 miles) inside the Soviet Zone of Occupation, West Berlin was isolated and vulnerable, surrounded by at least three hundred thousand Soviet troops and three thousand tanks. Although Stalin had signed in 1946 to formally grant the Allies access of supply into Soviet territory, the agreement could easily be thwarted if he so wished. Thus, on June 24, 1948, the Soviets mounted a blockade of the city, effectively turning the supply tap off from its western road, rail, and canal routes. He expected that either the city would starve or, ideally, the Allies would capitulate and withdraw from the city itself.

Under the leadership of General Lucius D. Clay, the military governor of the American zone; the commander of the USAF, General Curtis LeMay; and William H. Turner, the head of the Anglo-American Airfleet, the United States and her allies responded with a three-hundred-day airlift, the biggest in aviation history. Flying more than two hundred thousand sorties, delivering nearly 2.4 million tons of aid, with an Allied plane landing at Tempelhof Air Base every two minutes, the airlift kept the city alive.

Seventy-eight Allied aircrew and German personnel would lose their lives in the accidental crashes that occurred. Adolf Knackstedt was then a fourteen-year-old American-born Berliner watching the propeller-driven aircraft coming in to land, and remembers that "more and more planes could be seen flying in circles in the skies around Berlin. Many times, I stood on top of the ruins located in the flight path of the landing aircraft at Tempelhof admiring how the giant C-47s and C-54s glided in between the vast ruins of building façades still standing."

Knackstedt's parents had separately emigrated to the USA in the 1920s, met and married in 1929, and settled in a tight-knit German community in the Bronx, New York. Adolf would be born in 1934, the second son. The beginning of the Second World War brought confusion and separation for the family. The FBI's concerns over a German "Fifth Column" within the country allowed them to draw up a list of all Germans thought to be a threat to national security, and the Knackstedts were placed on it. Rather than be interned in the giant government camp called Crystal City, in Texas, Knackstedt's parents made the decision to return to the Fatherland in April 1941.

Dodging British officials trying to apprehend Adolf's father, who had absconded on his own, the family successfully managed to sail to Europe aboard a merchant vessel. Finding a home just outside of Brandenburg, the Knackstedts survived the war and were living in the small town of Brandenburg an der Havel. "At the end of the war," Adolf recalled, "the Soviet Army overran our town and it became a part of the Soviet Zone of Occupation. There, under the rule of the Soviets, we lived until February 1949." As the Berlin Blockade commenced, Adolf's father applied for a job at the Airlift Administration, and for the next four months, day after day, along with hundreds of other Germans, he was assigned to unload one aircraft after another. "Sometimes I waited at the gate for him to come out and we both walked home together," Adolf said. "The strain of this incredibly arduous work could be seen on his face, but he enjoyed his job and expressed that fact at a number of occasions."

On May 11, 1949, the official announcement finally came that the blockade was going to end the following day. The Russians granted Western access to the enclave once more, and crucially, both sides still permitted free travel across the zones of control of the city. By this point, a sea change at local and international levels had occurred that would yield long-term benefits to the Allies. The Berliners now looked on their British, French, and American occupiers as true protectors, and President Truman finally confirmed that American military might and money would stay in Western Europe for as long as necessary to encourage a rebirth of democratic rule in Germany. "We Berliners didn't fall into a frenzy of celebrations, because we were too suspicious about previous agreements signed by the Soviets," Knackstedt recounted. "May 12 was declared a holiday, which meant I didn't have to go to school, so I roamed the streets around Hallesches Tor with my pals. I witnessed the first truck filled with goods arriving from West Germany after the zonal barriers were lifted at midnight, bringing in desperately needed food. . . . There was no 'run' on the stores by the Berliners, even though they had suffered hunger for a very long time. It seemed as if they realized the standard of living in Berlin was permanently going to improve and the days of going without were coming to an end.

"When the Berlin Airlift happened, my brother Hansi and I were running more and more into trouble with the local Russian authorities, at one point being thrown into a prison cellar by the KGB. But now, as registered Americans, my family was assisted by their consulate in Berlin in getting us out of East Germany, and we settled in West Berlin." Two days after Knackstedt arrived in West Berlin, he would meet "the love of his life," Vera, for the very first time, where they played together in the rubble of the city. By 1952 he was eighteen years of age and, as a registered American living in the American sector, was thus due to be drafted into their armed forces. "My papers arrived telling me I had to register with the draft board in Washington, DC. I was also informed I had to be back in the United States before reaching the age of twenty-one, otherwise I would jeopardize my American citizenship. So, in February 1954, I packed my bags and headed back to the USA." He would return to play a major part in the Berlin story.

*   *   *

By the time Knackstedt was on his way to the United States, Margit Hosseini's German family had returned to Berlin to reestablish themselves, her father having served as a diplomat in France after the war and now believing that the city was safe to live in with a young family. He also longed to reconnect with his extended family, who were living in the Soviet Sector. Following her parents around the city, six-year-old Margit was stunned by the level of destruction from the war. "I found it frightening, and I didn't dare to ask my mother, Where have all these houses gone?" The family lived close to the Marienfelde refugee center. "We had a house with a large garden, and all the gardens around us when we arrived were all filled with vegetables, because people were hungry. Well, it slowly changed within a few years, as vegetables were discarded and replaced by flowers, as the economic situation improved in the Allied sectors."

Even as a young girl, Margit realized her world wasn't safe, as she heard the everyday worries from her family and their friends about what the Russians would do after the failure of the Berlin Blockade. "I remember distinctly 1953, the uprising on the 17th of June, and I heard the adults saying 'The Russian bear is coming!' and I thought, even as a little girl, They kept these big brown bears?" The brutal suppression by the Soviets of an East German–workers' revolt had reverberated throughout the western sectors of the city. "It was that kind of insecurity that was ingrained in all West Berliners, and no matter how small the incident, they felt it intensely, as we were surrounded by the Communists."

Five years later, Eastern Europe was still the vassal of Stalin's successor, Nikita Khrushchev, who was no more enthusiastic for the Allies to have access to Berlin than Stalin had been, but could never decide how far to push his claims without the conflict escalating to nuclear war with the West. And having so many Soviet troops in East Germany was a financial strain at a time when he needed to overhaul the Russian economy. The people of East Germany saw the Soviet occupation as a fact of life, especially the young, but there were still mixed views as to what benefit the Soviets brought to this newly created country.

Günther Heinzel, born in 1948 a few months before the beginning of the Berlin Airlift, lived in Waltershausen, Thüringen, and was lucky enough that his middle-class family could afford a cook and a nanny. Despite this, they still suffered hardships due to a lack of quality goods to buy, a chronic problem in East Germany. In 1953, in the days after the uprising across the country on June 17, the five-year-old Günther witnessed for himself how the Soviets imposed their will on the country. "Where I lived, they looked to quell any dissent through intimidation, by repeatedly driving through towns and villages in long convoys of armored cars and tanks, traversing their gun turrets in all directions."

But there was a sizeable portion of the country's population who felt comfortable under Soviet occupation if their needs for everyday living were met. Equally, for those whose families were part of the state apparatus and who believed in the paradise the Socialist Unity Party claimed it was striving to create, there was at the very least tacit support. Though all knew it came at a price. For Stefan Wolle—now director of Berlin's DDR Museum, which re-creates life in East Germany—day-to-day existence as a young boy in late 1950s East Berlin was both comfortable and politically driven. "My father and mother were members of the Socialist Unity Party, and my father also worked on the Central Committee of East German first secretary Walter Ulbricht's government. As a young boy, I believed in the system emphatically." A great many East Germans at the time, especially if they lived in Berlin or Dresden, looked at their still war-damaged surroundings and wondered if history would repeat itself if conflict with America actually did happen.

For Hans-Ulrich "Uli" Jörges, who later became the co-Editor-in-Chief of *Stern* magazine, and was born in 1951 in Bad Salzungen, a small town close to the border between East and West Germany, living under the Soviets did not seem oppressive at first. "I actually remember a happy childhood spent in East Germany. In the fifties, the war by then was a memory far away and people seemed to be enjoying life again after the shock of a Soviet invasion in 1945, occupation, and then the birth of the GDR in 1949. I vividly recall lots of family events. Birthday parties,

Christmas, and of course the coming of New Year would all be excuses in our village to organize a celebration. Once a year, in summer, there was a big festival at the lake in the center of the town with fireworks at night, which for any child is exhilarating! So, for me, as a youngster, the GDR meant normal life with no worries.

"There was still a *Kommandatura* of the Soviet Army in an old villa at the lake, and frequently we'd see Russian soldiers playing basketball in the garden, and as a child it was natural, I would be inquisitive and want to talk to them. They had settled into our area, and the boundaries of conquerors versus the occupied had fallen away. For the most part they were friendly and on occasion would even give us all sweets." As with Stefan Wolle, though, Jörges was reminded of darker times, too. "Another villa, close to the Russian one, was the headquarters of the Stasi [*Staatssicherheit*] which always seemed deserted and quite ghostly. When I passed it walking hand in hand with my grandmother, she would walk across to the other side of the street, lecturing on how I should stay away from this place as the screams of people being tortured could be heard during the night from the cellars of the building. Maybe this was just a rumor, but it sure as hell gave me nightmares." The simple life, with benign Soviet occupiers, would gradually change in the early 1950s, as the frontiers of this new Cold War started to be reinforced.

In early 1952, alarmed at the continued and rapidly increasing exodus of professionals and skilled workers from East Germany, Moscow flexed its muscles. Although initially pleased that this brain drain benefited the Soviet vision of the GDR by the departure to the West of potential opposition, it became obvious that this tap couldn't be left open much longer. The population of the Federal Republic of Germany was growing substantially as it incorporated those fleeing East Germany, which had economic consequences that might cause political instability. In April, Walter Ulbricht met with Stalin and his ministers in Moscow to discuss the situation and provide solutions. Knowing of his leader's fears of "infiltration" into the East by Western agents, Stalin's foreign minister, Vyacheslav Molotov, planned for the GDR to introduce a pass system for all Westerners coming into and out of East Berlin. By June 1952, *Republikflucht* ("flight from the republic") was a crime to be punished.

Not satisfied with this tool to sift out potential saboteurs, however, Stalin went one step further and ordered the entire demarcation line between East and West Germany to be officially drawn up as a hard border—thus preventing movement in either direction. For countless East Germans, this was yet another reason to attempt to flee—before the net tightened even more. This Inner German border, however, stretching almost fourteen hundred kilometers (close to nine hundred miles) from the Baltic Sea to the border with Czechoslovakia, was still not the impregnable barrier Stalin envisaged, a fact reflected in the name the locals living along its length gave to it, *die Grenze* ("the Border").

Hans-Ulrich Jörges's father decided to flee to the West in 1956, sending word to his family to follow him a year later. "We could leave," Uli recalled later, "because they were not interested in a single woman with two children. I do remember a house search by Stasi officers, who wore long Gestapo-like leather coats, when I was three or four years old. Of course, that was a terrifying experience. In West Germany we settled in a village close to the border in Hessen, not far away from Bad Salzungen. Every Sunday for many years, in a sort of Homeric ritual, we traveled to the border and looked across the fence into our homeland of Thüringen. My parents would stand there fighting back the tears, gripping our hands tightly, and talking to one another to offer some comfort."

For Uli's family, the frontier was perhaps in the mind. "Our border was marked with a simple fence that you could walk across fields to and stand right up against, without any concern as to the border guards on the other side harming you. It was almost like a fence for retaining cattle in their field. There was no 'Death Strip' at that time, and when the border guards in the East passed by, one could even casually talk to them. I recall a small man standing beside us who shouted out to them as they marched past us silently that they come over to eat some white bread [difficult to obtain in East Germany]—and they did."

For the Soviet politicians, there were of course bigger stakes than simply winning over an occupied population to prevent their escaping through a barbed-wire fence. For Khrushchev at this time, defending the Soviet

Union with missiles was the goal, even if the Soviet high command demanded an ever-larger budget to fight the Cold War with conventional weapons. To speed up the process, in November 1958 he announced that within six months either the Allies would sign a peace treaty with both the German states and the Soviets, or he would sign one himself with East Germany, thus giving the Soviets access to the supply routes into Berlin. Although his ultimatum created panic over the Allies' resolution to uphold their access rights to West Berlin, they stood firm. Khrushchev bowed to pressure and repeatedly extended his deadline.

As Walter Ulbricht tightened his grip on all facets of the GDR and the standard of living decreased under the economic constraints of a "command economy" through the latter half of the 1950s, so the migration to the West of the best of his workforce rapidly increased, escaping via the safest route—through the open borders of Berlin. The journalist and writer Stefan Heym, a committed antifascist who had relocated back to East Berlin from the USA in 1953, could see the writing on the wall. "The people in the East looked toward the West with longing. They would have liked to have had the same comforts, the same goods, the same chances in life. All they could see was a socialist system, which demanded great sacrifice for their efforts and nothing but promises for a better future. As long as the borders were open, it was relatively easy to get to West Berlin. All you had to do was board a U-Bahn and you'd be in another world. From 'socialism' to 'capitalism' in a two-minute ride. It was crazy."

There would be, of course, disagreements, even feuds, between family and friends depending on which side of the political fence you sat on in Germany during the 1950s. Margit Hosseini was also a child of this decade, and she undertook various visits to East Berlin with her family and witnessed firsthand the disparity in everyday living standards compared with her own life. "My French-born father was working for the government and had been transferred over to the French zone in 1949. The suburb of West Berlin that was my home was a world away from the life of my cousin in East Berlin. The only way my family crossed was by S-Bahn, and even as a child one immediately sensed and saw how quickly the atmosphere changed. . . . When one traveled across Friedrichstraße, there were big posters advertising socialism and the greatness of it. As you then moved farther into East Berlin, away from the center of town, it became grim; there were less colorful posters, and everything was gray. . . .

"In many places, the city was in ruins, and whole streets and large buildings were reduced to rubble—one could clearly see the tops of the cellars peeking out of the ground, and some bright souls even placed vases of flowers where their front doors had been. The sort of grayness was not just optical, in a sense the view of the town: It was also the people. . . . I don't know whether that was because of the kind of propaganda we had in the West, of course, as well, or whether it was a real fact. I do recall in my mind's eye the endless gray shuffling of people along the street, not talking a lot to each other. Whilst in the West, we were talking and laughing or making gestures.

"When we went across to see our relations, like every family from the West, we took lots of things: fresh fruit—oranges were unobtainable in East Berlin—nice clothes, soap, and such things. . . . And in those days, you must remember there was no Wall, so you didn't have your bags searched. In the S-Bahn they quite often did sort of random checks. And I remember once, my cousin came with her mother to stay with us for the weekend, and when they arrived both were in tears because they had been carrying oranges to give to us as a present—for them it represented a precious resource. Alas, they had run into a random police check and the oranges were confiscated. They were chided by the *Vopos* for this sort of Western influence, which the authorities in the East didn't want. And seeing their distraught faces as they explained their misfortune, it seemed to me so utterly absurd to make a political issue out of oranges!"

For Wolfgang Göbel, born in East Berlin before the war, in 1939, and later assistant head of transportation in West Berlin in the 1980s, the path from East to West was complicated. He was raised in a socialist family; his father was a metalworker and a committed supporter of the East German government who tried to imbue his son with a love of Marx and Lenin. The young Wolfgang would try to follow in his father's footsteps; studying hard to redeem himself he enlisted in the fledgling *Nationale Volksarmee* (NVA) for two years' military service. His love of the city, East or West Berlin, was seen through the prism of a rough-and-tumble childhood in the late 1940s. "When I was a child, it was exciting even when we crossed the street. I grew up in East Berlin and we could literally cross the street and we were in West Berlin and in a completely different world. The luxury of Coca-Cola, oranges, chocolate, and vegetables; you could buy all of this with your East money, you only had to put up with the exchange rate."

But by the late 1950s, Wolfgang was aware enough to see the disparity of life in the GDR compared to the West, and added to that, he had fallen in love with a girl who lived in West Germany. On an impulse he bought a round-trip flight to Hanover to be with her, and a short holiday turned into a desire to remain. The resultant pressure on his father by the East German authorities brought the boy back, where he was immediately arrested by the Stasi and imprisoned on trumped-up charges of military espionage. He would reside in the notorious Stasi-run prison at Hohenschönhausen, once run by the Nazis and then by the KGB and situated in the northeast of Berlin. "I was there from August 3 until October 10, 1960. Like at most totalitarian prisons, you were reduced to only a number. I was '50-2/49-2.' I shared a cell for a while with an actual agent who was German and had worked for American military intelligence. The prison cells underneath the original redbrick prison were called 'the Submarine' because they were in the basement. Most of them had no access to daylight, and neither was there a toilet, and it was very embarrassing when you had to relieve yourself, with everyone watching and listening, and the smell was terrible." There was no communication allowed between prisoners. Even if Wolfgang had encountered them when being taken for interrogation, all were ordered to turn to their faces to the wall so as not to have any contact.

"I endured nighttime interrogations, which were very hard. You were picked up at 9 p.m., then questioned all night into the early hours of the morning. Then you were released back to your cell, where they wouldn't allow you any sleep at all. If you do that for three weeks, you don't know who, or where, you are anymore."

Wolfgang had the advantage that the charges against him were fabricated. His father used an old wartime contact now high up in the Stasi to win his son's release. And within a few months Wolfgang would seize his chance and escape across the border at Friedrichstraße. This crossing point would later be known as Checkpoint Charlie.

By 1961, the tide of refugees seeking sanctuary in the West was reaching worrying levels. More than 2.1 million people in ten years, a sixth of the entire population, simply walked out of their front doors and never returned. West Berlin teenager Margit Hosseini would watch with growing concern as they flooded into her half of the city. "Everybody knew that something was going to happen. For weeks, thousands and thousands of people had come across into West Berlin, and everybody realized that in some way or another, East Germany would have to do something, because half of their labor force, well-trained young people, had left the country. . . . We didn't know what, but that there would be [a reaction], and soon." These young East Germans were the cream of the country's workforce—professionals who worked in essential industries, generally under twenty-five years of age: the nation's future.

Nikita Khrushchev was walking a tightrope of his own making by that summer—at home, in Asia, and in Western Europe. By denouncing Josef Stalin in 1956, he had unintentionally opened a Pandora's box of liberal nationalism across the USSR's satellite states that had taken Soviet tanks to quell, first in Warsaw and then in Budapest. He had not only to support Ulbricht but also to keep in check the growing power and influence of his Communist ally from the East—China. Mao Zedong had grown cold to Khrushchev's leadership for several reasons: his denouncement of Stalin's rule in 1956; his lack of ambition to take the revolution to the capitalist West; and, crucially, his decision to visit the USA when invited by Eisenhower in September 1959, before he had even gone to China to celebrate Mao's tenth year in power. The two leaders were now barely on speaking terms, preferring to communicate through their respective foreign ministries.

Closer to home, the thought of a West Germany led by the anti-Communist Konrad Adenauer being allowed tactical nuclear weapons by their NATO allies appalled the Soviets as much as it did the East Germans. Ulbricht began pressuring the Soviet leader for a solution to the growing problem of the refugee crisis, too. On June 15, 1961, in an international press conference, he uttered the prophetic words *"Niemand hat die Absicht, eine Mauer zu errichten!"* ("No one has the intention to erect a wall!") Perhaps he was telling the truth, but in reality he had, in January of that year, already set up a secret commission on finding a way to close the borders. It was also the first time the term *"Mauer"* ("Wall") had publicly been used by anyone.

The Russians initially believed they could do business with John F. Kennedy and had been pleased when he beat the more hard-line Richard Nixon for the presidency in November 1960. Khrushchev hoped the young Bostonian would usher in a new era of détente, allowing him to lower the Soviet military budget in order to bolster the Soviets' stagnating economy. But by 1961 the new administration's refusal to address the Berlin issue in step with Khrushchev's timetable had made the relationship increasingly fraught. However, Kennedy had suffered international embarrassment with the Bay of Pigs fiasco that April, and now required a big stage himself to establish his credentials with friend and foe alike. His administration had initially tried to treat Berlin as a sideshow in order to concentrate on both his domestic agenda and the insurgency growing in Southeast Asia, but events had overtaken them.

His first meeting with Khrushchev, in Vienna at the start of June, was a disaster. For once, JFK's legendary charm had no effect on a man who had survived the murderously capricious Stalin. Intent on defending the USSR's position, and unwilling to consider concessions, the Russian repeated his demands for a peace treaty that would settle the Berlin question, even if this meant it became a neutral "Free City," with neither side permitted to station troops within its boundaries. Kennedy, on the other hand, had come to Vienna hoping to discuss the arguments preventing both sides from signing a nuclear test ban agreement. The two leaders struggled to agree on anything, and the talks stalled when the Berlin question was raised again by Khrushchev. The bellicose Russian ominously threatened the young president, "I want peace, but if you want war, that is your problem!" A chastened Kennedy confided to his younger brother, Robert, that dealing with Khrushchev was "like dealing with Dad. All give and no take!" He flew home to head the intense debate going on in Washington: What to do with the Berlin problem? The hawks in his administration, such as Secretary of State Robert McNamara, pressed for a more robust approach. A first strike against Russia was deemed insane by many. Could a tactical nuclear war be winnable? The doves, or the "Berlin Mafia," led by the likes of Llewellyn E. Thompson, ambassador to Russia, wanted to keep the dialogue open to find a workable solution.

On July 17, Britain, France, and America formally rejected Khrushchev's ultimatum to change the status of Berlin to a "Free City"—and within seven days, nearly nine thousand refugees fled west. Something had to be done, or the East German regime would simply bleed to death. Over the weekend of July 22, a secret telegram from the US State Department was sent to its embassies in London, Paris, and Moscow discussing the Berlin situation and how best to respond: "We believe Soviets [are] watching the situation even more closely than we, since they are sitting on top [of a] volcano. Continued refugee flood could . . . tip balance toward restrictive measures."

Kennedy finally came off his fence in a televised speech on July 25. He reviewed the disastrous Vienna meeting and stated that West Berlin's pivotal position in central Europe—and the Allies' free access to it—was a cause to fight for, and that he would ask Congress for $3.25 billion to finance the call-up of 250,000 reservists and the conventional weapons with which to arm them. By then more than four thousand East Germans a week—the size of a small East German town—were arriving at the Marienfelde Refugee Reception Centre. At the same time, however, other messages were being put out that potentially offered another way out of this impasse.

On July 30, J. William Fulbright, chairman of the Senate Committee on Foreign Relations, was discussing the manpower shortage on ABC News. "I don't understand why the East Germans don't close their border, because I think they have a right to close it," he said. President Kennedy said nothing to counter this opinion. Staff working in the US Mission in Berlin certainly believed that their government was giving a green light for the GDR to take preventative action. Junior officer Richard Smyser, son of an American diplomat who'd spent part of his childhood in the city, viewed Fulbright's move as "a go-ahead. The Russians have told me that Ulbricht expected no military response."

The same day that Fulbright offered a possible solution, Walter Ulbricht was secretly flying out to Moscow. What he was hearing from the West gave him hope that events were turning in his favor to force a decision on closing the Berlin border for good. July had now seen 30,415 refugees reach West Berlin, of which more than 50 percent were under twenty-five years of age. After acknowledging that the Allies were not going to sign any peace treaty, Ulbricht and Khrushchev debated the various solutions. Bowing to what he saw as inevitable to save the GDR, Khrushchev seized the initiative and finally ordered Ulbricht to build a wall. "We will give you two weeks to make the necessary economic preparations . . . then you will issue the following communiqué: 'Anyone who wishes to cross the border can do so only with the permission of certain authorities of the German Democratic Republic.' " The Soviets were confident Kennedy would not react to "housekeeping" in their own zone. Had he not referred only to "West Berlin" several times in his televised speech a few weeks earlier? On August 3, Khrushchev rubber-stamped the decision on the Berlin "solution" at the meeting of the Warsaw Pact, allowing Ulbricht to present his plans to his Communist leaders. All were taken aback, but relieved that something was finally being decided; East Germany's weakness threatened them all.

Walter Ulbricht returned to Berlin on August 4 to begin preparations. Erich Honecker was the man to implement Operation Rose in two weeks' time. He and Ulbricht spent the next twenty-four hours working on the details of the operation, building into the plan how they could successfully build the barrier without causing internal unrest, and, if there was resistance, how they would handle it. Stasi chief Erich Mielke would now establish tight security on the planning and execution of Operation Rose. All three leading players of the SED (the GDR's

Communist party) were from the Stalinist school. Each had served his time on the political front line.

Ulbricht was the brittle-voiced, intransigent fanatic who believed faithfully that the Soviet model of government was the only one for the GDR to pursue—no matter what the cost. Honecker had joined the Communists in Germany as a teenager, battled the Nazis on the Berlin streets, and subsequently been imprisoned during the war. His rise to the pinnacle of the SED politburo by 1955 was his reward for absolute loyalty to Ulbricht. Rose was his brainchild, and he had handpicked the man to handle all aspects of internal dissension.

Erich Mielke was a political mercenary. He was a onetime Communist bullyboy in the 1920s, and there was still an outstanding warrant for his arrest for the murder of two Berlin policemen in 1932. He had somehow landed in the Spanish Civil War on the side of the Republicans, where he gravitated toward the Soviets. By 1938, this affinity had earned him a place at the KGB academy in Moscow before the outbreak of war, and it was believed by many he had been parachuted into Ulbricht's regime as a tool of the Kremlin. A teetotal fitness fanatic, he had run the security apparatus of the GDR since 1957, setting up one of the world's most efficient systems—overseeing 85,000 domestic spies and 175,000 informants. Except for soccer, his work was his life.

This was Mielke's crowning moment. He had personally briefed his cadre of officers the week before: "Whoever may confront us with antagonistic actions will be arrested. Enemies must be seized outright. Enemy forces must be immediately and discreetly arrested . . . should they become active." During the 1953 uprising, many police and soldiers had gone over to the protestors. Mielke had assured Ulbricht and Honecker this would not be the case now.

Ulbricht then returned to Moscow on the Sunday to reassure Khrushchev the operation could be successfully accomplished, with law and order maintained. The decision was ratified, and serious preparations could now begin. Despite a variety of warning signals, the enormity of the operation would catch the West completely by surprise.

CHAPTER TWO

The Spook in Berlin

The role Adolf Knackstedt played in the Berlin story of 1961, when Operation Rose was about to commence, was unique. To understand this significance one must first get to know the incredible journey he had undertaken over the previous years that finally placed him in the center of this seismic event.

His was a true American experience. He was originally born in the Bronx and then became a returning *Volksdeutscher* in the Second World War, a German refugee living amid the rubble of the Third Reich under Soviet occupation, a teenager who witnessed the Berlin Airlift and welcomed the "Candy Bombers'" gifts, and, finally, a spy for US military intelligence in Berlin who helped fleeing refugees and witnessed the Wall's construction and many of its tragic consequences. In his late teens Knackstedt had decided his future lay outside of West Berlin and away from the threat of a Communist takeover of his city. Enlisting in the US Army in June 1954, he underwent basic training and then advanced training as a combat engineer with a plan to serve in Korea. Then his life took an unexpected turn.

Knackstedt's German background meant he was pulled out of his unit, which was already shipping to the Rhine, and was instead assigned to the 513th Military Intelligence Group at Camp King, Oberursel, near Frankfurt am Main—which the Americans had used as a denazification center in 1945. From there he was attached to a small intelligence element and sent back to the USA for further training at the intelligence college at Fort Holabird, Maryland, where he finally became an agent, ready for duty in Berlin. "During my first stay in Berlin, there were no walls or barriers hindering the movements between East and West Berlin. The only indication we had leaving from one sector to another were signs. . . . I believe this was one of the reasons I was sent to Berlin, because I was well versed in knowing and identifying the border lines between the American and the Soviet Sectors."

During this first assignment to Berlin, he acted as an American civil servant, fooling his old German friends, who had no clue he was connected to the American military or its intelligence services. Knackstedt's own parents had no idea their own son was now serving in the city. After a period of settling in and knowing he was now securely established in Berlin, he decided to call on them. "At Christmas 1954, my buddy and I came to our house, and I can still hear my mother talking in the kitchen. I knocked on the door and it went quiet; then I heard my mother say, 'That's Adolf!' She read the knock, typical Mom." News of Knackstedt's being back in Berlin got around his old circle of friends, and he reunited with Vera Bobzein—now an eighteen-year-old who fortuitously dropped by with a girlfriend once she heard the rumor Adolf had returned. "We had grown up as kids," Knackstedt recalled, "like a brother and sister, but now as adults we were more than happy to see one anther again." Within a short time he was coming over for meals at Vera's parents' house, until it felt like a second home. For a "spook" operating in one of the most dangerous places of the Cold War, it was a welcome relief from the daily routine of covering one's footsteps and watching every word spoken.

For the next two and a half years Knackstedt lived a clandestine military life. Even though they were attached to an American military counterintelligence unit in Berlin, he and his men operated offline from the military, living in safe houses in German neighborhoods. He was a key figure, working with the West German police in processing the thousands of refugees pouring into West Berlin. "East German and Eastern Bloc refugees were screened by respective German and Allied interviewers at refugee reception centers, and those found to be of interest were questioned further at offices such as the one I was working at. Within my unit, I was responsible for convincing these refugees of interest to be our guests at Camp King, then manifesting them on

American military flights and escorting planeloads of refugees on a weekly basis to Frankfurt am Main air base. During this period, I flew on over seventy missions, returning via the American military train from Frankfurt am Main to get back to Berlin." He and Vera married and left Berlin in 1957, and she received American citizenship. When Adolf received new orders from his base at Fort Bragg, North Carolina, to travel back to Berlin in 1960, Vera would return with him.

In July 1960, Adolf was sent with his family—he and Vera now had two children—right back to West Berlin, where he assumed the same job he'd had during his first assignment in 1954. "While I was gone from Berlin, my office at Sundgauer Straße had been relocated to a villa located at Sven-Hedin-Straße, corner of Karl-Hofer-Straße, near Mexikoplatz. Space-wise, this facility gave us more flexibility in handling the increase of refugee traffic." The flow of refugees in 1960 had reached such a level that the West Berlin Senate simply couldn't handle the influx and made getting them out of Berlin a priority. Approximately 160,000 German refugees had to be taken care of, and this still didn't account for the Poles, Czechs, Hungarians, and Romanians who also were coming to the city. Since the West Berlin authorities had reached their capabilities, they requested assistance from their Allied occupiers.

"It was unbelievable how many refugees we flew out before August 1961," recounted Knackstedt. Every available aircraft of the USAAF arriving at Tempelhof Air Base (C-47s, C-54s, and C-97s) was filled up with refugees to be taken out of the city on their way to West Germany. "I was overwhelmed with the preparation of the flight manifests. . . . It didn't take long and we started to fill Pan American commercial flights to accomplish our mission." His unit still screened individuals for valuable information, and those of interest were sent to Camp King.

The work was relentless. "My wife never knew if I was coming home at the end of the day, or where I was. She never was able to prepare a timely meal. Frequently, I suddenly had to travel to locations within the Federal Republic without any prior notifications or preparation. We constantly had to work without any major breaks, which kept us moving twenty-four, thirty-six, and forty-eight hours at a time." Communications also hindered effective movement around the city. "We only had landline telephones to communicate. You had your home phone and then there were telephone booths located throughout the city. . . . We were responsible for keeping our duty officer informed when we left our home for more than two hours. He had to know how to reach us at any given time. And secondly, if we were on standby status—and that happened at least twice weekly—we had to be reached within twenty minutes."

By early August, Knackstedt's team were hearing worrying stories from refugees about large amounts of construction materiel being stockpiled at various locations near or along the sector and zonal borders. "Much of this materiel consisted of barbed wire and concrete poles. No one seemed to know the purpose of this. All this information was immediately reported through intelligence channels to our command, but it seemed as if no one was concerned or cared about these strange happenings along the 'Iron Curtain,'" he recalled.

On Saturday morning, August 12, he received a call from his duty officer instructing him to go to the office at Sven-Hedin-Straße and be on standby in case they needed him as an interrogator. An East German border guard lieutenant had been picked up at the West Berlin Anhalter Bahnhof S-Bahn station. The intoxicated officer had been observed by West Berlin police sitting on an underground platform bench, sound asleep. They themselves had no authority to arrest him, since the entire S-Bahn property, East and West, was part of the East Berlin sector. Allied authorities were the only ones who had the power to apprehend someone at these rail stations. "American military police had brought him straight to our office in accordance with 'Standing Operating Procedures' [SOP]. The officer sobered up quickly as soon as he realized where he was. He then became belligerent and wanted to be released back to the East German authorities immediately."

The *Grenztruppen*'s uniform identified him as a political officer, and his protestations as he came to his senses cut little ice with Knackstedt, who warned him that either he cooperated or he wasn't going anywhere. "That's when he nearly went to pieces. He was shaking all over and continued demanding to be released." During the subsequent interrogation by two of his team, Knackstedt became further convinced the *Vopo* knew much more than what he was letting on. "My commander, Captain Stewart, contacted IO-USCOB [Intelligence Office/United States Commander Berlin], asking for permission for enhanced interrogation, but the request was categorically rejected. Shortly thereafter, we received a call from the same office when Stewart was explicitly ordered and told how and when to take the East German to the Brandenburg Gate and have him turned over to our Soviet counterparts." Dumbstruck, frustrated, and angry, the American agents realized they had to comply, but instinctively knew they were letting the possible answer to this military puzzle slip through their hands. Within hours, they would be proved right, and Adolf's work would take on even greater importance and danger.

Knackstedt's adventures during the days and nights before the city was separated were not isolated incidents. The Allied command was gathering individual pieces of information hinting at what the East Germans were going to do, but they failed to see the big picture. Days before Adolf picked up the *Vopo* officer, on August 6, a functionary in the ruling Socialist Unity Party, turned by the CIA, provided the 513th Military Intelligence Group (Berlin) with the actual date when construction of the Wall would commence. Three days later, the Berlin Watch Committee's regular meeting saw the chief of the USMLM—the United States Military Liaison Mission—predict the construction of a Wall. As Knackstedt had reported up his chain of command, the Allies also knew of the huge amount of building materials being stockpiled in the city's hinterland—enough barbed wire to cover the 156-kilometer (100-mile) boundary of West Berlin. An intercept of SED communications on August 9 also informed the West that there were plans to begin blocking all foot traffic between East and West Berlin. The Watch Committee—an interagency intelligence group—surmised that this intercept "might be the first step in a plan to close the border." No one of seniority within the Allied command acted on it.

CHAPTER THREE

In a Mousetrap Now

"If I were you, I wouldn't leave Berlin this weekend. . . ." This cryptic advice from Horst Sendermann (an East German mid-level bureaucrat) rang in British journalist Adam Kellett-Long's ears as he slipped out of another tedious press conference at the *Volkskammer*, the "People's Chamber" in East Berlin. Another voice echoed in his brain, that of his informant from a government factory fighting group (*Betriebskampfgruppen*—armed government militia), who confided he wouldn't be able to see Kellett-Long in the next few days. Shouldering a full pack, rations, and a rifle, the informant had announced that he would be "going on exercise." Kellet-Long wondered what exactly that meant.

Back at his apartment, the journalist sat down at his typewriter and started to file his story. "Berlin is . . . holding its breath. . . ." That same afternoon, in the House of Ministries, the leader of the GDR, First Secretary Walter Ulbricht, informed his party security secretary, Erich Honecker, that Moscow had finally given the go-ahead for a long-awaited action. As the tactician and coordinator of the coming operation, he handed over the necessary authorization with a flourish and wished Honecker good luck. East Berlin was its usual subdued self despite the warmth of the evening of Saturday, August 12, 1961. The crowds were out in the west of the city, though, enjoying the bright lights that attracted so many of the British, American, and French occupying troops. The streets and parks buzzed; the bars were full. But the fate of the city was sealed.

At 1:11 a.m. on Sunday, August 13, the East German radio service interrupted their *Night-time Melodies* show for a special announcement:

"The government of the States of the Warsaw Pact appeal to the parliament and government of the GDR and suggest that they ensure that the subversion against the countries of the Socialist Bloc is effectively barred and a reliable guard is set up around the whole area of Berlin." The message was clear, but many in the West didn't hear it, as tuning into East German radio programs for enjoyment was unheard of.

The East Germans' first act was to extinguish the floodlights on the city's iconic Brandenburg Gate. The Berliners living nearest to the demarcation lines would then be stirred from their beds by the rising sound of trucks, boots, drilling, and hammering. More citizens were stranded coming home from a late night out as the S-Bahn was gradually closed and passengers were turned out of trains with nowhere to go. A barbed-wire barrier began to zigzag through key points on Bernauer Straße, Friedrichstraße, and Potsdamer Platz, and around the Brandenburg Gate. It even bisected cemeteries. General Peter Williams, who would serve with British Military Intelligence in Berlin during the 1970s, remembered, "At my [prep] school, for days afterwards, we discussed with both fear and incredulity, how could one possibly take a city the size of Berlin, which had existed since the days of Charlemagne, and simply park a wall through it?"

American military police watched the *Volkspolizei* at work from their positions at what would become Checkpoint Charlie, where they were on duty monitoring activity in East Berlin. The East German workers used giant jackhammers to break up the road and install the first fence posts. As American military police from the 287th studied their progress through binoculars, they discussed what would happen if anyone attempted this back home, in New York for instance. "A wall straight down Park Avenue?" questioned one MP. "It was a bizarre sight." The US military's security hut was located at the exact spot where the world's two dominant political and economic systems now collided. When they reported back into their command center, the order came back: "Do nothing!" *Feldwebel* Eduard Schram watched, too, from the other side of the divide. His role within the East German border police was ostensibly to protect the workers, and to deal with any immediate trouble from the Americans.

Along with five fellow border guards and a plainclothes Soviet officer, Schram scanned Friedrichstraße for sudden movement as his comrade Hagen Koch and his team went to work with their brushes and buckets of paint, marking the six-inch-wide white line that would come to define the frontier between East and West. It was a defining moment for Schram. "Hagen Koch was doing his duty. The task he performed that day was significant. There he was, at the fault line between our two systems—capitalist and socialist—with his pot of white paint, drawing the demarcation line. Like he was astride tectonic plates. I envied his role.

"In my opinion, the barrier was a means to keep the peace and quiet in Berlin. Since I was stationed at the border, I saw the problems of West Berlin with my own eyes. It wasn't just the incredible flow of people fleeing our country to the capitalists, but also the disparity of what the West offered to workers from my half of the city. Many of them were over there earning the more valuable currency, which bought three times more in our own East Berlin shops and markets. It would ultimately destabilize the country. Everyone could see that. I personally did not want a war. We wanted peaceful coexistence."

Schram and his fellow noncommissioned officers had known nothing of the buildup to this adventure. He was merely a cog in the machine. At noon the previous day, all units had been placed on high alert by the Ministry of Security. He was ordered to report to his unit outside the city by lunchtime. From there they were transported by truck into the Mitte district, where operations at the heart of the city would commence. Here they waited quietly in a large barrack-style office block. At 6 p.m. they were addressed by their commanding officer. "It was then that we realized something very big was about to happen. The older men in my company talked about the uprising of 1953. We all hoped it wouldn't be the same."

They tried to calm their nerves with cigarettes or by discussing what they had planned for that Sunday. Anything to distract them from what they perceived as imminent conflict. The authorities had put every East Berlin hospital on readiness for casualties. Dozens of civilians had died in the 1953 uprising. At 8 p.m., city commanders were given permission to open their sealed orders. Senior officers within the Berlin police and People's Army, at the commander in chief's Strausberg HQ, had already been briefed on the key details. The communiqué was then passed down the chain of command. Battalion commanders were briefed via telephone at 9 p.m. The plan had been printed in great secrecy the week before, at a Stasi-owned press near Potsdam. Drafted and approved by Ulbricht and Honecker, it stated, "In order to prevent the enemy activities of the vengeful and militaristic powers of West Germany and West Berlin, controls will be introduced on the borders of the German Democratic Republic, including the border of the Western sector of Greater Berlin."

Schram's unit was called for their briefing just before midnight. "Our commander stood before us and made a grand show of ripping open his orders. There was a long silence while he reviewed it and then he smiled and waved the letter. 'We seal the border tonight.' Without much fanfare we were ordered out into the night to board the trucks that would take us to our area." Despite his elation, Schram and his platoon still harbored some doubts. "We openly expressed our main fear amid the noise of the diesel engines so the officers couldn't hear us: 'What will the Americans do?'" By midnight, Honecker sat back at his base on Keibelstraße and basked in the revolutionary role he believed this to be. He gave the order over the phone: "You know the assignment. March!"

The 8th Motorized Artillery Division, comprising just fewer than four thousand men, one hundred battle tanks, and one hundred and twenty armored personnel carriers, drove straight to the center of East Berlin and took up their position at Friedrichsfelde. A further four thousand soldiers of the 1st Motorized Division, in one hundred and forty tanks and two hundred personnel carriers, departed their base in Potsdam to ring-fence the West Berlin boundary. Honecker gave detailed instructions to both sets of troops. They were to position themselves over one thousand meters (three thousand feet) behind their sector borders. Their role was to prevent by force any mass breakout attempts once news of the activity spread. There would be no repeat of 1953. Police units would then work with the construction gangs to build the barrier undisturbed. The twenty-five thousand men of the fighting factory units would be in reserve, should East Berliners resist.

The day-to-day traffic across the border would be the responsibility of the East Berlin People's Police, supported by almost ten thousand men of the 1st Brigade of Readiness (Riot) Police. Their role would be to quickly seal off all designated routes for civilians from East to West Berlin. Just after midnight, with the Brandenburg Gate and nearby Potsdamer Platz now shrouded in darkness and transport crippled, Operation Rose kicked off in earnest.

Eduard Schram's detachment had now reached their destination at Friedrichstraße. From this jumping-off point, all official traffic between the Cold War adversaries was documented, reported, and spied upon. "Dismounting from our vehicles, we were marched down *Unter den Linden*, and gradually units tailed off from the column as our commanders gave out orders for which group would be stationed where, each unit comprising two squads of six men. We then began double-timing down to the border, with the troops in their trucks already appearing. One of my comrades guessed our destination was the official Allied crossing point into our city, Checkpoint Charlie. We could make out the bright lights of the US Army post in the distance. Despite all the bodies of men and equipment on the move, it felt eerily quiet."

Speed was of the essence. Honecker had to catch the city unawares in order to prevent serious opposition. The majority of East Berliners were asleep in bed, and that's where Honecker wished them to stay. Schram's unit took up positions that West Berlin security monitors would observe later, in daylight. The troops and police turned their backs on the actual border in order to protect the construction workers—from their own people. This was a sealing-in operation, not an invasion.

As Schram's unit was closing down Friedrichstraße, Adam Kellett-Long was motoring toward the Brandenburg Gate. At 1:11 a.m. an anonymous voice had called out of the blue to advise him not to go to bed that night, and then the radio announcement had been aired. His office teletype suddenly spluttered into life as it received the GDR's official declaration of border closure. He pored over the type as it spilled out, taking in key phrases: the Warsaw Pact member states offering a "safeguard" to the territory of West Berlin and reassuring NATO Allies that West Berlin's routes of access would not be touched. The scoop was on. He needed to witness this.

His route took him through a deserted city until he came to the roadblock at the Brandenburg Gate, the giant columns of the monument eerily clothed in darkness as the sounds of men digging echoed in the distance. The East German guards waved him away abruptly: *"Die Grenze ist geschlossen!"* ("The border is closed!"). He turned down *Unter den Linden*, where he was again halted as more trucks roared past him. He raced back to his office and filed the first report to the world. "The East-West border was closed early today. . . ." It was 2:30 a.m.

Half an hour earlier, the military police commander at Friedrichstraße had been growing increasingly anxious. He watched several soldiers position themselves some eight hundred yards back from the Soviet control zone. He could tell by the way they carried themselves that they were not *Vopos*—nor were they Soviets, as their uniforms looked new. What concerned the Americans most was that whoever these troops were, they were armed with a heavy machine gun, which was now set up on the corner where Zimmerstraße intersected with Friedrichstraße. These soldiers were clearly following a plan, but the Americans couldn't ascertain whether the Communists meant it for them, or something else going on inside the East German border.

Operation Rose was an immense logistical undertaking. Eighty-one crossing points were reduced to thirteen. The twelve underground (U-Bahn) and overground (S-Bahn) city lines were to be severed at the sector border. The main target for clearance and shutting down travel by the authorities was Friedrichstraße, a key railway hub where the majority of refugees and international travelers aimed to cross from East to West Berlin. Finally, and essentially, all 193 streets across the border sector were to be closed off. No detail had been left to chance by Honecker's team. Honecker even drove himself around Berlin all through the night, dropping in on various local units to judge their progress and encouraging his commanders on the ground.

Just outside the city boundary, the surprise was again total. At 00:30 hours the two-man Royal Military Police border patrol—"Bravo 3"—

to see what was going on. Smyser then alerted his fellow junior officer, Frank Trinka, and together they made their way out into the night in an open-topped Mercedes. They arrived at Potsdamer Platz, where trucks were parked, men scampered everywhere in the half-light, and coils of barbed wire and other obstacles were already in place. Smyser got out and walked toward the crossing and was stopped by a young, spotty-faced *Volkspolizist* who asked for his identification. The American pointed to his car's registration plates, denoting he had diplomatic status and thus free access. The young policeman shined his flashlight toward the car, studied the plates, frowned, and told Smyser and Trinka to wait where they were while he marched across to his officer by a nearby truck. Smyser couldn't hear what they were saying above the noise of hammers and drills, but the boy returned and gestured for them to drive through, pulling the coils of barbed wire back to allow the car access.

The pair then spent the next few hours driving in and around the East-West checkpoints, noticing various *Volkspolizisten* and factory fighting units everywhere. They witnessed hundreds of civilians, including women and children, many in tears, attempting to gain access to the U-Bahn stations and being forcibly ushered back. As they continued, they encountered side streets jammed with armored cars and trucks carrying more barbed wire and concrete posts. Two things both diplomats noted: the East Germans hadn't brought artillery or heavy weapons with them, and where were the Russians?

Meanwhile, Assistant Provost Richards watched the ever-increasing buildup of forces at the Brandenburg Gate area and the increase of Berlin civilians angrily demanding to know what was going on. He decided he had to find out more. "I reported back to the GOC and political adviser that I was about to enter the Soviet Sector and would radio brief observation reports if possible." He would be taking a risk, for a foreigner using a radio in East Berlin was strictly forbidden, but Richards was keen to establish Soviet intentions in order to give London a clear picture of what was happening. The threat of conflict breaking out was uppermost in his mind. After much debate with East German guards at the crossing point, where he argued the case of free access as part of the Four Power Agreement, Richards and his driver started touring the Soviet sector.

commanded by Corporal Michael Blakey was halfway through its normal twenty-mile route where the old Berlin-Hamburg Route 5 departed from the outer perimeter of the British Sector. They had already encountered the homeward bound patrol, who had nothing unusual to report, and then been greeted at the checkpoints manned by West Berlin police and customs officers. All seemed as it should be. Blakey and his partner, Lance Corporal Bray, drove up to the British Sector border with the French. They reported that all was well and began the circular route that would take them back to headquarters.

Halfway back to base, their night turned upside down. The scene they witnessed had transformed from quiet countryside, hamlets, and train crossings to one of frenetic activity on the East German side. Coming toward the border crossing at Staaken station, they immediately noticed that the lights had been mysteriously turned off up ahead. The headlights of their vehicle now started picking out figures stumbling along in the darkness. They were Berliners who said they had been passengers on the train up ahead, which had been stopped and ordered emptied by heavily armed East German and Soviet soldiers. More worryingly for the MPs, the terrified passengers ominously told of seeing many Soviet tanks hidden by the bridge. Corporal Blakey immediately decided he needed to directly contact his commanding officer, Assistant Provost Marshal Richards. Roused from his slumber and briefed by Blakey, Richards immediately got dressed, jumped into his staff car, and roared off toward Staaken, covering the eight miles in a matter of minutes.

While they waited for his arrival, the two British NCOs quietly moved toward the Staaken bridge, using the border demarcation line as their guide to find their way in the darkness. They could now hear a great deal of noise: engines turning over and many voices of men—fighting men. Suddenly, the whole site was illuminated as the station's lights were switched back on again, revealing hundreds of heavily armed Soviet troops and East German border police, three of whom were standing just yards away from the British military policemen, submachine guns pointed in their direction. As Blakey stared in shock at the sight before him, wondering what the hell he was going to do now with a Russian submachine gun pointing at his chest, he was reassured by the familiar sound of a British bullet going into the chamber from the magazine of his partner's automatic pistol. Both sets of men stared at one another in the glow of the station. What now? Their fears eased as they heard the distant rumbling of their CO's staff car speeding toward them, its headlights picking out yet more Soviet troops massing on the border line. Was this an invasion? It didn't seem like one to Richards.

As Richards was briefed on the spot by a very relieved Blakey, more armored vehicles and trucks hove into the arc of light from the station—disgorging not only more East German guards but also civilian workers who busied themselves unloading barbed wire, concrete posts, slabs, and building equipment. The British watched in shocked fascination as the barriers started to be assembled. Richards got on the radio-telephone to speak with the General Officer Commanding (GOC), Major General Delacombe, who agreed the RMPs should now move back toward the Brandenburg Gate and monitor what was going on there. It was 2 a.m. and the British car quickly covered the fifteen miles into the heart of the city.

During the night, the West Berlin police force would mobilize thirteen thousand of its officers under the orders of Chief Superintendent Hermann Beck. Reports of military trucks and armed *Vopos* at the Brandenburg Gate and elsewhere, plus the S-Bahn being closed, had caused panic at his headquarters at Tempelhofer Damm. Initially struggling to comprehend the unfolding situation, Beck deliberated with his subordinates whether he should open the envelope from the safe containing instructions that would set in motion the official "Defense of Berlin" and thus send panic throughout the governments of the West. But on hearing that the East German movements were all within their own territory, he decided to scale down the alarm. "At first, we thought they were going to overrun us and march into West Berlin, but they remained precisely within one centimeter inside the sector boundary."

Adolf Knackstedt's team was also alerted. Very early in the morning, the telephone rang in his bedroom. "With a very stern voice, the duty officer told me to report to the office immediately. First, I thought it was a routine monthly training exercise drill. I got dressed and leisurely drove

down Argentinische Allee in the direction of Mexikoplatz, enjoying the beautiful balmy summer morning with its blue sky and beautiful sunrise. I played around with the radio looking for the Armed Forces radio station [AFN], but it seemed to be off the air. Just then, a buddy of mine, Henry Otten, came roaring up from behind, honking his horn and giving me hand signals to speed it up. That was the moment I started to realize this was not a routine exercise drill. I sped up and followed Henry's car until we got to the office. We opened the main door to the villa and stopped in our tracks. Our offices were converted to a military command-and-control center and everyone in there seemed to know what they had to do. Captain Stewart then briefed us on the situation at the border during the night."

Knackstedt was informed that the East German military was in the process of systematically sealing off the east sector to West Berlin and the zonal border to the Federal Republic of Germany. Streetcars, subways, regular rail, and public traffic had all been halted in both directions; telephone lines had been severed; and sector border foot crossings had been sealed off. All German and foreign national border crossers were being aggressively denied transit by East German border guards and auxiliary forces. Only Allied occupation forces (American, British, and French) weren't hindered in their movements within all sectors of Berlin. Captain Stewart issued orders to the team. Knackstedt remembered, "I was tasked to scout the American Sector border and furnish situation reports to my unit. For the next few days I was to roam along the border and intermingle with the Germans, acting as if I was one of them."

Like the Americans on the ground in Berlin, the British and their French counterparts tried to react with calm, find out what was going on, and relay what information they could gather back to their respective governments in Paris and London. The British minister to Berlin, Geoffrey McDermott, phoned his ambassador to West Germany in Bonn, knowing full well the Stasi would be eavesdropping, and then dispatched cables to the Foreign Office. Meanwhile, at the US Berlin Mission, junior officer Richard Smyser received orders from his duty officer, George Muller, to drive out into the city and "take a look around" commanded by Corporal Michael Blakey was halfway through its normal twenty-mile route where the old Berlin-Hamburg Route 5 departed from the outer perimeter of the British Sector. They had already encountered the homeward bound patrol, who had nothing unusual to report, and then been greeted at the checkpoints manned by West Berlin police and customs officers. All seemed as it should be. Blakey and his partner, Lance Corporal Bray, drove up to the British Sector border with the French. They reported that all was well and began the circular route that would take them back to headquarters.

Halfway back to base, their night turned upside down. The scene they witnessed had transformed from quiet countryside, hamlets, and train crossings to one of frenetic activity on the East German side. Coming toward the border crossing at Staaken station, they immediately noticed that the lights had been mysteriously turned off up ahead. The headlights of their vehicle now started picking out figures stumbling along in the darkness. They were Berliners who said they had been passengers on the train up ahead, which had been stopped and ordered emptied by heavily armed East German and Soviet soldiers. More worryingly for the MPs, the terrified passengers ominously told of seeing many Soviet tanks hidden by the bridge. Corporal Blakey immediately decided he needed to directly contact his commanding officer, Assistant Provost Marshal Richards. Roused from his slumber and briefed by Blakey, Richards immediately got dressed, jumped into his staff car, and roared off toward Staaken, covering the eight miles in a matter of minutes.

While they waited for his arrival, the two British NCOs quietly moved toward the Staaken bridge, using the border demarcation line as their guide to find their way in the darkness. They could now hear a great deal of noise: engines turning over and many voices of men—fighting men. Suddenly, the whole site was illuminated as the station's lights were switched back on again, revealing hundreds of heavily armed Soviet troops and East German border police, three of whom were standing just yards away from the British military policemen, submachine guns pointed in their direction. As Blakey stared in shock at the sight before him, wondering what the hell he was going to do now with a Russian submachine gun pointing at his chest, he was reassured by the familiar sound of a British bullet going into the chamber from the magazine of his partner's automatic pistol. Both sets of men stared at one another in the glow of the station. What now? Their fears eased as they heard the distant rumbling of their CO's staff car speeding toward them, its headlights picking out yet more Soviet troops massing on the border line. Was this an invasion? It didn't seem like one to Richards.

As Richards was briefed on the spot by a very relieved Blakey, more armored vehicles and trucks hove into the arc of light from the station—disgorging not only more East German guards but also civilian workers who busied themselves unloading barbed wire, concrete posts, slabs, and building equipment. The British watched in shocked fascination as the barriers started to be assembled. Richards got on the radio-telephone to speak with the General Officer Commanding (GOC), Major General Delacombe, who agreed the RMPs should now move back toward the Brandenburg Gate and monitor what was going on there. It was 2 a.m. and the British car quickly covered the fifteen miles into the heart of the city.

During the night, the West Berlin police force would mobilize thirteen thousand of its officers under the orders of Chief Superintendent Hermann Beck. Reports of military trucks and armed *Vopos* at the Brandenburg Gate and elsewhere, plus the S-Bahn being closed, had caused panic at his headquarters at Tempelhofer Damm. Initially struggling to comprehend the unfolding situation, Beck deliberated with his subordinates whether he should open the envelope from the safe containing instructions that would set in motion the official "Defense of Berlin" and thus send panic throughout the governments of the West. But on hearing that the East German movements were all within their own territory, he decided to scale down the alarm. "At first, we thought they were going to overrun us and march into West Berlin, but they remained precisely within one centimeter inside the sector boundary."

Adolf Knackstedt's team was also alerted. Very early in the morning, the telephone rang in his bedroom. "With a very stern voice, the duty officer told me to report to the office immediately. First, I thought it was a routine monthly training exercise drill. I got dressed and leisurely drove down Argentinische Allee in the direction of Mexikoplatz, enjoying the beautiful balmy summer morning with its blue sky and beautiful sunrise. I played around with the radio looking for the Armed Forces radio station [AFN], but it seemed to be off the air. Just then, a buddy of mine, Henry Otten, came roaring up from behind, honking his horn and giving me hand signals to speed it up. That was the moment I started to realize this was not a routine exercise drill. I sped up and followed Henry's car until we got to the office. We opened the main door to the villa and stopped in our tracks. Our offices were converted to a military command-and-control center and everyone in there seemed to know what they had to do. Captain Stewart then briefed us on the situation at the border during the night."

Knackstedt was informed that the East German military was in the process of systematically sealing off the east sector to West Berlin and the zonal border to the Federal Republic of Germany. Streetcars, subways, regular rail, and public traffic had all been halted in both directions; telephone lines had been severed; and sector border foot crossings had been sealed off. All German and foreign national border crossers were being aggressively denied transit by East German border guards and auxiliary forces. Only Allied occupation forces (American, British, and French) weren't hindered in their movements within all sectors of Berlin. Captain Stewart issued orders to the team. Knackstedt remembered, "I was tasked to scout the American Sector border and furnish situation reports to my unit. For the next few days I was to roam along the border and intermingle with the Germans, acting as if I was one of them."

Like the Americans on the ground in Berlin, the British and their French counterparts tried to react with calm, find out what was going on, and relay what information they could gather back to their respective governments in Paris and London. The British minister to Berlin, Geoffrey McDermott, phoned his ambassador to West Germany in Bonn, knowing full well the Stasi would be eavesdropping, and then dispatched cables to the Foreign Office. Meanwhile, at the US Berlin Mission, junior officer Richard Smyser received orders from his duty officer, George Muller, to drive out into the city and "take a look around" to see what was going on. Smyser then alerted his fellow junior officer, Frank Trinka, and together they made their way out into the night in an open-topped Mercedes. They arrived at Potsdamer Platz, where trucks were parked, men scampered everywhere in the half-light, and coils of barbed wire and other obstacles were already in place. Smyser got out and walked toward the crossing and was stopped by a young, spotty-faced *Volkspolizist* who asked for his identification. The American pointed to his car's registration plates, denoting he had diplomatic status and thus free access. The young policeman shined his flashlight toward the car, studied the plates, frowned, and told Smyser and Trinka to wait where they were while he marched across to his officer by a nearby truck. Smyser couldn't hear what they were saying above the noise of hammers and drills, but the boy returned and gestured for them to drive through, pulling the coils of barbed wire back to allow the car access.

The pair then spent the next few hours driving in and around the East-West checkpoints, noticing various *Volkspolizisten* and factory fighting units everywhere. They witnessed hundreds of civilians, including women and children, many in tears, attempting to gain access to the U-Bahn stations and being forcibly ushered back. As they continued, they encountered side streets jammed with armored cars and trucks carrying more barbed wire and concrete posts. Two things both diplomats noted: the East Germans hadn't brought artillery or heavy weapons with them, and where were the Russians?

Meanwhile, Assistant Provost Richards watched the ever-increasing buildup of forces at the Brandenburg Gate area and the increase of Berlin civilians angrily demanding to know what was going on. He decided he had to find out more. "I reported back to the GOC and political adviser that I was about to enter the Soviet Sector and would radio brief observation reports if possible." He would be taking a risk, for a foreigner using a radio in East Berlin was strictly forbidden, but Richards was keen to establish Soviet intentions in order to give London a clear picture of what was happening. The threat of conflict breaking out was uppermost in his mind. After much debate with East German guards at the crossing point, where he argued the case of free access as part of the Four Power Agreement, Richards and his driver started touring the Soviet sector.

"It was a scene of intense activity and great tension," he recalled, "with uniformed men everywhere, all heavily armed; everybody seemed to be involved—the *Nationale Volksarmee* [NVA], the *Volkspolizei*, the *Grenzpolizei*, the *Betriebskampfgruppen* [factory fighting units]; even the *Freie Deutsche Jugend* [Free German Youth, FDJ] movement were seen to be in command of armored vehicles." Richards noticed that the vast majority of East Berliners seemed as scared and confused as the civilians in the British Sector. But though he was still unsure of what the actual intention of all this activity meant for West Berlin, he came to the conclusion it didn't mean an invasion. "Had they wished to do so, they could have rolled straight in at two o'clock that morning." He radioed his conclusions directly to GOC and made one further tour of the area opposite the British Sector.

As he dodged *Volkspolizisten* chasing him through the side streets back toward the British border, Richards found himself coming out onto the main boulevard to the Brandenburg Gate and driving past the East German Ministry of the Interior. He eyed the mass of people milling around hoping to get to the Eastern border to see for themselves what was going on. He spotted members of the FDJ handing out pamphlets to passersby and ordered his driver out to get one and bring it to him. Studying the official proclamation of an "anti-fascist barrier being constructed to protect the GDR," he realized that in his hand he had all the information necessary to comprehend what they were witnessing, and what it meant for the city, the people, and the Allies. The East Germans were constructing a fifty-mile barrier to encircle the East Berliners themselves, cutting the dozens of crossing points to a handful. What they had witnessed at Staaken station was the actual encirclement sealing the whole city in, more than 130 miles of barbed wire. This evaluation from Richards was immediately dispatched to the Foreign Office in London, and Prime Minister Harold Macmillan was reading it hours before the American commander on the ground in West Berlin had even woken up.

The previous evening the staff at the Marienfelde Reception Centre had drawn up their total number of refugees from East Berlin for the day: 2,662, the second-highest figure the center had ever recorded.

How many would there be the following day? The mayor of West Berlin, Willy Brandt, had relaxed with a drink on the train shuttling him around West Germany on the campaign trail as he sought to be elected chancellor in that year's national elections. He reviewed the day's activities. The election campaign, which had Brandt facing his wily, veteran opponent, Konrad Adenauer, had for both men been a tough one of mudslinging and vicious arguments. But it was almost at an end, and Brandt mulled over the speech he was about to give in Kiel, on the Baltic coast. Nikita Khrushchev had been preparing for that October's party conference at his luxurious resort in Sochi, along the shores of the Black Sea. President Kennedy was himself spending a few days at the family's summer residence in Hyannis Port, Massachusetts. He had planned to take his wife, Jackie, and their children sailing on Nantucket Sound that weekend.

But for the 3.3 million Berliners waking up on that sunny Sunday morning, things would never be the same. *"Die Grenze ist geschlossen"*— "The border is closed"—was about to become an all too familiar mantra. The first stage of sealing off the border had been achieved without a shot being fired, or the East German population protesting to stop it. Surprise had been on Honecker's side. He turned to his weary staff and smiled. "Now we can go home."

Robert Lochner, head of RIAS, the US-sponsored radio station in West Berlin, heard the very first announcements. "I was alerted at one minute past midnight that the East Berlin radio, which of course RIAS monitored, had started to announce not the Wall as such, but that communications within the city were cut." He instructed his staff to overhaul the weekend's programming of rock 'n' roll music in order to provide regular news updates. RIAS owned the largest transmitter in Europe, so it would be to their station that the world would tune for news. "We carried [bulletins] every fifteen minutes." As the next day dawned, "we could hear jackhammers tearing up the street and see the construction crew members, each with a soldier with a gun behind him to prevent him from defecting, laying these rolls of barbed wire. On the other side, one yard away, hundreds, if not thousands, of frustrated West Berliners were shouting their outrage and demanding that the wire be removed."

Lochner needed to be out in the streets of East Berlin to see what the security forces were up to. His State Department plates would afford him access to the border crossings, and, he hoped, some protection, too. "It was a very warm summer night, but because we didn't know what reception we would get, I hid a tape recorder under a coat. There was nothing heroic about it; at worst they would have turned us back . . . [but] when they saw the license plate, they waved us through." RIAS had the lead on every European radio station that night. Lochner's recording of the human misery he encountered alerted the listening world to the city's desperate plight.

Walter Ulbricht, meanwhile, was content that the initial phase had been successful. Troops had shown little appetite to interfere with Rose in the American, French, and British Sectors. Just as significantly, their respective governments had also said little. Like many of his comrades in the 287th Military Police, one young officer at the time was left incredulous at his superiors' inaction. "We had passed down the line in our reports of what was happening on the ground days before they sprang into action. Now we had *Vopos*, border police, and their regular army out in front of us, building a barrier. We did nothing in response. Our command didn't even issue a protest letter. I was continually upbraided by the locals for staying inside my hut. It was demoralizing—for both them and us."

That didn't mean the garrison was not ready to repel and protect the city. Private First Class Wayne Daniels from California spoke for many ordinary Allied soldiers when he said he believed the whole command was ready for action. "We had obviously had practice alerts. But on the morning of the 13th of August, the alarm went off in our barracks for an alert, and we were moaning: 'Oh, we just had one of those the other day. We don't want to do this!' And then our company commander burst in. 'This is no drill. I repeat: no drill. Fall out, and full combat gear!' We were looking at each other in shock. The term was always: 'If the balloon goes up, start fighting.' And we did feel ready to go. The morale of the American soldiers that I worked with in the 287th Military Police company, the patriotism, and the feelings about the war—we were ready to protect the German people, period."

The only physical resistance East Germany faced was from West Berliners, who fiercely demonstrated their anger and disgust. John Wilkes, an enlisted airman from Santa Cruz, California, was a Russian linguist stationed at the radio monitoring center at Tempelhof Air Base. He had pulled the graveyard shift the previous evening and heard the news going around his base past midnight of something big happening in the city center. The border was being sealed and crowds were gathering at the Brandenburg Gate. The urge for a thrill and the invincibility of youth drove his desire to witness history. He whistled up a Mercedes cab and reached the Brandenburg Gate at 8:30 a.m. "When I climbed out of my cab, wearing civilian clothes, the first thing I noticed was a crowd of four hundred young Germans, mostly men. They were loosely gathered in the wide boulevard about fifty yards away. They were chanting 'Schweine! Schweine!' Many of the young boys were shaking their fists at the Volkspolizisten who faced them in a line that extended across the boulevard between the crowd of demonstrators and the looming gate. The impassive soldiers were standing about four feet apart, each holding a rifle or a submachine gun diagonally across his chest."

They were following the three key orders of Rose: not to allow travel from east to west, not to react to Western provocation, and not to open fire with live ammunition. Each sector followed the same set of instructions. The barbed-wire fence was to be set back from the actual border where possible. The soldiers and Vopos were to act as a shield as well as monitor the workers constructing the barrier. Wilkes summarized: "Behind the line of soldiers and along the face of the Brandenburg Gate, crews of workers were unrolling wide, six-foot-high rolls of barbed wire. Following them were men with long steel rods, which they thrust under the strands of wire and twisted the strands into a tangle. As the crews rolling out the wire moved on, fresh teams with more rolls of wire took their place, followed by more men with iron bars who twisted the tangle higher."

By 9:30 a.m. the crowd of young Germans had grown, surrounding Wilkes, as ever more people poured into the street from the west side of the gate. With the new arrivals, the chanting began to get very ugly. Fearing a bloodbath, the Western authorities felt compelled to act. Several dark-blue trucks appeared, carrying West Berlin riot police. "On each flatbed they sat back-to-back, ramrod straight on a bench that ran fore and aft; about twenty men to a truck. They were bigger than the average German man and looked especially formidable with their tall-crested helmets and knee-high jackboots." Before their vehicles stopped, the riot police had pulled out their long batons and launched into the crowd, hitting anyone within reach, mostly across the shoulders.

Wilkes ran for his life. "When one of the riot police started heading in my direction, I decided I had seen enough. But I hadn't yet looked through the Brandenburg Gate to find out if a similar crowd was gathering on the East Berlin side. I had to know whether young East Berliners were as willing to protest as the West Berliners were. After all, the East Berliners had much more at stake than the West Berliners around me. I positioned myself to see between two of the grand columns. When the barbed-wire crews moved aside, I saw nothing but a wide, empty street leading into the center of the city. The usually crowded boulevard in the heart of Berlin was utterly deserted." Honecker's detailed planning had again borne fruit. The factory fighting units and regular army had done their job—clearing the streets while the barrier was erected.

Back in their homes, many Berliners began to panic about loved ones they might never see again. The teenaged Margit Hosseini sprang out of bed as her father came bursting into her room. "'They have closed the border,' he said, and I didn't understand what he meant. It was incomprehensible. Then my mother came in, weeping hysterically, followed by my older sister. We were all thinking the same thing: How do we get my Gabi [my younger sister] back?"

The Hosseinis tried to use their telephone but discovered what the rest of the city was realizing—that all communications had now been severed. The family sped to their local police station for help. "After many frantic inquiries, they told my parents to go to Friedrichstraße to try to sort this out. So, we all took the S-Bahn, and it was complete chaos." The U-Bahn had been severely hampered by the East Germans stopping scheduled trains after midnight. Now the system was functioning again, but only sporadically. "People were crying and shouting—some were frightened, some were very angry." The station was overrun with Berliners from both sides of the city—westerners wishing to find loved ones in the east, and easterners who had been out for the evening or at work simply wanting to get back home. Clinging to her parents' hands as they pushed and shoved their way through the throng, Hosseini was overcome with emotion. "I just remember being bereft, thinking, *We'll never see my sister, she's lost.*"

To her shock and delight they were given extraordinary news by the official her father was berating. "We discovered that my aunt had had the same idea as we had, and was actually in Friedrichstraße, too, thankfully with my sister, trying to get her home." Overwhelmed with relief, the family still had to attempt to work their way safely through the confused and frantic crowds back to the U-Bahn again. After an hour of queuing and clinging to her young sister's arm, Hosseini and her family boarded a train. "You had to go through two stations that were still in East Berlin, where the train didn't stop, and we could see many soldiers with such fierce faces and armed with machine guns. It was very frightening, really frightening. And only when we arrived in Papestraße, which was officially in West Berlin, did we feel safe."

By midday Robert Lochner was driving through the border for a third time, recording what he saw and trying to get a clear picture of what was going on. He finally managed to get through the police barriers and parked outside Friedrichstraße station. "The vast waiting hall was full of thousands of people milling around with desperate faces, cardboard boxes, some with suitcases." He moved past the entrance and made his way up the staircase to the U-Bahn platform. "The black-shirted *Trapos*, the transport police, who vaguely reminded me of the SS, stood locked elbow to elbow blocking access to the staircase going up." Lochner spotted an old woman walking up to them and standing on her tiptoes to ask when the next train for West Berlin was due. "I will never forget the sneering tone in which the guy answered: 'That is all over now, Granny. You are all sitting in a mousetrap now.'"

A shocked and livid Mayor Brandt, now back in the city, had been forced to use water cannons to break up demonstrations such as the one Wilkes saw at the Brandenburg Gate. But Phase One of Rose had achieved its objective. Provoking military conflict had been specifically forbidden by Khrushchev. Commander-in-Chief Ivan Konev's tank divisions encircled the city as a display of force, nothing more. This was Ulbricht's show, and he would dictate the pace of Phase Two. On August 15, along the border of the US and Soviet Sectors on Zimmer-straße, workers began to erect a more permanent structure. The men of the 287th, at what would soon be officially titled Checkpoint Charlie, looked on in both fascination and disgust. "As they replaced the barbed wire with concrete cinder blocks, even then it was apparent to me how disaffected these so-called 'loyal socialists' were to their leadership," Lieutenant Vern Pike recalled.

The Wall now stood six feet high, topped with barbed wire, and it zigzagged for twenty-seven miles through the city. Another seventy miles of it would separate West Berlin from the Soviet zone in the north, west, and south. Pike gave the ordinary soldier's verdict on what that August had brought not only to the city, but to the Allies themselves: "The Wall was the ultimate and seemingly permanent reminder that our own top spooks had gone up against the KGB on the front lines of the Cold War—and lost."

PART II

A TALE OF TWO CITIES

The building of the Wall split families apart and, in the first months leading up to Christmas 1961, tragic scenes such as this one would be commonplace along it's length as Berliners would do their best to see relatives and friends.

"At all costs we must avoid any kind of dispute in the Allied ranks at this time as to what we would and what we would not fight for."

—Telegram from British ambassador
in Bonn to Foreign Office, London,
August 14, 1961

CHAPTER FOUR

Split Asunder

The shock of events on that first night quickly turned to anger and heartache as families and friends attempted to connect across the city during the many days that followed. A palpable sense of dread, shock, and abandonment lay over Berlin like a shroud—and not just across the western half, either. East Berlin citizens were recorded by the regime openly criticizing the operation to build an "anti-fascist protective wall," and harsh reprisals were meted out in order to prevent a repeat of the 1953 uprising. It still didn't prevent people from sabotaging industrial output, making jokes about the regime, and committing acts of civil disobedience, such as the slogan painted on the factory works wall at OWL, Treptow, in the southeastern part of the city: "Berlin is now a prison!"

Many East Germans were also caught out by being abroad on August 13, having taken advantage of the summer holidays to apply for permission to visit relatives in West Germany. With the sudden announcement of the Wall being constructed, they wondered if normal travel rules and regulations still applied on their return journey, or would a harsher fate await them? Günther Heinzel's parents faced that scenario. Because his family had a lot of relatives dotted about West Germany, they applied each summer for twenty-eight-day passes, and since their names weren't on any Stasi list, they got them. Previous trips had been fraught: "It was still a terrible experience to get oneself through the border controls, though. One was treated as if you were the enemy, with the guards armed with machine guns, standing there with dogs, shouting out orders for everybody off the train. They would be herded into a kind of barracks, where all suitcases had to be opened and thoroughly searched. Then, if all was in order, back on the train we'd all go, and within a few minutes a sense of relief would ebb its way through the carriages as one by one they crossed into the west. There, the Allied checkpoint had an unarmed guard, no dogs, and a polite request to hold up one's identification and travel pass. There you knew that you had arrived in a civilized country. The return journey a month later was horrible, with the guards at the GDR control even worse than before. It was a dreadful, humiliating atmosphere, and it was clear how bad our situation was and what a run-down state the country was in. It took days until you got used to everything again." And that was before the Wall.

On August 13, the family was again holidaying in West Germany. A boy from Heinzel's neighborhood ran up to him announcing the news of the Wall. "As someone from the GDR, I immediately thought of the 17th of June, 1953, and thought there might be another uprising occurring, and so I ran to my parents to tell them the news, but they were skeptical and said, 'Let's wait and see,' and turned the radio on to listen for the next news bulletin. When it was officially announced, we were all horrified. What do we do now? Our main fear was that the Communists are walling us all in and will not grant any future inter-zone passes.

"My parents had always been of the opinion that they wanted to finish their working lives in our hometown [Walthershausen], and once I had reached adulthood and completed my education, then they assumed I would want to leave, and we might well relocate to the West. Over the course of a few days that month, however, they argued back and forth as to what was the best thing to do: go home to the GDR, or stay in West Germany? I was thirteen; my attitude was to remain in the West even though I worried about the rumor that if one was under eighteen years old, then the West could repatriate you back to the East. We decided, unfortunately for me, to return home." However, the welcome home they received wasn't a warm or happy one. "Our friends looked at us as if we were crazy, and I was bullied at school as a suspected traitor. We had to write essays thanking our Soviet 'protectors' for allowing us to come home."

Back in Berlin, Adolf Knackstedt was now undercover and busy systematically scouring the city for news of what the East Germans were really up to. "Never have I seen so many tears flowing down cheeks of grown-up men and women as I saw during those days," he emotionally recalled. "Mothers, fathers, grandparents, kids, as well as curiosity seekers stood at the border, looking over the newly constructed fences and barriers in the hope of seeing or being able to communicate with a relative or friend.

"Somewhere along the southeastern border of the city, in the borough of Neukölln, I ran across a young couple who just gotten married, with the bride still in her white wedding gown, standing at the west side of the fence and waving to her mother and father, who were standing approximately one hundred meters [three hundred feet] on the other side of the barriers, guarded by indifferent and aggressive-looking border guards, keeping everyone away from the crudely and hastily created barriers. The parents were hindered from attending the wedding of their daughter. They even were blocked in their attempt to get closer to the fence and to their children. A little boy standing on our side asked an East German border guard to give the flowers he was holding up to his *Oma* [grandmother], who was standing approximately fifty meters [150 feet] from the fence in the east. An East German officer took the flowers and, instead of passing them to the old grandmother who was leaning against a building and sobbing, he dropped them on the ground and stomped on them. Everyone was shocked, especially that little boy, who started to cry profusely. His father took him into his arms, but the boy couldn't be consoled. Both walked off after their grandmother was forced to leave the blocked-off border area."

It wasn't just Berlin wedding parties that found themselves in the middle of an international crisis. Funeral processions were also hindered from crossing the border, even if the cemeteries were in the opposite part of the town. During the early stages of the Wall's construction, people were still escaping in smaller numbers by jumping over barbed wire fences or swimming across the Spree and Havel Rivers or the Landwehr Canal. By August 24, the first fatality had occurred—a young tailor from the East Berlin borough of Weißensee, Günther Litfin, was shot and killed by East German transportation police while trying to swim to the west via a small canal that branched off the River Spree. A *Grenzgänger* ("cross-border commuter"), he had recently found an apartment in West Berlin, in Charlottenburg. Anxious to get back there once he knew he was really trapped by the new barrier, Litfin took the fateful decision to escape via navigating the small canal networks linked to the city's arterial rivers. Although the Stasi would attempt to manage the news of his death, his family and friends soon spread the word that he had been killed trying to flee to the west.

Slowly but surely, the tension evolved into anger among the West Berlin spectators. They couldn't understand what was happening, and they demanded action to stop this insane division of their city. They couldn't understand the ineptness and non-presence of the Western garrison troops, especially that of the Americans. It seemed as if the West agreed with what was happening.

Adolf Knackstedt remembered that for the first few days the East German border guards were carrying their weapons but had no ammunition. They were under strict orders from the Soviets to retreat immediately should they be confronted by Allied military forces, but such a confrontation initially didn't come. "Every hour or so, I called my office and gave them a status report. I watched West Berlin being sealed off more and more from the eastern part of the city. Most Berliners and the US military now expected a second blockade of their city, but this luckily didn't materialize. All traffic from West Berlin was channeled through East Germany to West Germany on specifically identified roads, rail lines, and barges along certain specific rivers. Air service was unhindered but had to traverse through three designated air corridors. The Germans living in East Berlin and in the eastern zone, however, were denied travel outside of the Soviet-controlled East German territory. Since we didn't know what the East was up to, all the military had to stay at their assigned stations during the first night [Sunday to Monday]. Most of the time we played pinochle."

But alarms were continually raised due to the nature of the sporadic news coming in from all parts of the city. Shortly after midnight, Knackstedt's team received word that border crossers were reporting concentrations of East German NVA (National People's Army) units close to the West Berlin border. Others reported that an attack on West Berlin was imminent. Rumors were quickly being taken as fact. "Suddenly, live ammunition appeared on top of our desks. We remained at the ready all night and expected the worst. All preparatory plans I made to warn Vera for the eventuality that she and the kids had to get out of the city before trouble started were in vain (we had a code word set up, a word that was seldom used). There were no flights out of Berlin during the night—we all were trapped." Finally, dawn broke and Knackstedt's unit witnessed a surreal and very beautiful sunrise, which relieved the tension that had been building during the night. The men turned in their weapons and ammunition and returned to their assigned duties.

In East Berlin, the young Stefan Wolle was seeing firsthand how many of his fellow citizens of the GDR were coping with the stress of their newly built jail. "I was a ten-year-old Pioneer—belonging to the *Freie Deutsche Jugend* [Free German Youth, FDJ]—and we were on a weekend camp in the hinterland of Berlin. The FDJ were promoting physical activity, but always with an undercurrent of socialist indoctrination. At lunchtime on August 13th, we were listening over the camp loudspeaker to a program from *Rundfunk der DDR*, the regime's official station, when the news of the situation in Berlin and the building of an 'anti-fascist barrier' was announced."

That Sunday happened to be a visiting day for parents, but Wolle's mother and father were on holiday in Czechoslovakia, leaving the shocked young Pioneer alone with no one to confide in or ask what all the fuss was about. "As we mingled together with the grown-ups, I could hear from their discussions with their sons what was really going on and watched as many of them broke down in tears. It did make me question what I was being taught by my parents, who were so deeply committed to the Party. Later on that year, my father took me to the Wall. We would travel by U-Bahn up to the sector crossing points, and he would walk with me right up to the last white line denoting the start of the American Sector. Pointing across to the Americans, he would then explain to me, 'On that side are the imperialists. We do not step into this territory, it is forbidden.' At ten years of age I believed in my father and trusted him."

Families, loved ones, and colleagues were all searching across the newly barricaded border for some news of what was going on on the other side and what it meant for their future. East German police would aggressively stop people taking photographs of the barrier being constructed, shouting, "This is Free Berlin, taking photographs is not allowed here!" Worshippers were prevented from walking the fifty yards across a road in order to attend their church service; schoolchildren waved to their classmates across coils of barbed wire; mothers wept as they held up their children to wave hello to their grandparents across the divide; and gleeful factory fighters hurried up in their work of erecting concrete posts and nailing down yet more wire into the ground. At any point, an armored vehicle or a crane could have swept these obstacles aside, but nothing was done. Allied soldiers were ordered to watch, report what was going on, and not to interfere. On the eastern side, official vans toured the border broadcasting propaganda and news of the closure over loudspeakers.

By the end of the first day of the Berlin Wall's life, the Ministry of the Interior reported to Ulbricht that there had been only fifteen attempted escapes from the GDR into West Berlin, of which seven of the escapees had been captured and detained. Meanwhile, at the Marienfelde Refugee Centre, new arrivals totaled just forty-one people—a true picture of how West Berlin was sealed off from the outside world. By Tuesday, August 15, the East Germans had stepped up their plans to intensify the border closure by banning West German cars from entering East Berlin.

The Allies were still holding their positions and not encroaching on the erected barriers, and were seemingly under no urgency to respond aggressively to the East Germans systematically preventing any of their citizens finding routes out to the west. It was a matter of time before the next phase would begin, but ordinary East Berlin citizens did not know how permanent or formidable the barrier would become.

Somehow, people still found ways to contact loved ones in the west of the city, such as by standing on the roofs of cars near the border crossings to send signals. Rosemarie Platz, a young physiotherapist working at the Charité Hospital on the eastern side of Checkpoint Charlie, was one of them. She had enjoyed a blossoming romance since the winter of 1960 with a medical student from West Berlin whom she had met in the Friedrichstraße U-Bahn station. They had spent a beautiful and romantic summer together excitedly discussing their hopes for the future, where they would live and work if she left the GDR. All was well until the barrier's sudden creation tore them apart.

Rosemarie noticed over the next few days that various hospital colleagues had not returned to work, and when a friend asked her why she remained, she began to plan her escape. Her first attempt to cross the fortifications at the Sophien parish cemetery turned out to be too dangerous. Border guards were patrolling the grounds. A man had just been arrested. Then someone suggested she try to cross through the back courtyards of Bernauer Straße. Her heart was hammering as she approached the first guard, who was controlling access to Brunnenstraße. She was turned away both there and on the other side of the street. But the third guard, a policeman, on the next cross street, was convinced by her tale of an appointment with a bedridden patient, backed up by her Charité ID. Armed guards stood in the doorways of the buildings along Schönholzer Straße. Only one doorway was unmanned. She headed through it into a courtyard, only to discover that the archways leading to Bernauer Straße had already been bricked up. When she knocked at the doors on the ground floor, there was no response, so she went up to the first floor, where one door was locked. She knocked urgently and heard footsteps coming, and was greeted as the door opened by a woman. Rosemarie made her case, this time pretending to be pregnant and pleading that she needed to be with her husband in the west. The woman said she would need to wait for her own husband to return from work. He in turn advised Rosemarie to wait until it became dark. Then, with a picklock, they led her into an empty first-floor apartment and quickly disappeared again. She found her way through the dark apartment and sped to the window leading to Bernauer Straße. "I opened the window, threw out my bag and umbrella, climbed onto the windowsill, and simply jumped onto the street. On the other side of the street I was in safety, and I cried my eyes out as the tension of the ordeal finally broke over me."

Tense, exhilarated, and uninjured, she made her way to her boyfriend's apartment. "We were supposed to meet at Checkpoint Charlie, but I didn't know where that was from where I had escaped into West Berlin." When she arrived, her boyfriend took her to a hotel, because as a lodger he was not allowed to have female guests overnight.

Margit Hosseini's family, now safely back together after the drama of August 13, feared, like all West Berliners, for the future of their city. In a wider political sense, many questioned the Allies' response, and more significantly what America would now do. Just as worrying was what the Russians intended. Would they attempt a second blockade of the city? Or would they simply invade and capture it? As Hosseini remembered, "There was very little reaction coming first from America, as President Kennedy was on holiday. Equally, neither Britain nor France seemed to want to raise a hand to protect us. None of the Allied powers in the city had issued any objection or strengthened their garrisons. Our Mayor Brandt was livid, and there was real anger in the city. We all felt 'They are dropping us like a hot cake. They don't care about us; they don't do anything.' All this sort of talk about West Berlin, the sort of 'frontline island,' was just a propaganda thing, and now they are turning away because it's too risky to do something. This explains the totally different reaction later in 1963 when President Kennedy eventually did visit West Berlin. People were jubilant. But these first few days of that August of '61, we thought, 'That's it; we will now be part of the GDR.'"

*   *   *

As the realization of the finality of the sudden splitting of the city set in, the residents of West Berlin started to adapt their lifestyles to living with the Wall; whether through changing travel routes across the city, communication to the outside world, or simply buying necessities to live. "We listened to the radio, and Willy Brandt did try to calm people down and try to say, 'We are safe. America will come to our aid,'" recalled Margit Hosseini. In general, the political establishment in West Berlin tried not only to calm the population but also to organize what to do next. "We were constantly told, therefore, through television and radio, that we are not lost and there will be help and something will happen. But in a way, although people wanted to believe, they were not convinced that this might happen."

The Berlin Allied commanders could do very little but issue letters of protest to the Soviet commander of the city. West Berlin was not under threat, so in essence the principles agreed to at Potsdam in 1945 had not been violated: for Allied troops in the city, free access to East Berlin had not been prevented yet, and the right of self-determination by the West Berlin population was not under threat as such. But the West's tepid response to the barbed-wire barrier emboldened Ulbricht that he could now transform the wire fence into a concrete wall. Even though there had been daily escape attempts, those that succeeded amounted to fewer than a hundred a day. What was more concerning to the regime was the report compiled by the Stasi that listed the eighty-five *Volkspolizisten*, border guards, and militiamen who had bolted for the freedom of West Berlin. The most famous of these escapes had been captured three days into the Wall's construction by Peter Liebling's camera and became the photograph that summed up the futility of Ulbricht's plans.

It was at this point that Adolf Knackstedt came into his life. "After the successful defection," Knackstedt recalled, "Private Schumann was turned over to JROC(B) [Joint Refugee Operations Centre (Berlin)]. He underwent a short interrogation and was then turned over to me. At this point, I didn't have the impression he was in shock. Far from it." It was now Knackstedt's job to look after the escaped border guard and get him prepped for a new life in West Germany. "It was well past 10 p.m. when I took him to a clothing sales store. I had special arrangements with the store's manager for purchasing civilian clothing last-minute for cases such as this. The store was open for business 24/7 to help with our work. I put him up for the night at a safe house and we flew him out to Frankfurt am Main for further assessment the following day. By then his photograph had circulated to all major news agencies around the globe—it was big news. The sooner we could get him out of Berlin the better, as the Stasi would have been after him."

The blocks lining Bernauer Straße now became the front line of the conflict. Their windows on the western side looked down on the French zone of control. Over the coming days, residents kept the West Berlin fire department busy. Paper notes floated down, with details of which floor and window the escapee would use, and what time he or she would be jumping to freedom.

By August 18, the entrances to all the blocks overlooking Bernauer Straße had been nailed shut or walled up, replaced by doors that led through rear courtyards. Ida Siekmann, a nurse who lived there, waited another week before committing to her escape. She could no longer bear being separated from her younger sister, Martha, who lived three streets away in the west. Early the next morning she threw her belongings out the window of her third-floor apartment and then three eiderdowns to cushion her landing. As *Vopos* attempted to break in, and before the firemen had a chance to stretch out their rescue net, she jumped. She died of her injuries on the way to nearby Lazarus Hospital—one day short of her fifty-ninth birthday. Her death—the first due directly to the imposition of the Wall—was met by outrage in West Berlin. The press reported it in detail. Following an official memorial service, a wreath was placed in front of Bernauer Straße 48. It bore the inscription: "To the victim denied freedom." A few days later a monument was erected at the site.

For every death, there would be a small glimmer of victory, of thumbing one's nose at a totalitarian regime imposing such a violation on this beautiful and cultured city. Much like the photograph of Conrad Schumann vaulting to freedom, so seventy-seven-year-old Frieda Schulze would unwittingly become a symbol of West Berlin resistance, and an international story in her own right. She would find herself in a dramatic tug-of-war, dangling from her window, arms held firmly inside her room by East Berlin officials who had arrived to take her away, and legs gripped tightly by West Berlin firemen on the street below.

Frieda had lived at Bernauer Straße 29 since the end of the Second World War. Three days after the barrier was installed, she was forced to move from her ground-floor apartment into one above. The elderly widow fled when the large-scale evacuations began on September 24, 1961. Firemen spread out a net beneath her window. She launched her cat into it, and a few small personal possessions. She then clambered onto the sill. Despite a large crowd's encouragement, she was too scared to jump. The local media filmed her predicament. West Berlin teenagers climbed up and tried to help her. One managed to hang on to her leg for a few seconds. In the meantime, East Berlin policemen had broken into the apartment and were trying to pull her back inside. They also threw tear-gas grenades at their rivals. Just when it seemed she would be hauled back by the *Vopos*, Frieda Schulze finally tumbled into the rescue net, to a gleeful cheer from the locals. Ulbricht soon ordered the windows bricked up. That avenue of escape, much like the city itself, was now closed.

By the second week, despite fierce mass protests by West Berliners, the East Germans now began to transform the barbed-wire barricade into a more physically imposing structure. More troops and workers were drafted in, and the barricades were strengthened. There was no going back—the city was to be entombed.

The Berlin Wall
August 1961–November 1989

N

FRENCH ZONE

Tegel

Chausseestraße

Bornholmer
Straße

SOVIET ZONE

Staaken — Heerstraße

BRITISH ZONE

Invalidenstraße

Prinzenstraße

Friedrichstraße
Checkpoint Charlie

Oberbaumbrücke

Gatow

AMERICAN ZONE

Tempelhof

Sonnenallee

Dreilinden
(Checkpoint Bravo)

Drewitz

Waltersdorfer
Chaussee

EAST GERMANY
(RUSSIAN ZONE)

Airports

✕ Checkpoints open to Germans only

⊗ Checkpoints open to Germans and non-Germans

© MDL Design

CHAPTER FIVE

A New Border to Patrol

Before it was designated "Checkpoint Charlie," the crossing was one of many created and agreed upon by the military planners ruling over a defeated city in 1947. It was located at the junction of Friedrichstraße with Zimmerstraße and Mauerstraße (whose historical name ironically means "Wall Street"). Almost two weeks after the East Germans had erected the barrier, on August 23, 1961, their Ministry of the Interior announced that among a group of border crossings, this checkpoint would be the only one where the Allied military would be allowed entry into their sector of the city. Before, the city had used eighty-one official crossing points, and the Friedrichstraße junction had been an open gateway to military traffic without hindrance other than a perfunctory, if not haphazard, check of papers. Now the city would have to make do with limited entry and exit points, for along the new border 192 streets had been cut in two; 97 of those streets had given the population access into East Berlin, while 95 had run out of the city itself into the GDR.

For anyone studying the new map of the city for exit points, their options would now be thus: Bornholmer Straße, farthest to the north in the city, was ostensibly for the use of citizens of the Federal Republic of Germany when crossing into East Berlin. Chausseestraße served as the crossing for West Berliners entering into and exiting out of East Berlin. The border crossing at Invalidenstraße was located east of the Sandkrugbrücke, a bridge over the Spandauer Schifffahrtskanal near Berlin's central train station. The Friedrichstraße S-Bahn station was the last station before the West Berlin border for trains running from east to west. When the border was sealed off, this through station became a terminal and a border crossing point for travelers from both parts of the city. The pavilion was taken over by border control for clearance and aptly named the *Tränenpalast* ("Palace of Tears") due to the heartbreaking farewells occurring there. It would also be under heavy surveillance by the Stasi. Heinrich-Heine-Straße was designated for goods and postal transport between the two halves of the city and was one of the largest border crossings. West German citizens would also be able to enter East Berlin from this crossing point. The Oberbaumbrücke crossing was situated by the bridge that spanned the River Spree between the city districts of Kreuzberg and Friedrichshain. Sonnenallee attracted little attention due to its location in the south and the limited amount of human traffic it processed.

Checkpoint Charlie would be formally distinguished by the Four Powers as the single crossing point (either by foot or by motor vehicle) for foreigners and members of the Allied forces. Members of the Allied forces were subsequently not allowed to use the other sector crossing point designated for use by foreigners at the Friedrichstraße railway station. The name "Charlie," though it would become quite catchy to fans of spy novels and films over the years, had a more prosaic backstory. The Allied checkpoints covering entry into East Germany, and then into Berlin, derived their names, simply, from the letters in the NATO phonetic alphabet. The Allied checkpoints on the Autobahn linking the city to the West were Checkpoint Alpha at Helmstedt/Marienborn and Checkpoint Bravo, its counterpart at Dreilinden/Drewitz in the southwest corner of Berlin. Soldiers of the US Army's 287th Military Police Company would man this new crossing in shifts around the clock beginning on August 23. This small unit was then formally expanded, and a desk was placed in a nearby building on Freidrichstraße to serve as the official checkpoint, complete with a radio system. Now that it had a radio, it needed a call sign, and thus "Charlie" was attached to it. Within a few weeks, the US Army moved a trailer to the center of the road to act as the new control point on the Allied side. Checkpoint Charlie was now designated the major crossing point for Allied personnel, foreigners, and diplomats in the heart of Berlin. The Russians simply called it the "Friedrichstraße Crossing Point," and their East German cousins the *Grenzübergangsstelle* ("Border Crossing Point") Friedrich/Zimmerstraße—which was geographically where the checkpoint was located.

The checkpoint was oddly constructed at both ends. During its twenty-eight-year span of service, the infrastructure on the eastern side evolved into a grand affair—as we will see further into this story—and would be expanded to include not only the first, second, third, and fourth generations of the Berlin Wall, with its watchtowers, chicane driveways, and cement barriers, but also a multilane shed where cars and buses with their occupants were checked. However, the Allied side was pointedly simplistic, and always would be. The Allies purposely never erected any buildings to match this, and rather made do with what is now the iconic wooden shed. Their clear message was "This hut isn't permanent," as neither was the establishment of the GDR on the opposite side, where no international agreements had yet been signed. The checkpoint hut was anonymous and quite small, with light-gray or white-painted wooden panels, accessed by a door facing rearward toward the American positions, with a sandbagged bunker looking out toward the east. A window with a hatch that opened out on both sides to address passengers and vehicles coming through also offered some protection from the elements in wintertime. Draped in the American flag, and later in the 1960s the three flags of the Allies, it sat atop a small traffic island to allow it to process vehicles moving to and from the GDR. A very basic horizontal pole was regularly lowered and raised as vehicles traversed the checkpoint.

Next to the checkpoint would be built a large white hoarding sign on which the message "You are leaving the American Sector" was clearly, and loudly, spelled out in English, French, German, and Russian Cyrillic. An observation platform would also be constructed nearby that would soon become famous in the early days of the Wall's being erected as families made their way to the border crossing to try to catch a glimpse of their loved ones and, if they were lucky, exchange a message or a sign. The Café Adler ("Eagle Café"), opposite the checkpoint, would, over the coming years, entertain not only Berlin locals, but a host of military personnel, generals, agents, policemen, and reporters. For the price of a coffee, you could sit right next to the border where East meets West, taking in the everyday passage of human traffic, whilst all the while noticing East German *Volkspolizei* and *Grenztruppen* monitoring your every move through their binoculars—not one hundred yards away.

Over the years, the wasteland separating the two superpowers would be cleared of the rubble strewn everywhere from the damage from the Second World War, but the actual space was left as a reminder to all and sundry that it was an international no-man's-land. On the western side, the buildings would be renovated to a degree, to be inhabitable, or in the case of the Café Adler, to serve the thousands of visitors who entered it for food, drink, or to get out of the winter weather. The Americans had an observation post built into one of the apartment buildings on Zimmerstraße, overlooking the wasteland and the Soviet positions, and as time went on, allowing perfect access to view the Wall and the watchtowers.

The main duties now for the military police would be to monitor and control Allied movement through the crossing, verify documents required for entry into the GDR, and advise those wishing to visit the eastern side of the local laws as well as what procedures to follow in order not to fall foul of any officials. When necessary, they could also escort important dignitaries into the GDR and bring them back.

As we shall see later, the East Germans designed and built a grandiose series of buildings to emphasize the sovereignty of the GDR. Checkpoint Charlie would create a myth and legend all its own, but the people who lived, worked, and escaped through it, and the Wall itself, would reveal what life was like during the Cold War, when at any moment a flash point could lead to a single death, or to untold catastrophe for Europe and the World.

The thousands of men and women who served in the military police of the Allies, whatever nationality, in whatever formation, will tell you unequivocally that their DNA is in the very concrete of the Berlin Wall. From when the Allies took control of the destroyed city in May 1945, at the war's end, to the eventual collapse of the GDR in 1990, the constant assignments that were maintained, twenty-four hours a day, seven days a week, 365 days a year were: the transportation network must be secured; the Allied sectors must be policed; and the Wall (or, at first, "the Wire") needed to be guarded. These duties ranged from securing VIPs to guarding headquarters and supply depots to keeping the road, rail, and sea links open to checking the border around the city, policing their own troops in their own sector, and, of course, processing civilians and military personnel through the checkpoints into the GDR.

While many British Army and RAF formations were rotated in and out of the city, the Royal Military Police (247th [Berlin] Provost Company) of the 2nd Regiment Royal Military Police and elements of the Royal Air Force Police based at the airfield of RAF Gatow were a constant presence in the British Sector. The Royal Military Police had a continuous presence in the city (and at Checkpoint Alpha) from July 1945 until their departure in April 1994, having arrived with British troops after the Soviets finally captured Berlin, following heavy and costly fighting (more than eighty thousand killed). Immediately postwar, the RMP would establish a policing presence with the other Allies. Colonel Jeremy Green OBE, Regimental Secretary RMP and director of the Royal Military Police Museum, concurs: "The first two Allied noncommissioned ranks to arrive in Berlin after Germany's defeat were two military policemen who escorted Major General Lyne CB DSO (commanding the British 7th Armoured Division and appointed as Field Marshal Montgomery's initial representative to the Soviets). The military police forces of the three Allied occupying powers combated the plague of black marketeering and other serious and petty crimes. In the late 1940s and 1950s, general policing was the norm, the exception being during the Berlin Airlift, when US and UK military police and French gendarmes would escort convoys and help with traffic control, distribution of supplies, and fostering good relations with the population."

For the Americans, after the creation of the Berlin Brigade in 1961, the 502nd Infantry would be the recognized formation to garrison their Sector, with the role of policing it left to the US Military Police Corps.

The French garrison also consisted of permanent units in situ with personnel rotated in and out as time dictated, their Gendarmerie Berlin overseeing the same roles as their British and American counterparts.

For all three countries, their joint occupation of West Berlin for such a length of time would be their longest recorded presence on enemy territory in modern times. All three formations were unique in their training and approach to the delicate job of policing a city like Berlin, where the slightest miscommunication or argument might easily conflagrate into an international incident—as we shall see later. As policemen first and foremost, their role was to handle and resolve disputes, calm down provocative actions, and assist where needed those in need of help. Ensuring they retained control without recourse to a military solution was paramount—that they succeeded in this across the twenty-eight years of the wall's existence, and if one measures their stay from the time the Allies arrived to the time they departed Berlin in 1994, across almost fifty years, is an incredible achievement. But what were the men and women who undertook this unique job like—whether they policed the city, monitored the wall, or guarded and maintained the links back to West Germany?

For Private Tom Ables of the 287th US Military Police, from West Virginia, the opportunity to escape the drudgery of small-town life and working in his town's glass factory (owned, ironically, by German émigrés) to experience travel and adventure abroad in the late fifties was too good an opportunity to pass up. Tom joined the army, and with his language skills he volunteered to serve as a military policeman in Germany, where he was stationed in Frankfurt starting in January 1961, before being selected for the Berlin unit on September 16 of that year—right after the Wall went up. He would see firsthand how the GDR attempted to portray to the world the health of the country. "On traveling by train to get to Berlin, we would sit there and look out the window while they were hooking up the West German train, to finish taking us to the western sector. The place was busy, and the cars were there driving around, giving the impression of a bustling, vibrant Soviet sector. But we studied the scene over a period of minutes, and we noticed the same make of car and the same driver passing by, again and again. They were going around in circles to give the impression of affluence."

Private Ables would serve at first with the railway police but was taken for processing at his barracks. "My first day I suffered the initiation of being served my first German beer—very strong, and once I'd drunk two of them to please my new MP comrades, I passed out! The following morning, I went to work on the train, where I met more American personnel, as well as the German service workers who maintained the train itself. One guy would come in and change his clothes and start cleaning the trains and sweeping the floors and stuff. So they introduced me. 'Joe, this is one of our new MPs, Tom Ables.' He put out his hand, and said, 'Oh, Tom Ables, you goddamn son of a bitch!' I stare back in shock and ask the others, who were by now laughing, 'What did that guy say?' 'We're just teaching him English,' came the reply from my sergeant. The joke was on me again."

For a US military posting to a hot spot such as West Berlin, one had to have a record of good conduct and exceptional service. Tom had impressed his superiors with his eagerness to take more language courses, but a transfer to Berlin came with good and bad news. "The US Army cannot, and will not, try to rescue any unit, or anyone else," said his lieutenant, "if war breaks out in Berlin. Two things can happen to you if the Russians decide to take Berlin. Neither one of them is good." Then he smiled at Tom and added the good news: "'The town itself—when refugees come from the eastern sector, they'll send the men to West Germany. The women are usually allowed to stay on. So if you go up there, there's going to be about twenty young women for every one man in Berlin!' That sounded like something that might not be a bad idea," Tom added. "My patriotism overcame my emotions. 'Well, sir, when can I leave?'

"'How about the next train this evening?' He smiled."

But when Tom walked down the hallway of the barracks for the first time, he was asked, "'Hey, Ables, did you get stuck with that "twenty women to every guy in Berlin" story they give you?'

"'Yes, I was,' I said.

"He laughed. 'Welcome to Berlin!'"

With the construction of the Wall, the situation in the city may well have been very tense, but to Tom, it was a part of his everyday life and he wouldn't lose sleep over it. "Being from West Virginia—a coal-mining area—it wasn't unusual to have relatives who were killed in the mines, which gave one a fatalistic attitude. . . . With that thought in my mind, going to Berlin, to me it was practically the same thing—even though I wasn't going to a coal mine. . . . If the Communists attacked, we knew our chances of survival were slim, if nothing at all. Our favorite bar for the MPs was Lulu's, and we partied hard when off duty, as we had this thought that any moment now World War Three could commence."

The American and the British units always had friendly relations, both on and off duty. Both nationalities regularly shared their facilities, and the British especially loved shopping in the US garrison's PX store and attending their cinemas and bars. The American troops found the British bars equally interesting, having never tasted warm beer, though a lack of air-conditioning in the heat of a Berlin summer was not welcome. They toasted the Queen on royal anniversaries, but the one thing all American personnel found fascinating about their British colleagues was that they had an escape plan if things got ugly with the Soviets. As Private Wayne Daniels recalled, "We were in one of their bars one evening talking to some British soldiers, and they said, 'What are you guys going to do when the balloon goes up? We're ready for it.'

"I said, 'What do you mean—you're ready for it?' They laughed and took out a piece of cloth from their top pocket.

"'What we have is a little silk handkerchief. This is what the British airmen wore and carried with them in World War Two.'

"We studied the handkerchief, which had a picture of Berlin and the surrounding areas, with basic sentences in German, such as 'I am a British soldier. In case of war, we'd appreciate if there was any help you give.' It was like something from a spy movie!"

All American personnel, like their British and French counterparts in Berlin, believed that they were just a trip wire; they were not there so much to defend the city, as to be the first ones the Warsaw Pact nations would take in case of war. "We would always talk about it," recalled

Daniels, "sometimes laugh about our position, but we never had any answers for what we could do, like our British cousins. What was our best way out of Berlin? Our idea for escaping from the city was to change uniforms with the street cleaners—because they always had a uniform, they looked sort of snappy—and get one of their brooms and tell them we were sweeping our way back to the West! It sounds ridiculous now, and it sounded ridiculous then, but that was probably the only thing we felt we could do to try to get out of the city."

Every Sunday the Allied police would attend the ceremony at the Soviet War Memorial within the British sector, by the Brandenburg Gate. On those rare days in a Berlin summer when the temperature could hit at least ninety degrees, much like at the "Trooping of the Colour" in London, there were always ceremonial casualties among the British soldiers. Recalled Tom, "They only had one type of heavy, woolen uniform, which would have been incredibly hot and uncomfortable. We would bet on how long it would take before one of them would pass out from heat exhaustion. We'd see them lying in the bushes and their comrades would come and drag them out and put a replacement into line. I admired their discipline."

Interaction with the local population was an everyday occurrence in a city surrounded by a wall and divided into three sectors of control. Unlike their counterparts in the Federal Republic to the west, US MPs Ables and Daniels both found the Berliners friendly and welcoming— thus creating a special bond. "My time stationed in Frankfurt often made me think the people there were like sculptures," recalls Daniels. "They were very polite and businesslike if you needed to converse with them, but generally, they wouldn't even want to talk or look at you. They would just go on about their way. But when you went to Berlin, it was a different story. They were very nice, very receptive, and if you made comments about their kids, they loved that. The overall impression was they knew why we were all there and appreciated our service."

Working his shift on the US Army train commuting between the FRG and West Berlin was an eye-opener for Tom Ables. Tensions were still running relatively high, and the MPs were vigilant to ensure there were no infractions by the East Germans or Soviets at the border crossing points when the engines and personnel were changed over. "We had an interpreter who spoke Russian, and another guy who spoke German," Tom recalled. "Usually, there were probably about ten to twelve cars overall—most of them for passengers, and the remainder for freight, which was attached at the far end. When the train stopped at Marienborn, at the Russian Checkpoint, an East German train conductor would then climb aboard, too, in order to ride in the command car, where he was obliged to stay, but not move through the train. We would get onto the back of the command car to make sure that no one jumped onto the train. There would be about twelve to fifteen Russian soldiers walking around the train itself to also check that no one got on and no one got off. One of them would usually take his station by our position, and that is when the bartering began! . . . The three things the Russians were desperate for were pornographic magazines, those ballpoint pens that revealed a naked lady if you turned them upside down, and watches. You have to remember that these guys, when not on duty, were confined to barracks, so couldn't mix with the locals, who wouldn't have had these anyway."

Despite this low-level fraternization, the Allies knew, if given the order, the Communists would kill them, and vice versa. "Although," said Wayne Daniels, "we were just a bunch of young, twentysomething soldiers who were just doing what young soldiers do. We were the only unit in the American military that had eye-to-eye contact with the enemy every day. I mean, we were so close to them, we could hit them with a rock. In appearance, these Russians looked poor, with only one uniform, poor equipment, their food and supplies weren't great, and they were mainly confined to their barracks." Private Ables's inquisitive nature and skill with the German language enabled him to find out a little of what life was like for the Soviets. What he heard shocked him. "There was one Russian soldier that the authorities had billeted in a little town to direct traffic for the many Soviet convoys coming through. He was there for three days, and he hadn't been supplied with food or water. The townspeople became so concerned about him that they ended up feeding him in order that he wouldn't starve or pass out. His superiors didn't care."

Just as with the problems Lieutenant Corbett of the Irish Guards had endured with the East German guards crossing the border, so, too, the Americans frequently had issues with the changeover of trains. Tom said, "One time I was listening on my portable radio to the second Sonny Liston–Cassius Clay heavyweight fight, which famously would last about thirty seconds. I had the carriage window down, and the commentary from the radio floated out into the night. Suddenly a *Vopo* appeared and sternly ordered me to put my window up, to which I actively disagreed with him! I quickly had quite a few of them shouting at me, when suddenly Clay knocked Liston out in the first round. I shouted back at them all, 'Hey, fight's over!' He still wanted the window up, which wasn't going to happen, and instead he got the international gesture of defiance." This sort of typical altercation with the guards did not blind Tom or his buddies to the plight of the ordinary East German. "When our train stopped at the border, as you looked outside, you could tell from their downcast eyes that they were afraid to look at you. I always believed they were terrified to show any emotion to anybody from the western side, thinking that one of their own might be watching them, as if there was some sort of secret communication going on. If you caught the eye of a young East German girl—she was not going to smile back at you. She'd turn her head away. It was very sad."

By the autumn of 1961, however, Tom and the rest of the American and Allied garrisons would have more important things on their mind, as Ulbricht and Khrushchev again upped the stakes for who controlled access to and from the marooned city.

CHAPTER SIX

Who Blinks First?

In late October 1961, with the Allies increasingly at odds among themselves as to how best to respond to the barriers going up in Berlin, a
series of incidents ratcheted up the tension even further. Walter Ulbricht
was in Moscow along with thousands of other Communist delegates
attending the XXII Congress of the Soviet Union. Brimming with confidence at pulling off his masterstroke of building the Wall, he was now
critical of his Soviet masters for not signing the long-promised treaty
that recognized GDR sovereignty. Nikita Khrushchev, on the other
hand, had bigger issues to attend to. He was battling with Chinese disaffection at his further denouncements of Stalin's rule (the ex-dictator's
coffin would also suffer the indignity of being relocated from Lenin's
mausoleum that October), and this tension would run right through
the conference. Equally, his desire to keep the pressure on Kennedy
led Khrushchev to gleefully announce to the world's press that Russia
was testing the first hydrogen bomb. The rules of the game with the
Americans had changed—in his favor, he thought. In various offhand
conversations he held with British and French officials, he warned them
about how few hydrogen missiles it would take to obliterate each country. This mixture of bombast and brinkmanship perhaps caused him
to take his eye away from the crisis escalating in Berlin. He believed
he had lanced this annoying boil, but it was about to erupt once more.

President Kennedy had bowed to the "Berlin Mafia" in the White
House who despaired that the Berliners' morale was plummeting due to
inaction and felt that the United States must make a significant public

gesture of support to shore up those fearing capitulation, none more so than the city's mayor, Willy Brandt. His correspondence with JFK was blunt, to the point, and intended to get a response with leakage of the letters to the press. Stung into action, Kennedy, to the city's relief, ordered his vice president, Lyndon B. Johnson, to accompany the hero of the '48 Berlin Airlift—General Lucius D. Clay—to the arrival of the US Army's 1st Battle Group. Despite Johnson's initial misgivings, his antenna for political opportunity quickly had him playing the part of conquering hero. Amid public adulation and relief at their presence, both men toured the city with wide press coverage, and eventually welcomed the 1,500 American soldiers who finally made it to the city after an arduous four-day trip covering a mere 110 miles. The city received them like the Seventh Cavalry, with Johnson taking the salute as they paraded through the city center. The Kremlin made no comment on these events, but Kennedy was laying the groundwork for a further surprise.

West Berlin erupted in jubilation once more with the return of General Clay, only this time he took up permanent residence in the city as the president's special envoy. No one knew better how important a free Berlin was to the overall Allied strategy in Europe now that the Cold War was running hot. Clay's relationship with Berliners was almost paternal, and the gesture of sending him to the city's aid gave them the confidence boost the White House desired. There would be limits placed on his authority this time, as he was Kennedy's man on the ground, reporting directly to him, though he had no official position within the overall US Army command in Europe, or within NATO. On arriving, he conveyed nothing but an aura of authority, stating that his job was to "demonstrate United States strength and determination" to reinforce the Potsdam Agreement and to establish the continuity of the Soviets running their own sector. He would not recognize the East Germans. West Berlin mayor Brandt accompanied him as they drove in an open-topped limousine through the heart of the city, hailed by hundreds of thousands of people lining the streets.

By this point, the physical wall was taking shape. Haphazard in design and crude in construction, it had been built by the East Germans using whatever was at hand, which in their part of the city meant utilizing the rubble strewn everywhere, left over from the war. Broken glass was even cemented into the top of the Wall. New building material allocated for construction of accommodations for East Berliners was also requisitioned for this purpose, causing long-term housing issues with the locals. The infamous *Todesstreifen* ("Death Strip") was now being set in place, separating the two sides by one hundred meters (about three hundred feet). Wooden watchtowers were erected in that space, with more barbed wire added, along with steel hedgehog anti-vehicle traps spread across famous squares such as Potsdamer Platz and dazzling searchlights that aided armed guards scanning the border. The Soviets had not been involved in the planning, but the East Berliners were now erecting their own prison, which the West German press bemoaned, in the equal measure that they celebrated the East German workers who chose to attempt escape instead. Despite some successes, however, people were still dying—twelve shot by the end of 1961.

Now established in the American sector and pondering his options, General Clay could see shades of 1948 as the city was slowly being strangled by the Communists. But instead of having the full support of President Harry Truman, which he had relied on during the successful airlift, he was now uncertain what his superiors in Washington were prepared to do to establish Allied rights and protect the local population. He believed he had President Kennedy's backing—to a degree—but he was eager to test the resilience of the East Germans taking over Soviet control of the borders—which he was steadfastly against. The US Army in Berlin had increased its training—whether for defending the city, smashing down the Wall with bulldozers, or civilian riot control. All of this to assuage the West Berlin civic authorities that the US garrison was actively looking at options to tackle Communist aggression, a message that mirrored the strengthening of US and NATO troops farther afield in Western Europe. Clay was keen for an opportunity to flex American muscle and reassert the freedom of the city.

On October 22, E. Allan Lightner, the senior US diplomat in West Berlin, was stopped by East German *Vopos* at Checkpoint Charlie as he and his wife, Dorothy, were on their way to the state opera house in East Berlin. Lovers of art, ballet, and opera, the Lightners were regular visitors into the Soviet zone to attend many high-profile events, to the point that many East Berliners recognized their car as it traveled through the zone. That evening was to be a similar excursion, and they were running late as they drove through Checkpoint Charlie and onto the border control in the East. The Allied leadership in Berlin were on notice that the *Volkspolizei* had instigated a formal process of checking Allied papers, and though the British government had not protested, to the American leadership in Berlin, this was a step too far that should be firmly rebuffed. Lightner himself was a fan of General Clay, believing he would have prevented the barriers going up that August, and so he was willing to support this newly aggressive policy toward the East Germans.

The game began. As the Lightners' Volkswagen came to a halt at the Soviet checkpoint, the *Volkspolizei* at the crossing demanded to see their papers, which, following standard protocol, he insisted only Soviet officials had the right to check. A young *Vopo* officer stalled for time to have a Soviet official come to resolve the issue, and the scene degenerated into a shouting match lasting several minutes. Finally, an angry Lightner refused one last request to show his papers, and with his wife now joining in the argument about a breach of the Four Power Agreement, he turned the car around and started to return to the US checkpoint.

On receiving this news, Lucius Clay and the garrison commander, General Watson, ordered the mobilization of a full platoon of soldiers from the 2nd Battle Group, supported with armor. One of them was Private Daniels of the 287th Military Police. "Sitting in Andrews Barracks, the alarm went off for another alert. It could have been the guys in front of me selected, it could have been the guys behind me, but the first sergeant on duty pointed at me and my buddy, barking, 'Daniels, you and Malloy go pick up a jeep with a blue light, go to Turner Barracks, pick up the tanks and some APCs, and escort them to Checkpoint Charlie.' We rushed down, requisitioned the jeep, and I drove over to McNair, and off we went toward Checkpoint Charlie."

What followed was epic theater. Lieutenant Colonel Sabolyk, the US provost marshal, had arrived and looked on at the scene developing a hundred yards from his hut at Checkpoint Charlie. He was acutely aware he had to intervene to retrieve the Lightners before the reinforcements he had been informed were coming arrived on the scene. He didn't want civilians—or senior diplomats, for that matter—becoming entangled in what he feared could be a serious confrontation. Sabolyk found his staff car and drove at speed toward the Soviet checkpoint, then screeched to a halt by the Volkswagen. Having diverted the attention of the *Vopos*, one of Sabolyk's officers followed on foot and persuaded Mrs. Lightner to vacate the car and retreat back to the American sector. As she did so, Allan Lightner spotted in his rearview mirror eight heavily armed infantrymen, carrying rifles with bayonets fixed, double-timing to stop alongside his car. With American armor now trained on their position and armed infantry on top of them, the *Volkspolizei* backed away and allowed the US diplomat's car entry through the checkpoint. Not satisfied with merely reaching this goal, Lightner then decided to drive into the city for half a mile with his armed escort, before turning around and returning to the American sector. No armed American soldier had ever set foot this far into the territory before; the Rubicon had been crossed.

Much to the excitement of the growing gallery, including the press now taking up positions on Friedrichstraße and Zimmerstraße, Lightner decided he wanted to pursue the point, and with an American press official accompanying him, he repeated his journey, again backed up by his armed guard. By this time a Soviet official had finally appeared to apologize for the error of his East German cousins, but still issued a curt objection to the armed Americans entering the Soviet zone. The standoff dissolved into a blame game, as Lightner drove back to Checkpoint Charlie, exhilarated that he had proved General Clay's claim of obstruction at the border by the East Germans themselves—which ran completely against the Four Power Agreement. On the Monday both sides issued press statements: Clay reiterating his stance on infringement of Allied access into the Soviet zone, and the East German authorities making it clear that henceforth any foreigner traveling through checkpoints into their capital *must* show ID, unless the foreigner was in uniform. Further confrontation was in the cards. The Allied garrison knew it, the international press knew it, and a vexed president in Washington, DC, was aware, too.

Clay was pushing his authority beyond his remit set by Washington, and he knew it. In a personal letter to President Kennedy, he laid out his frustrations at the lack of decision-making he could wield in Berlin, and his need to show support to the West Berlin population. He went as far as he dared in also criticizing the president's handling of the barriers going up in the first place that summer. Minor infractions against the Allies' right of access were stepping-stones to ultimately losing Berlin, which could therefore destabilize NATO, he believed, and he asked for more power to handle the situation on the ground should it escalate. The moment mirrored the crisis that had come between Douglas MacArthur and President Truman in 1951—when the former had wished to have a greater say in US policy toward an aggressive China during the Korean War. Truman had reined in his soldier with great difficulty, forcing him to resign and suffering the biggest slump in any US president's approval ratings. The question was now whether Kennedy could keep Clay in check, too. At the same time, he knew some of his key allies (France and West Germany) advised being as tough with the Soviets as Clay envisaged. It was a delicate balancing act of international diplomacy, with the crucial drama being conducted across one hundred yards of ground at Friedrichstraße.

Back in West Berlin, the American command wondered which side would blink first. General Clay decided to press ahead and ordered another excursion, resulting in two US Army officers in civilian clothes being stopped at the Soviet crossing point, their identification demanded by the East Germans. Clay repeated his move of supporting the men with armed troops to escort them, and backed that up this time with ten American M-48 tanks and three armored personnel carriers (APCs) lumbering up to the crossing point. Faced with such point-blank fire-power, the *Vopos* again backed down. This act was repeated again the following day, with the American armor positioned some one hundred yards from the border, noisily revving their engines and sending plumes of black diesel smoke into the cold evening air, attempting to reassure the West Berliners and intimidate the East German border guards.

After two days of this, the Soviets, possibly taken by surprise at how quickly events had escalated, felt they now needed to respond. Khrushchev knew he had to either back Ulbricht's stance on sovereignty for the GDR or back off. He instructed the commander on the ground, General Konev, to match this "American aggression" tank for tank and send Russian T-54s rumbling to face down the Americans. They, too, ground to a halt, their barrels facing toward Checkpoint Charlie. Lieutenant Vern Pike stared in disbelief as they arrived, knowing through experience that the chance to test the resolve of the Communists should have been taken during the first days of the barriers going up. "One evening after the 13th of August, while on duty at Friedrichstraße," Pike recalled, "I watched intently as East German workers slowly constructed the barricade with cinder blocks and mortar. Suddenly, one East German looked up from his task, glanced in my direction, and in German exclaimed to me, 'Lieutenant, look, I'm working as slow as I can. What are you waiting for?' A few moments later, standing behind the worker, a *Vopo* with a submachine gun strapped across his chest glanced nervously left and right before yelling over to me, 'Lieutenant, look—my machine pistol is empty, no ammo. Why are you waiting?' The drama of those moments was not lost on me." Many in the Berlin Brigade believed the East Germans had fully expected that the Allies would cross the border and destroy the barbed-wire barriers. Now the barrier was here to stay, and the Soviets were adopting even more aggressive tactics.

Lieutenant Pike's own armor had just withdrawn back to Tempelhof Air Base less than an hour before—having shepherded the latest American drive across the border, leaving the checkpoint unprotected. "It was a great view for us right down the Friedrichstraße. We were taking a smoke break when I spotted a column of tanks approaching us from the Soviet Sector. Major Thomas Tyree ordered me to bring our tanks back." Pike immediately jumped into his official white Ford and raced down the road toward Tempelhof to recall the tanks, using his car horn to disperse the Berlin traffic. "There we were in the late afternoon coming through rush-hour traffic, racing down Mehringdamm back toward Checkpoint Charlie, and me sitting in my little white Ford, horn blasting and lights flashing!"

In a curious if ultimately unsuccessful effort to preserve deniability, Khrushchev had instructed Konev that his tanks' national markings be obscured and that his tank men wear unmarked black uniforms. Clay, of course, needed to ascertain whose they were—if they were Soviet tanks, then an escalation could lead to war, and the Allies needed to be wary. But if they were East German, then their actual deployment was a direct violation of the Potsdam Agreement of 1945. Clay issued a directive for Pike's commander, Lieutenant Colonel Sabolyk, to get across to the GDR side and ascertain who actually was inside the tanks. "Sam McCart [the driver] and I jumped into a US military sedan," Pike recalled, "and drove into the Soviet Sector. While they appeared to be Soviet T-54s, I couldn't tell because they had their vehicle markings painted out. I was surprised by how they were parked. The formation they were arrayed in [2-3-2] meant that the rear vehicles couldn't actually fire in support of the lead ones. It also made them easy targets for our guys."

Quietly parking behind the tanks, the two MPs walked up to the last tank and observed no one in or around it. Pike decided that he needed to get inside one of them to positively identify the crew as either East German or Soviet. "With my heart pounding, I climbed up and into the tank and found the crew compartment empty. Inside I saw Russian lettering on the instrument panel, as well as a copy of a Red Army newspaper that I took when I exited the tank." After climbing down and out of the tank, Pike noticed a group of approximately fifty tankers in a meeting behind the lead tank. The two Americans silently approached the large group to eavesdrop on what they could. "I had a basic understanding of Russian," recalled Pike, "and the leader was speaking Russian. These were Soviet tank crews!" Suddenly, the Soviet officer spotted the American MPs and barked out orders as the others turned to see what he was looking at. Pike and McCart hastily returned to the sedan and sped back to the American sector.

"I told Sabolyk the tanks were quite definitely Soviet. The colonel at first didn't believe me. After I explained how I knew, he exploded. 'You did what!?' I handed him the Red Army newspaper to prove my point. The ashen-faced colonel then handed me the phone and directed me to report to General Clay himself! When I did, there was stony silence on the other end of the phone. General Clay then asked to speak with Colonel Sabolyk."

Opposite the Soviets at the checkpoint, the Americans now had four M-48 Patton tanks, with two around the corner on Friedrichstraße and four more farther back. Supporting them were five APCs and the unit from the 287th Military Police, armed to the teeth in bulletproof vests and fixed bayonets. Clay had also placed the entire garrison of more than six thousand men on alert. The British garrison had joined in with two anti-tank guns stationed farther along at the Brandenburg Gate. Studying the Russians across the divide through his binoculars, Pike couldn't get the thought from his mind: *What happens if one of those young idiots takes a potshot at us, and this becomes one big shootout?*

A large crowd of perhaps five hundred West Berliners had now gathered at Checkpoint Charlie, with the world's press anxiously waiting by the phone or on radio mics to describe the sight of two wartime allies, for the first time, facing off, guns loaded. The cold night air was illuminated by searchlights on both sides of the border, and the usual hum of everyday traffic was broken by the loud rumblings of engines as the tank crews tried to keep warm. The Russians had by now brought up more tanks, aligned in a side street with engines running loudly. In the wider world, both sides had by now alerted their forces across the globe to "stand to" for possible conflict. All eyes were on Checkpoint Charlie. At about midnight in Berlin, Kennedy reached Clay on a secure line in his frenetic map room in West Berlin. "Hello, Mr. President," Clay said.

"How are things up there?" Kennedy asked in a voice that was attempting to be relaxed.

"We have ten tanks at Checkpoint Charlie," the general calmly replied. "The Russians have ten tanks there, too, so now we're equal." An aide then handed General Clay a note. "Mr. President, I've got to change my figures. I've just been told that the Russians have twenty more tanks coming up, which would give them exactly the total number of tanks that we have in Berlin. So we'll bring up our remaining twenty. Don't worry about it, Mr. President. They've matched us tank for tank. This is further evidence to me that they don't intend to do anything," Clay said matter-of-factly.

Kennedy could do his own math. Should the Soviets escalate their numbers further, Clay lacked the conventional capability to respond.

Kennedy scanned the anxious faces of his advisers in the room. He propped his feet up on the table, attempting to send a message of composure to men who feared that matters were spinning out of control. "Well, that's all right," said the president to Clay. "Don't lose your nerve." The general scanned his command room, looking at the faces of his officers studying him intently for what was being said by their commander in chief.

"Mr. President, we're not worried about our nerves. We're worrying about those of you people in Washington."

The American president was indeed unnerved, and US officials were now forced to intervene in the escalating crisis. General Clay was informed by Secretary of State Dean Rusk that Berlin was not so crucial an interest to be worth risking a global conflict with Moscow. Unbeknownst to everyone (including Clay), and only recently discovered, the president's brother Robert Kennedy, the attorney general, had spent the previous six months establishing a back channel of communication with the Kremlin (through the Soviet spy Georgi Bolshakov) in order for both sides to find a way to back off from the brink of potential Armageddon.

On the morning of October 28, Konev began to withdraw one T-54 from the eastern side of the border at Friedrichstraße. Minutes later an American M-48 departed, too. So this armored dance continued until all the armor was withdrawn. Like his young American counterpart, Khrushchev did not want a war over Berlin. In return for Kennedy's assurance that East Berlin was now established and the integrity of the Wall agreed, the Soviet leader acknowledged that Allied officials and military personnel would have unimpeded access to the East German capital. From that point on, the Western Allies and the Soviets freely dispatched diplomats and military personnel to travel in the divided city. Lieutenant Pike was full of admiration for his commanding officer, and thankful a war had not broken out. At the back of his mind was not only his own mortality, but the life of his pregnant young wife, who would soon give birth to twin sons in a West Berlin hospital.

"I still marvel at my luck that there wasn't an armed Soviet in that tank. I realize to this day that a Soviet tanker shooting an American officer inside his tank in the Soviet sector could have created an international incident." It had been a small victory for the Allies, but it demonstrated that the Soviets were indeed responsible for the security of their sector of Berlin and not the East Germans. The tank confrontation proved to be one of the decisive moments of the struggle in Germany during the Cold War. It had clearly shown that the real military power still lay with the Soviets, and Moscow was in overall command. General Clay was to respect the authority of the East Germans at the border, and his "D-Day" plan to have bulldozers knock down sections of the Wall was mothballed, too. All military escorts for civilians were now prohibited as unnecessary, though one vehicle per day would be allowed to gain access across the border to test that the agreement was still adhered to.

Private Tom Ables of the 287th Military Police was also relieved the situation had been brought under control. "The tank standoff at Friedrichstraße was the most dramatic thing that I was ever involved in. It was the closest that we ever got to World War Three. We didn't know if they were East German or Russian tanks for a while, and we were actually locked and loaded. General Clay was our hero, and he really took on the Russians and wouldn't take a step back, but after the tanks eventually pulled back, that was pretty well the end of him, because I think that he knew about 90 percent of American officers and men thought that what he was doing was on the dangerous side." Indeed, Clay would last only a further seven months in his role before heading back to the United States. As a government memo indicated, "For the time being nothing further can be done on the spot since the matter has now moved to the highest government levels."

Adolf Knackstedt, monitoring events from afar as he toured Berlin, was pleased with how the West had stood up to this act of aggression but knew the consequences didn't bear thinking about. Like Pike, he, too, had a young family, as well as many local relatives in the city. "This crisis nearly got us to the brink of World War Three! Finally, the interference of Allied traffic by the East German border guards came to a sudden halt. The Russians must have put a stop to Ulbricht's willingness to risk a conflict with the West." The incident was one of the most iconic and certainly dangerous moments of the Cold War, as the fifteen-hour standoff had the world watching to see whether the USA and the Soviet Union would actually start World War Three over Berlin. That December the commander in chief of the United States Army, Europe, General Bruce Clarke, decided to bring all the garrison's units under one roof of operational command. A fresh battalion would now be rotated into the city every three months, which would continue for the next four years—the Berlin Brigade was born.

The East Germans kept themselves busy, too, as the second generation of the Wall began to take shape in June 1962. In a chillingly thought-out campaign, whole blocks of buildings adjacent to the border were now demolished in order to shape a one-hundred-meter-wide (three-hundred-foot) control zone. On either side stood a wall, the outer one facing the West bigger and stronger, the inner one lower but still a challenge to get over. Defoliants were used to maintain the smooth, sandy soil now separating the barriers, with an asphalt road constructed to run between the two for motorized patrols traveling from the watchtowers spaced every thousand meters (three thousand feet). Concealed in nearby buildings, the East Germans also created new observation posts to watch the Allies and monitor human traffic. Razor-sharp barbed wire topped both walls on steel arms. To thwart vehicles crashing through, ditches were dug, more steel hedgehogs were implanted, and concrete blocks were added. In areas where space limited what could be constructed, forests of tangled wire were placed behind minefields. Runs were also established for the hundreds of trained attack dogs brought in to be housed in the zone itself, attached to horizontal cables allowing them to run freely along their section and attack any would-be escaper. For greater shooting accuracy for the guards, both sides of the Wall were now painted white, thus illuminating any person climbing it. The odds had now increased for the defense and limited the chances for the East Berliner rash enough to try his luck and risk being wounded, captured, or killed. The world would see how deadly it was later that summer.

CHAPTER SEVEN

Elvis Is Dead

On August 17, almost a year to the day since "Barbed Wire Sunday," the warm mid-afternoon tranquility of life passing through Checkpoint Charlie was shattered by multiple rifle reports from the GDR side. An escape was in progress.

Two boys were frantically scrambling across the "Death Strip" near Zimmerstraße and attempting to scale the final six-foot-high wall, topped with its deadly barbed-wire crown. The eighteen-year-olds were the only participants left in what had been a planned breakout by a gang of like-minded rebellious boys. Dodging obstacles and the more than thirty-five shots fired at them, they faced their final barrier to freedom, and their luck ran out. Crouching for cover, Peter Fechter watched as his friend Helmut Kulbeik scaled the wall—with bullets thudding into the brickwork only inches from his flailing limbs—and disappeared. His turn now came. But as he threw himself forward, he was hit by bullets to his back and leg—the latter severing a main artery. The heartrending scene that followed shocked not only those watching from Checkpoint Charlie but also the thousands of West Berliners who came out to see what was going on, some even standing on their car roofs for a better view as Fechter's lifeblood oozed away and he groaned and cried out for help, which didn't come.

Bookseller Margit Hosseini, who had grown into adulthood amid the chaos of living in the now-divided city, was horrified. "I was staying with friends near Friedrichstraße as we had enjoyed a party the night before in the flat that overlooked Checkpoint Charlie, and we heard the shouts and realized that something was happening. We went out to look, and in the sunlight saw him lying there in no-man's-land. It was a surreal atmosphere as the minutes went by. The American soldiers gathered on one side were not doing anything, and on the GDR side, the *Vopos* looked on, too. Time seemed to be standing still for everyone. And I could clearly see this young man now huddled against the Wall. He was lying in an 'S' shape and first he screamed, cried, and pleaded for help. As time elapsed, slowly, his voice got weaker and weaker, until he stopped. It was so heart-rendering [*sic*] that in the middle of nowhere was a human being dying, and two groups were facing each other, too worried to act, because they didn't know what the other one was going to do.

"You felt anger and sadness at the same time. Lots of onlookers like myself were crying or shouting 'Murderers!' at both the Americans who stood motionless and the *Vopos* who stared blankly back at us holding their machine guns close to their chests. Some of the *Vopos* even climbed up and stood on the Wall itself as if daring us to challenge what they had done. I felt shame, endless shame. But on the other hand, rationally, I knew that we couldn't do anything, but my emotions told me 'You should.'"

With the American soldiers at Checkpoint Charlie refusing to intervene or even offer any real help, it was left to the West Berlin police to scramble atop the Wall and throw a first-aid kit to the lifeless Fechter. Amid rising tension and anger, the *Vopos* who had been shooting at the fugitives (or "border violators" as the Stasi report would later label them) decided to act. Egged on by a senior officer arriving at the scene, they fired off ten smoke grenades to mask their movements and cautiously made their way to Fechter's motionless body. There arose a chant of "Murderers! Murderers!" from the audience of West Berliners as the West Berlin police responded with their own fusillade of tear-gas canisters, too.

Fechter's limp body made a pitiful sight, dressed in the "rockabilly" style made famous by Elvis Presley with skinny blue jeans, sneakers, and a striped bomber jacket and sporting the telltale hair forelock—he looked every inch the boy he was. His legs crumpled underneath his bloodied torso and the whole site by now saturated in his blood, the four guards shouldered their weapons and manhandled him like a sack of potatoes back across the wasteland to his jumping-off point—all under the watchful glare of the media at Zimmerstraße, as well as the West Berliners who hadn't been driven off by the tear gas. The whole episode had lasted less than an hour, but to many who witnessed Fechter's death, it seemed like an eternity. Peter Fechter would later be pronounced dead on arrival at the police hospital, and the many photographs taken of his ordeal would circulate around the globe, guaranteeing his martyrdom.

Holding a handkerchief while she stumbled away from the scene, a stunned and upset Margit Hosseini made her way home, trying to come to terms with what she had witnessed. "Later, when I had time to process my thoughts back at the flat, I did think, *What if the Americans had barged in to help him? What would have happened to us, and to the rest of West Berlin?* And I am sure the other side thought exactly the same. I think both sides didn't know quite how to handle the situation. But it made you realize that a personal action is sometimes not good, for the good of everyone else, so there is a difference between a political action and a personal one.

"I was so worn out, very, very tired, and I didn't talk to anyone about that for a long time, and I couldn't. The next day all the papers were full of this photo of this poor young man lying in barbed wire. It left such an impact. But you also then realize that there are situations where everything is taken out of your hands. That I couldn't have rushed forward, and I don't think it ever occurred to me, rushing forward, because it wouldn't have made the slightest difference. But this feeling of total passiveness—that was dreadful, and I've never ever forgotten it. And I've kept that shame. Sometimes I think of the Jews who talk about having survived camps and suffer survivor's guilt. Maybe it's a little similar, that shame—which is totally irrational, but you still feel it."

Riots in West Berlin would follow, and world condemnation was not far behind—the *Vopos* accused of murder and the American GIs tainted as cowards for not assisting Fechter. Finally, the brutalism of the Wall was there for all to see. President Kennedy discussed the incident at the cabinet level, as did Ulbricht and Khrushchev. The patrol commander and the two guards who shot and killed Fechter were personally awarded a flag by Ulbricht himself for their action, but this became an act seen around the world as shameful, and one the GDR would never recover from.

For weeks afterward, the tension in West Berlin was palpable. Adolf Knackstedt would find himself caught up in the fallout. "After the Peter Fechter incident, Vera, the children, and I drove home after visiting Oma and Opa at Baerwaldstraße, Kreuzberg. We decided to take a detour and drive along a road that ran parallel to the Wall. Near Friedrichstraße we ran into a large crowd of German demonstrators. We couldn't back out; we were stuck! The angry demonstrators didn't give an inch for us to get through, so we had to stop. We were totally wedged in by the demonstrating crowd, who just stared at us. Needless to say, we didn't feel comfortable at all. Finally, a couple of West Berlin policemen showed up and got the mob to move a little bit away from our car, but only by inches. It was just enough space for me to start moving forward slowly again. I still shudder thinking what could have happened if I had touched one of the demonstrators. We drove straight home while quietly saying our prayers. We never made this mistake again."

It didn't take a rocket scientist to realize that the Western Allies had no intentions from the beginning to take risks, or drastic counter-measures, to stop the building and subsequent policing of the Berlin Wall. Nikita Khrushchev and Walter Ulbricht appreciated the Western Powers' weaknesses and were inspired in initiating "Step Two" of their plan. All border guards were now issued live ammunition with orders to shoot if they were threatened. The only limitation placed on them was when Allied military personnel were involved; then they were prohibited from using or threatening with their weapons. Soon after these shooting orders were issued, the ante was raised to include "shoot to kill" individuals attempting to escape or defect through the GDR fortifications. Peter Fechter was one of the first killed only because he wanted to leave and live in a free society.

"Deadly incidents started accumulating, and they popped up at many places along the Wall and zonal border," said Knackstedt. "One day, it must have been sometime in 1962, I was on a duty mission near Checkpoint Charlie and afterward drove over to the checkpoint. An American MP informed me about a shooting incident that just had happened in the French Sector at Bernauer Straße. Someone had been shot while attempting to escape to the West. My colleague and I jumped into our duty car and quickly drove up to the place of the shooting. Bernauer Straße was already prominently known in the world as the place for heartbreaking escapes by people of all ages, who'd been jumping out of three- and four-story apartment windows. The buildings stood in the east, but the entire street belonged to West Berlin. These folks were jumping into nets or blankets that were stretched out by West Berliners and by fire department personnel. A number of people survived these daring and dangerous jumps, but some were not so fortunate; they dropped to their deaths by missing the nets or blankets. These horrible scenes could be witnessed daily until all the windows were bricked up. The main entrance of a church also was sealed because its main entrance led directly into West Berlin. Eventually all the buildings and the church were torn down and the first floor of each building became part of the initial Wall."

White wooden crosses started to accumulate along the sector wall and zonal border defenses, indicating the places where people had been killed while attempting to escape. One more cross would soon be added to Bernauer Straße. An East Berlin railroad employee, approximately fifty years old, decided to escape to West Berlin. He walked along the top of a brick wall separating two cemeteries. This wall led directly to the western border. A *Grenztruppen* soldier in a watchtower one hundred yards away warned the man to stop. He wanted him to turn around and go back, but the railroad worker disregarded the warnings. Just after he reached the actual Wall, two crackling sounds of streaking bullets ended his life. Adolf Knackstedt witnessed the aftermath. "With two holes in his temple, the guy tumbled off the wall, hanging with his head downward in a pile of barbed wire. He was hanging there like a butchered hog with blood still dripping out. His cap dropped on the ground in the western sector. A French officer was so infuriated he climbed on top of the Wall and protruded his fist toward the guard tower. He was screaming his head off, but it was all in French and I couldn't understand what he said! The border guards were so well protected we couldn't even see them standing inside the tower. Because of the massive barbed wire strung all over, no one could get to the victim in an attempt to help. It took a few hours before the East Germans finally removed the body, and only after a large contingency of armed border guards protected the perimeter. It was an ugly spectacle."

The railwayman's and, of course, Peter Fechter's deaths, although tragic and ugly to a watching world, would not be the last, by any means. Twelve Germans died in the last five months of 1961, and Fechter's death would be among the list of twenty-two people killed in 1962. While the city mourned its dead, Berliners continually looked to the West for protection, and to the White House for inspiration and hope, embodied by its young occupant. The question on every West Berliner's mind, discussed in cafés and restaurants on the Kurfürstendamm, bathing in the lakes of the Grunewald, or waiting for a train on the U-Bahn, was would John F. Kennedy come to save them?

CHAPTER EIGHT

Let Them Come to Berlin!

Over five thousand miles separated East Germany from Cuba, but both countries' futures were entwined, driven, and endangered by the Cold War. In both capitals, hostile confrontations between their respective governments and the United States could have led the world to the brink of World War Three. Thirteen days in October 1962, however, finally proved to the world that John F. Kennedy had the mettle to go head-to-head with the Soviets, debunking the myth that had grown up around the disastrous Vienna superpower summit of 1961. Nikita Khrushchev had played a strong hand since that eventful meeting, convinced he faced a weak-minded ditherer whom he could push and prod into submission. Reducing his defense budget by focusing on nuclear arms, overhauling the country's ailing economy and dire social infrastructure, and maintaining Russia's hegemony within the Communist sphere were Khrushchev's main concerns. This balancing act was underpinned by what he believed he could win from the Allies, whether that meant shoring up the security of the GDR by fencing in its population or flexing Russia's rights in Berlin itself. Kennedy's actions in the first half of 1962 only reinforced the Soviet leader's assessment of the Bostonian: "[Kennedy] would make a fuss, make more of a fuss, and then agree."

By that April the Kennedy administration was embroiled in a transatlantic row with their West German allies. A working paper on the "Berlin Question" the White House was discussing was sent to the chancellor, Konrad Adenauer, to assess. To Adenauer, it seemed as if

Moscow itself had drafted it. Control of access to the city would be handed over from the original Four Pwers to a new ruling body. This body would have limited control, as both the Russians and the East Germans could block any person or group they saw fit, as long as they still agreed to grant Allied rights to remain in West Berlin. Of more pressing concern to Adenauer, there was no mention in this working document of Germany ever being reunified via the ballot box. To the West Germans, this was impossible to accept, and abhorrent to contemplate. A disgusted Adenauer deliberately leaked the paper to the press, knowing it would bring down vitriol on the Kennedy administration, not only for showing weakness to the Soviets but also for displaying a degree of callousness toward the Berliners themselves as dozens of young people still risked their lives to attempt escape through the border. The proposal died in its infancy, not helped by the Soviets' rejecting it out of hand a few weeks later.

As this debate raged for the next few months, with other solutions being floated by both the USA and the Soviets, Khrushchev himself was orchestrating a completely different and more dangerous plan. Kennedy had come to the Vienna Summit in 1961 to meet with Khrushchev for the first time in the shadow of problems in Cuba and his calamitous decision to green-light the Bay of Pigs invasion. The failure of the CIA-backed operation to overthrow the Communist regime of Fidel Castro had haunted Kennedy, placing him in a weak position with the Russians, which arguably had brought about the Berlin crisis a few months later. The Allies had not reacted to the Berlin Wall going up or resisted the Soviets' allowing the East Germans to take control of their own borders within the city, but the Russians still coveted a military-free West Berlin, thus taking away the threat deep within their borders.

Now Khrushchev formulated a plan to boost Communism abroad, as well as shift the balance of power in Soviet nuclear capabilities against the United States and NATO. The Americans had placed their Jupiter ballistic missile system in Italy and Turkey, within easy striking distance of Soviet targets. Despite the boasts of their leader, the Soviets had at best a mere seventy-plus intercontinental ballistic missiles (ICBMs), of which only twenty had the capacity to reach North America from inside

Soviet territory. The Americans, on the other hand, were confident of their "first strike" capability, with more than 180 ICBMs. The Russians knew they were outgunned. At the same time, the USA's desire to crush Castro's regime was ongoing and constantly being updated. The Bay of Pigs had failed spectacularly, but the Americans launched an embargo of Cuba that February, as part of a timetable of economic pressure on Castro that analysis dictated would ultimately result in his overthrow that autumn. The Russians now decided in July to support the Cubans as part of a grand strategy to win more concessions in Berlin and redraw the missile imbalance, harking back to Khrushchev's assessment of Kennedy as a man who would bark but ultimately not bite at this Soviet initiative. It was a calculated risk.

Under the disguise of an agricultural delegation, Soviet missile specialists traveled to Cuba to finalize the plan and prepare the way for the installation of short-range nuclear weapons, agreed to by Castro, who was won over to support the overall socialist strategy and wanted to also protect his country from the Americans. Under the utmost secrecy and deception, Operation Anadyr commenced in July, as the Soviets transported thousands of workers to Cuba under the leadership of Sergei Biryuzov, head of the Soviet Rocket Forces, to install R-12 medium-range ballistic missile systems capable of striking civilian and military targets throughout the United States. Despite assurances they were simply supplying conventional weapons as part of a long-term agreement with the Cubans, and with varied and numerous diplomatic and press announcements, by October 16, Kennedy had been shown proof of the missile sites via photographs taken by high-altitude U-2 spy planes.

Over the following thirteen days, the world held its breath as the Americans and Soviets went back and forth with claim and counterclaim while Kennedy's administration evaluated the cost of air strikes, an invasion, or a naval blockade of Cuba. How strong a response should he make? On the evening of October 22, the president spoke to the American people to say he had ordered a naval blockade, placing all US forces around the globe on DEFCON 3. As the days progressed, international pressure mounted—by October 25, US forces were set at DEFCON 2, with B-52 bombers in the air 24/7, 145 ICBMs ready to launch, and an invasion force on standby. The Americans, mindful of Pearl Harbor in 1941, refused to countenance a surprise air attack. As Russian ships sailed toward Cuban waters and the US Navy prepared to repel them, secret negotiations—as had been seen in October 1961 with the tank standoff at Checkpoint Charlie—had been opened by Khrushchev and Kennedy via back channels. In return for the Soviets' removing the missiles, the United States would issue a statement that it would not invade Cuba. This would evolve within a day to the Soviets' demanding the removal of the Jupiter missile sites from both Italy and Turkey—still as the container ships steamed toward Cuba, and the Americans prepared for invasion.

Both leaders were aware that the cost of a thermonuclear exchange would be at least a third of mankind being killed, devastating both countries and all of Europe and parts of China. A radio broadcast by Khrushchev on October 28, after much backroom wrangling via third parties representing each government, finally brought the crisis to a close. By November, the missiles had been dismantled and were being shipped back to the Soviet Union. The United States had shown its strength of will, and the Soviets had succeeded in a certain level of brinkmanship in reducing the threat of a missile strike to their borders.

The world rejoiced, but as Kennedy confided to Presidents Eisenhower and Truman in private phone calls, he fully expected the Soviets to now focus more on the Berlin question and push for more concessions. However, the balance of power was shifting in his favor because of how the Soviet leadership now perceived him. Khrushchev for one had been shocked at the display of strength shown by Kennedy during the Cuban crisis, having been convinced he had the man's measure. The American president's European allies were now resolutely behind him, with De Gaulle, Adenauer, and British prime minister Harold Macmillan all congratulating Kennedy on his handling of the Soviets. Some critics, however, believed the situation would never have arisen if Kennedy had shown more intolerance of Communist aggression in the first place—specifically by not allowing the division of Berlin.

Some good had come out of the crisis for both sides. Kennedy pushed for high-level talks to commence to negotiate a ban on nuclear testing and potentially for the Russians to bring an aggressive China to the table, too. It was agreed that a "hotline" would be set up between the Kremlin and the White House to ensure future communication was speedy and clear, to avoid another calamitous scenario. However, the question of what to do with Berlin remained, and it was now decided Kennedy needed to shore up his European allies if a test ban treaty was to succeed. He would undertake his first presidential tour of Europe to meet his NATO allies in Britain, Italy, and West Germany. He would also go to Berlin.

The trip to West Berlin was scheduled for June 26, within the itinerary of the president's ten-day trip. The eight-hour visit would live in the minds of Berliners for decades to come as the glamour, excitement, and hope that encapsulated the Kennedy presidency lived up to its legend. Air Force One landed at Tegel Airport in the French Sector, delivering the American president, accompanied by Secretary of State Rusk, mayor of West Berlin Willy Brandt, and chancellor of the FRG Konrad Adenauer. Thousands were crowding the tarmac, held back by a phalanx of police officers as Kennedy's security detail eyed the scene with concern. The president paused to give a few positive words to the waiting press, expressed his delight at being in the city, and reaffirmed the Allies' commitment, which, he said, was "written in rock." He then got into the presidential limousine, bedecked with pennants of both the United States and the Federal Republic of Germany. Brandt, Adenauer, and Rusk joined him to stand in the back of the vehicle, and with an enormous vanguard of police outriders they set off toward town, waving to the one million Berliners who came out to see the US president. The level of adulation that greeted Kennedy's motorcade shocked all who witnessed it, with the president confiding to his military aide, General Godfrey T. McHugh, "If I told them to go tear down the Berlin Wall, they would do it." The *New York Times* reported, "Along the route from Tegel airport to the United States mission headquarters in the southwest corner of Berlin, waving, cheering crowds lined every foot of the way. . . . The crowds must have nearly equaled the population of the city, but many persons waved once and then sped ahead to greet Mr. Kennedy again."

For many Berliners and American personnel in the city like Adolf Knackstedt, the appearance of the commander in chief was a much-welcomed shot in the arm. "The more the East Germans improved their fortifications along the sector and zonal borders," Knackstedt said, "the more the West Berliners lost faith in America's promises made to defend Berlin, even though Vice President Johnson and Robert Kennedy had visited the city and passed on greetings and promises made by the president. These visits were appreciated, but the Berliners needed more. They needed assurances to be given directly by the leader of the free world, and those only could come from President Kennedy."

Kennedy's schedule took him first to Checkpoint Charlie, where he walked past the border control hut as crowds ten deep cheered him on and an entourage of military and civilian personnel followed in his wake, including General Clay. Kennedy then stood on the observation platform constructed especially for his visit to view the East German border, perhaps imagining what it must have been like for the American tankers as they faced Soviet T-54s eighteen months earlier. Whatever he thought, he kept it to himself, but it was clear to all who observed him how affected he was by the reception he received all along the route, and also by the resilience of the city's people on display—the smiling faces, the children on the shoulders of their parents, the wave of feeling that surrounded him at every turn.

From Checkpoint Charlie, the motorcade moved on to the Brandenburg Gate, where Kennedy now took in the spectacle of the wall for the first time—trying to catch a view of the East German side despite the red banners the Communists had draped through the gate's Doric columns to prevent this. Discussing and debating what to do after August 13, 1961, in the safety of the White House was one thing, but now he could see the monstrosity for what it was, and the human toll it had already exacted. Was it at this moment he decided to amend the speech that had been prepared weeks before in Washington? Possibly, for it stirred in him a desire to confront what the barrier stood for and pledge support to the people who were forced to endure it.

The motorcade drove on to Schöneberg City Hall, where JFK was to give the first of his two speeches that day. It would go down in Cold War history as one of the great presidential speeches, much copied by others but never bettered. The crowd there to receive him was once again enormous. Well over three hundred thousand people jammed into what was a medium-sized square. Many of them had camped out the night before on mattresses in order to obtain the best view, with those at the front opening their umbrellas to shade them from the hot sun now beating down. Kennedy and other dignitaries stood on a grand platform, approximately twenty feet above the crowd, draped in a giant Stars and Stripes flag and flanked by the smaller flag of West Germany and the emblem of the city itself—the black bear. As he smiled and waved to the crowd, Kennedy felt the expectation and marveled at the scale of the event and what his visit meant to the city. Sections of the prerehearsed speech that would not offend the Soviets in their own backyard were now quickly replaced with his desire to speak from the heart instead:

> There are many people in the world who really don't understand, or say they don't, what is the great issue between the free world and the Communist world. Let them come to Berlin. There are some who say that Communism is the wave of the future. Let them come to Berlin. And there are some who say in Europe and elsewhere we can work with the Communists. Let them come to Berlin . . . !

The crowd roared their approval as the atmosphere cranked up to a frenzy—as if Elvis Presley were in town. Bookseller Margit Hosseini experienced excitement and terror in equal measure. "It was so scary. My bookshop I worked in was in Rheinstraße, where the Americans were based, and was near to the Schöneberg Town Hall. All the shops were closed as we all walked up to the square. It wasn't very far. We went fairly early, but still it was already really crowded. I was standing with my colleagues when Kennedy stepped up to speak, and then there was a human wave as thousands of people moved forward to shout, because all of the West Berliners were so anxious to hear his words. I lost my feet and was suddenly vertical, carried by these people and in such a frantic state. I was fighting, biting, scratching to get back down again onto the ground, and I managed to fight my way out to one of the side streets. I was shaking, but it was an experience I will never, ever forget."

A young Michael Howard, twenty-one and straight out of Cambridge University, who would go on to be leader of the Conservative Party in Britain in the 1990s, was in the city for a week attending a conference as a member of what was called *Königswinter*—an annual get-together of the Anglo-German Association, which linked people in politics and business from the two countries. "I was in the audience, standing by *Rathaus* Schöneberg looking at the small figures in the distance on the podium. I didn't feel frightened at the size of the crowd. I thought it was really inspiring. I was quite a long way from Kennedy . . . but there, in the distance, was this slim young man on whose shoulders the future of the Western world rested—the future of the world rested."

Kennedy had been practicing a specific line he hoped to use depending on how his words were received, enlisting the help of RIAS head Robert Lochner, who himself had witnessed the Wall being erected in August 1961. Now, swept along by the crowd before him and glancing at his index card where he had scribbled the correct phonetic pronunciation he desired, the president uttered his famous words:

All free men, wherever they may live, are citizens of Berlin, and there-fore, as a free man, I take pride in the words, "*Ich bin ein Berliner.*"

The explosion of noise was deafening as sections of the crowd rushed toward the stage. Kennedy was on a roll and carried on in the same vein, decrying the wall and Communism, and going so far as to imagine what a reunified Germany within a peaceful European continent could look like. He then turned to gesture toward Lucius D. Clay:

I am proud . . . to come here in the company of my fellow American, General Clay, who has been in this city during its great moments of crisis and will come again if ever needed.

Clay strode to the front of the stage to stand alongside his commander in chief, the man whom he had openly questioned whether he had the stomach for the fight against the Soviets. With huge smiles, both men raised their hands to wave at the vast, ecstatic audience. The Berliners gave Clay an even bigger ovation.

Law student Dietrich Weitz had grown up in the Soviet-occupied zone. His father was an academic, and thus the son was deemed unreliable to be admitted to secondary school. Taking his future in his own hands, he moved to Berlin and enrolled in a school in the Steglitz district with the ambition of earning a diploma that would get him into a university. "We felt that his visit was long overdue," Weitz said, "two years after the Wall went up. . . . But Kennedy gave us hope in the end—and he gave us courage: the courage to keep going, the courage to endure our fate as a locked-in city. '*Ich bin ein Berliner*,' he said that day, and we knew what he meant: 'I'm one of you!' " The American leader admitted to Rusk that the moment had gotten to him as they continued on to the next destination, the Free University of Berlin in Dahlem, where he would give a second speech.

Schoolgirl Eva Quistorp was fortunately on a school trip from her home in the Lower Rhine when Kennedy arrived at the university campus. "In our youth hostel we were listening to the radio and were all very excited," she said, "when we learned that the president of the United States was in the city." President Kennedy's limousine came to a stop at the front entrance to the Henry Ford Building, where he was to give his speech. "I was completely spellbound when I saw what a handsome, elegant young man got out of the car. We weren't used to that among German politicians. Kennedy came right up close to us and smiled at me, but I didn't dare to stretch out my hand. As the daughter of a pastor whose family had resisted the Nazis, I had been taught not to admire stars or those in power. At that time I was also a little shy. Since I was so close to him, when he smiled at me, I followed President Kennedy's speech in somewhat of a trance. On that lovely summer day, everything seemed so light and cosmopolitan. It seemed to be the beginning of a new era, after the Holocaust and World War Two, which had ended just eighteen years previously."

The second speech, albeit in an academic hall, surrounded by the great and the good of the city, was more considered and tempered to the Soviets, with Kennedy stating reconciliation might be possible down the line with a "people or system, providing they choose their own destiny without interfering with the free choice of others." Wolfgang Göbel, who had escaped East Berlin before the Wall went up and had been a guest of the Stasi prison in Hohenschönhausen, said, "I experienced both of Kennedy's speeches. His speech in front of the students of the university was a completely different one than the one he delivered to the vast crowd at *Rathaus* Schöneberg. Firstly, he hinted at the policy Willy Brandt wished to pursue, what would become *Ostpolitik* ["East Policy"]. He hinted that he agreed with talking to the Russians despite all difficulties, that talks are more important than anything else. Cuba was just one year ago, and that the relationship between America and the Soviet Union has to become a completely different one. In my view, this speech at the University was more or less the breakthrough Brandt took forward to create relations with the GDR."

Again, Kennedy's words met with riotous approval. It was a momentous occasion, and one the president looked back on fondly. After the motorcade returned him to Tegel Airport, Kennedy informed the waiting press (and crowd) that he would leave a letter for his successor in the White House, which would say, "To be opened at a time of some discouragement." In it, the note would read, "Go to Germany." On the plane taking him to his next stop in Dublin, Kennedy further confided to his speechwriter Ted Sorensen, "We'll never have another day like this one as long as we live."

Khrushchev and Ulbricht attempted to save face by holding their own high-profile meeting in East Berlin a few days later, and uniquely, Michael Howard, having witnessed Kennedy's historic speech at the *Rathaus* Schönberg, now watched the Communist response. "I went over with a couple of my colleagues to the East to listen to Nikita Khrushchev speak in East Berlin. He turned up with Walter Ulbricht in an open car. It was a very heavy day—quite an ominous portent. And there were quite big crowds, which had fairly obviously been told to come along. And Khrushchev and Ulbricht spoke, and then they drove away in their open-topped limousine. So my colleagues and I—it was just one or two of us—walked back. And I'll never forget it, because it was very dramatic. As we walked down *Unter den Linden*, the skies opened, and there was the most fantastic downpour. And the flags, the red flags, fell down from their mountings, and the *Volkspolizei* scurried into the street to pick them up. *Unter den Linden* is a very—or was then—a very sandy street. And the sand whipped into our faces. And by the time we got back to Checkpoint Charlie at Friedrichstraße, we were absolutely drenched. But anyway, we made our way back to West Berlin."

Although the test ban treaty made some progress at the negotiation table, within five months Kennedy was assassinated in Dallas, and by October 1964, Khrushchev himself had been ousted by conspirators within the Soviet Central Committee. Too many failures at home and abroad, as well as the ambition of his successor, Leonid Brezhnev, forced him into retirement, stripping him of his dacha and awarding him a desultory pension of four hundred rubles per month. Suffering depression and on prescription drugs, he became a "nonperson" in Soviet history and would waste away until his death in 1971. The country under Brezhnev would take a harder line going into the 1970s.

By this time, Willy Brandt—the Wall's fiercest critic, who had become the chairman of the SPD (Social Democratic Party of Germany) in 1964, was now his country's foreign minister under the chancellorship of Konrad Adenauer's successor at the CDU (Christian Democratic Union of Germany), Ludwig Erhard. In 1969, Brandt would win the election to become chancellor himself of the FRG. As leader of the country, Brandt now pushed through a policy of *Neue Ostpolitik* ("New Eastern Policy")—a rapprochement toward the GDR, as well as a closer relationship with the Soviet Union and its satellite states Poland, Czechoslovakia, and Hungary. While signaling the official end of the Second World War and admitting that reunification of the whole of Germany was on ice, *Neue Ostpolitik* also opened up possibilities for expanded visiting rights of West Germans into the GDR. For a man who had seen close up in 1961 the heartache of families separated by the

Wall, Brandt knew this would bring some relief to tens of thousands of West Germans. Politically, while many of his opponents saw this move as selling out to tyranny with Berlin still divided, geopolitically it did succeed in easing tension throughout Europe and strengthening diplomatic relations between the two Germanys.

In Berlin, the Wall and the intra-German border itself evolved into a yet more brutal edifice beginning in 1965. This "third-generation" barrier was constructed of vertical concrete posts, or steel I-beams set in concrete, with precast concrete slabs, twenty-five centimeters (ten inches) thick and measuring one meter (about three feet) high by three meters (ten feet) in width. Like giant dominoes, they were stacked one on top of the other in batches of four or five to create what we would now think of as a vertical climbing wall. To prevent any chance of an escapee gaining a handhold, should they succeed in climbing this barrier, a reinforced sewer pipe ran the length of the Wall's top. All other security measures were reinforced, too.

The original Four Powers that had occupied Germany and Berlin in 1945, together with the governments of the Federal Republic of Germany and the German Democratic Republic, signed a treaty that now paved the way for the United States to officially recognize the sovereignty of the GDR, but also for the East Germans and Soviets to recognize the rights of the Allied garrisons to remain in West Berlin. The city itself was now undisputedly linked culturally, politically, and economically to the FRG, with its access routes to the west honored, although as some in the White House feared, this situation could change at any time. In whatever way it was received, the treaty worked on many levels. The one thing the treaty couldn't alter was that the Wall was still in place. As one American reporter based in Berlin concluded, "Even the most grotesque situation becomes normal if you live with it long enough."

PART III

THE INTELLIGENCE WAR

Their power and monitoring may have been all encompassing, but East Berliners' humor still came to the fore if they encountered what they believed to be Stasi surveillance in their midst.

"Espionage generates its own rules."

—L. Garthoff, *A Journey through the Cold War*

CHAPTER NINE

The Secret Army

As the Cold War hardened in the 1960s and '70s, the existence of the Berlin Wall became an accepted geopolitical fact. And life carried on, on either side, for Berlin's residents and the Allied soldiers stationed there. Meanwhile, through Hollywood films and bestselling spy novels, the public came to be both fascinated and intrigued by how Berlin became a city of spies. On either side of the Wall, Berlin and its surrounding area was now a huge militarized camp, as the Allies monitored the threat posed by the Warsaw Pact forces that surrounded them. The fear of invasion and their destruction if the Communists invaded Western Europe was a very real one—the city expected to fall quickly. If hostilities erupted, then they were the trip wire that would alert NATO. However, there were other top-secret "assets" in place, known to only a few senior American commanders. The US Army had installed an elite team of Green Berets who would act as sleepers, waiting for the moment when they would go into action. In effect they were willing participants on a suicide mission, that of attempting to stall a Warsaw Pact juggernaut heading westward. They were trained to create mayhem, target key locations for demolition, and, if possible, eliminate key enemy personnel. They were the best the US Army could train and make ready for World War Three, and their life expectancy was figured at just seventy-two hours. They were the cream of Special Forces. They were Detachment A.

Special Forces were created, or re-created, in the footsteps of the Office of Strategic Services (OSS) from World War Two, but that was an elite infantry unit using conventional tactics and armed with light weapons—as the public would see when watching the 1962 movie *The Longest Day*, in which a US Ranger unit storms the cliffs at Pointe du Hoc. The antecedents of what we now see today derived from the OSS after the war and would evolve into the Central Intelligence Agency (the CIA). Founded by Colonel William "Wild Bill" Donovan in 1941 and copying the principals of British Special Operations Executive (SOE) units, the OSS operated deep behind enemy lines in the European, Balkan, and Pacific Theaters of war. Postwar, the OSS, along with other elite units such as the Rangers and Merrill's Marauders, were disbanded, as the Pentagon now believed that conventional warfare—mechanized troops and armor, supported by massive airpower from land and sea—would be the most successful method of conducting a successful campaign.

Chief Warrant Officer James Stejskal (now a historian and the author of *Special Forces Berlin*), was a veteran of two tours in Berlin in the late 1960s and early 1970s, and recalled the skepticism of many American military planners about the formation of the Special Forces units. "The military was really focused on the grand fight, the big battle, conventional warfare, and not only that, the threat of a nuclear war. So, the infighting for resources within the Pentagon was really intense, with a lot of conventional military officers believing that finance going into Special Forces would detract from their main goal. Why should they siphon off resources to a specialized unit and the army not benefit from it?"

The coming of the Cold War had radically changed US strategic thinking by 1947, forcing military leaders to plan to combat the Soviets in unconventional warfare across the globe. This concern intensified with the start of the Korean War in June 1950 and accelerated army plans to recruit and build up new units with Special Forces capabilities, to mirror the "behind the lines" skills their OSS forefathers had achieved. They would comprise fifteen-man teams (later reduced to twelve per unit) with six such teams to a company, with three companies forming a battalion. As the US Army now drew it, a Special Forces group could therefore in theory muster three such battalions. Each twelve-man team would be led by a captain supported by a lieutenant and ten NCOs—all twelve men would be proficient in light and heavy weapons, communications, combat medicine, intelligence operations, and demolition. They could operate as a complete unit or break up into smaller units to work independently behind enemy lines and train local guerrilla groups.

In 1952, Ranger battalions were to be deactivated and chosen personnel reallocated to three new battalions, thus creating the first Special Forces regiment, under the direct command of the US Army, not the CIA. Infiltration of Eastern European countries was the established goal, and the speedy passing of the Lodge-Philbin Act of June 1950 allowed the US Army to recruit foreign nationals into its Special Forces who would easily assimilate into this theater of operations. At least 50 percent of the regiment would consist of Eastern European émigrés; if they served five years and had an honorable discharge, then they would win US citizenship.

The 10th Special Forces Group came into being in May 1952 and was based at Fort Bragg, North Carolina. Recruitment proved difficult in those early months, as they faced a backlash from regular commanders anxious to retain their best men, but pressure from above enabled the new unit, by the spring of 1953, to number more than 1,700 fully trained men, each capable of parachuting into enemy territory and operating either on his own or as part of a small team. Their training mirrored the type practiced by the OSS and Allied Jedburgh teams of World War Two, until they were deemed ready to be activated for front-line service in the European Theater.

Events in the GDR by 1953 had made the Allies' need for Special Forces capability to infiltrate the ever-threatening Eastern Bloc a necessity. The Soviet response in putting down the East German uprising of 1953 had laid bare the inadequacy of Allied power in Berlin as they sought to influence events and to support any resistance to the Communist leadership of Walter Ulbricht. The events of that summer had caught commanders at SHAPE (Supreme Headquarters Allied Powers Europe) on the wrong foot with their suddenness and intensity, and had very nearly toppled the SED (Socialist Unity Party) until Soviet tanks crushed the rebel population, killing more than two hundred and imprisoning thousands.

To attempt to thwart the juggernaut of more than 170 Eastern Bloc divisions, NATO could muster 75 divisions, including heavy armor, backed by superior air and naval forces. But it was no illusion to think that even inflicting heavy losses would not prevent the Warsaw Pact from reaching the Pyrenees within the first month of fighting. As this steamroller advanced through Western Europe, nuclear weapons would be used, as would hidden units of the Soviets' own Special Forces (Spetsnaz), trained to "stay behind" and disrupt NATO's command structure and logistical pressure points in the vacuum a Soviet advance would leave in its wake.

By 1955 Allied commanders in Berlin had already agreed upon the strategy of not only attempting to slow down any Warsaw Pact invasion but also attempting a breakout themselves, back to the West. For this, they would need demolition teams as well as special units to undertake reconnaissance and sabotage work to create confusion and allow the Berlin garrison time to react. Six teams were deployed from their base at Bad Tölz in Bavaria and forward to Berlin in 1956, designated as Special Forces A teams (Detachment A or, more commonly, Det A) attached to the US Berlin Command, to range more than one hundred miles deep into Communist territory and ready to take the fight to the Soviet armed forces. It was the Allies' secret weapon should World War Three commence in Europe.

This top secret force, based in McNair Barracks, situated in the southwestern corner of Berlin, was initially commanded by Major Edward Maltese, previously a D-Day veteran with the 82nd Airborne who had later fought in Korea in 1951. His men traveled incognito, in small groups, as civilians on the US Army duty train from Helmstedt—Checkpoint Alpha—with their weapons and equipment being shipped to them in closed trucks via the Allied autobahn. All, except the officers, were volunteers, and only a dozen or so senior officers within the US Berlin Brigade command knew of their existence.

The average American serviceman in Berlin saw the men of this newly arrived unit as a "security platoon," and nothing more than that. They would move again several times before relocating to what would become their permanent home at Andrews Barracks, which in the Second World War had been the headquarters of the Führer's personnel body—*Leibstandarte* SS Adolf Hitler. The barracks was the home of the 297th Military Police, 298th Army Band, the Army Security Agency, and the 20th (later designated the 42nd) Combat Engineers Company, as well as the Berlin Brigade's motor pool, laundry services, a maintenance division, and a treatment plant with deep well pumps. With such huge facilities, Andrews Barracks offered more space to accommodate the full complement of Special Forces, as well as to ensure security was tight.

Purely on a cultural and language level, the unit must have been one of the most international and colorful of any formation based in the city, thanks to the benefits that the Lodge-Philbin Act had afforded them. Each team within Detachment A seemed to have its own culture based on ethnicity, with English, in this instance, not the universal language. Every member of Det A had the same five numbers at the start of his ID tag—10-8-12—which served as the title of the unit's own club that would come into being upon their arrival in Berlin. A veteran member of the unit who would rise from a team sergeant in the late 1960s to commanding Det A by 1978, Master Sergeant Bob Charest, celebrated this ethnic mix: "Many of these troops still had families behind the Iron Curtain. . . . In later years during the Cold War another breed of men was joining the Special Forces originating from all over Europe."

For the lower ranks, the experience of enlisting and then joining and being accepted by such a close-knit group of men as Det A was life-changing. Before boarding at Bremerhaven, they would have undergone a thorough check of their belongings to ensure they carried nothing that identified them as Special Forces. At the other end, they would then be met at the West Berlin station at Lichterfelde West by a senior NCO from the unit and driven in unmarked cars to Andrews Barracks to receive their security briefing and be introduced to their team. There were few regulations they had to observe, but there were punishments for those that they did infringe. Anyone who came to Det A intent on causing trouble or not toeing the line was quickly put on the train back out of the city. As Lieutenant Colonel Darrell W. Katz summarized, "In Berlin I think we had a higher standard of intolerance for some matters of misconduct. Our mission was important."

James Stejskal recalled how he felt coming into West Berlin for the first time. "It was slightly surreal. I obviously thought about what would happen if World War Three kicked off, but at the same time I was thrilled to be living in the most exciting city in the world." As he established himself in his unit and grew accustomed to the city, the routine became enjoyable. "Being able to walk around Berlin in civilian clothes, knowing who I was serving with, walking down the street with my buddies, all conversing in German, and no one suspecting anything. When we would be eating with the locals in a café or drinking in a bar, you would have this wonderful opportunity to be right in amongst ordinary Berlin life and be a part of what I have always called an existential struggle between two different philosophical entities. It was a very good experience."

Living in barracks and then getting out into the city and into the hinterland of the GDR itself while dressed in civilian attire wasn't as cumbersome as one might assume, according to Stejskal. "A lot of folks lived out in the city, with their wives, in what the locals called the 'American Ghetto.'" Where the unit was housed was within a very long building, part of which was sectioned off for Field Station Berlin, the area security agency, where they collected intelligence and signals. Detachment A inhabited the middle section where their main barracks were, and at the far end space was allocated for their headquarters and communication staff. In the basement below was an old shooting range left over from the war, which was used for training, and the unit had use of an Olympic-sized swimming pool for scuba training, too. Much as there was suspicion as to who Det A were and what they were actually doing there, they were left alone by other units based at Andrews. "We would usually be in civilian clothes," Stejskal recalled, "and anyone could see us coming and going, but we dressed in Western clothes and were allowed to have our hair at a suitable length in a non-military style, so we'd be amongst the civilians right away. Once you got away from the barracks you were just another person."

The teams would need to be proficient in navigating the city without the support of maps; one of the favorite tests was traveling to an out-of-the-way bar or café to rendezvous with a senior colleague. With only a small amount of currency, the soldier would need to arrive at various locations plotted around West Berlin to gain the next set of instructions in order to continue his journey and reach his ultimate destination. The teams also practiced their tradecraft in the city, performing "live drops" of documentation (direct contact with another member of the team), "dead drops" (leaving messages between members of the team without their actually coming into contact with one another), "primary meetings," "brush pasts," and "shadowing" of one another. Detecting enemy observation was a vital skill required by all members in the field, as the city was full of spies, never mind local criminals. The goal was to evolve street sense and an instinct for avoiding potential confrontations and arguments unless absolutely necessary. Despite this, like countless soldiers abroad, various members did find themselves in the odd street fight with an unsuspecting local down a dark Berlin side street, or sparring with members of another Allied unit or the West Berlin police.

Many Vietnam veterans rotated from their tours of duty to Europe in order to volunteer for Detachment A, one such being Lieutenant Darrell Katz, who had won the Silver Star for gallantry while under fire in Tien Phouc in September 1967. He described the structure of the unit. "We had some administrative people that were Special Forces–qualified, but all the operational personnel had to be Special Forces–qualified, and they had to have a secret clearance as well as be eligible for top-secret clearance. They couldn't have any prior serious disciplinary actions. There were six teams of eleven men, and the rest served as our headquarters staff—radio fitters, parachute riggers, etc. Each team was identical in the fact that it had one officer and ten enlisted men. Each man would be fluent in German and a weapons specialist, and trained in demolition, radio, first aid, scuba, and the like."

Det A teams were administered by areas of operations across Berlin as a whole—two teams per area, or a "task group." These were designated North, Central, and South. "North" would cover the French sector of West Berlin and into its hinterland; "Central" entailed the aforementioned "stay behind" role of conducting urban warfare on Soviet forces once West Berlin had fallen; and finally, "South" Task Group would jump off into East German territory from the American sector. All groups needed to be completely attuned to what was going on with regards to border control and where the best places to gain access to the GDR incognito were at any one time. "We [would] cross the Wall as small teams of two or four," recalled Katz, "but generally we would plan on operating alone and only come together for specific operations, and those would be worked out through short-range communication devices or through, if you were in the city, undercover contacts."

James Stejskal described the work that went into planning every mission. "Only our commanding officer and his intelligence staff were aware of the overall picture of where each task group was headed. Each mission was extremely straightforward in terms of answering three main questions: How essential was the target to the Warsaw Pact forces? Could it be reached without hazard and thus destroyed? And, how difficult would it be to be replaced or repaired?" These were the questions discussed, analyzed, and updated constantly.

Once each unit had achieved its principal target, they would then revert to their long-term goal of "staying behind" in enemy territory to cause as much distress and destruction as possible to hinder the enemy's movement and strength. To support and stir up local civilian resistance, Det A operatives had the ability to train and, if possible, arm them in order to carry out further operations. The men of Det A were fatalists about the success of their mission and their chances of surviving. James Stejskal spoke for many when he said, "Nobody really thought about it to a great extent. Essentially, we all thought we could get out and do the mission, which was to give NATO twenty-four to seventy-two hours of time, but after that, all bets were off on how long exactly we were going to be alive. The targets were not that far out of the city—the railway, some of the key headquarters. We thought we could get to those and do what we needed to do; well, at least give them as much grief as we possibly could and then go from there."

To support the units in the field, which would have little hope of resupply, arms caches, known as "mission support sites," were carefully established throughout the city, such as in the Grunewald Forest, in weatherproof containers filled with explosives, fuses, igniters, submachine guns, pistols, ammunition, radios, and medical gear. Their existence and their whereabouts were classified and all written documents detailing their exact location were kept in a locked safe at Andrews Barracks, though to bypass any concerns personnel had of losing this information, quite a few men maintained illegal caches of their own. Also secretly squirreled away in the Det A safe were a great number of gold coins, for the teams to use in case of an emergency with no access to the local currency. Known as the "Bluebird Fund," it could help pay for their survival if an invasion was looking likely.

The men of Det A were incognito for the first few years of their residence in West Berlin, but toward the middle of the 1960s, after the Wall had become bricks, cement, barbed wire, and machine guns, their presence—if not their faces—was very much recognized by the Soviet security and armed forces. Yet the East Germans posed the biggest danger. Colonel Darrell Katz confirmed, "We concluded that our biggest threat would be the Stasi and the ordinary police, because they were so effective. We did not believe that elite military forces would be used to target us but that all of us were well known, and that the Stasi and the police, the *Volkspolizei*, would be looking for us."

James Stejskal said, "They started to figure out that we were in the city in the early 1960s, as far as I can tell from the East German papers I've read, and by around 1968 they figured out that we were indeed Special Forces. From there the Stasi extrapolated what our mission would be basically from the open-source paperwork. Seemed a lot of their intelligence with regard to Detachment A looks like they just took existing documents and translated them into German and said, 'Okay this is what these guys are doing.'" It was far easier for the Stasi and the KGB to infiltrate West Berlin, due to the lack of security around the city's transportation networks that led to the east. During the Cold War, more than thirty thousand assets worked for the Stasi in the Federal Republic, and a great many of them filtered through to or via West Berlin, which as a military city was chock-full of targets the Warsaw Pact would require intelligence on. This would explain the all-pervading atmosphere of paranoia and heightened security in the city, as well as within the US Berlin Brigade and in the British and French garrisons, too.

Targets for the teams to identify within the city were easy enough, but getting out into Berlin's hinterland to locate, assess, and plan attacks on installations was more problematic. Even the CIA itself could not assist, as the East German security and counterespionage apparatus proved an extremely hard nut to crack, offering very little in terms of recruiting local agents to assist them. Recognized sites and installations of value could be identified from aerial reconnaissance, but they were limited due to the areas the Allied planes were permitted to fly. There was one loophole, as Stejskal detailed: "We were traveling into East Germany, both on our own to a small extent, but also alongside the US Military Liaison Mission [USMLM] as part of their people, which was the best way to get out and see sites we needed to see and to get familiar with the geography of the country. The East Germans or Soviets may have suspected, but it was sanctioned intelligence collection, which they did themselves in the west. They fully expected we were spying on them, and we were. But I think they were more concerned with our work around their bigger units. I don't think that they had grasped the idea that we were reconnoitering the targets that we endeavored to sabotage."

As the Cold War progressed, the role of Detachment A evolved from one of "stay behind" to actively becoming involved in counterterrorism as an "immediate response team" and developing further arms skills, including sniping or "close-quarter-battle techniques." By the 1970s, various terrorist organizations were roaming across Europe looking to bomb, rob, assassinate, and kidnap targets—whether they were the Black September Group, the Irish Republican Army (IRA), or, in West Germany's case, the Baader-Meinhof Group.

At the 1972 Munich Olympics, Black September claimed the lives of eleven Israelis it had captured in the athletes' village—killing the first two when the group stormed the compound. Without any specialized teams of snipers or commandos (West Germany's constitution forbade armed soldiers on its soil) there followed a botched security rescue operation organized by the West German police in which two policemen, all five kidnappers, and nine athletes were killed. The massacre and subsequent inquiry precipitated the West German authorities' setting up their own counterterrorism force—GSG-9—an elite tactical unit. Detachment

A members would share training with this new unit, with teams being regularly assigned to GSG-9 in the FRG. The Baader-Meinhof Group was operating across the Federal Republic in their terror campaign against capitalism, reaching their peak in 1977 with the murder of Hanns Martin Schleyer, a high-profile German industrialist and leading figure in the Christian Democratic Union, during what became known as the "German Autumn." American military authorities in Berlin were thus concerned with American planes coming into and out of the city being hijacked, and their protection fell into the unit's sphere of influence. Eventually this task was widened to cover all European flights. Pan Am would allow their aircraft to be used by the teams for training purposes, to practice tackling a suspected terrorist team on board.

In November 1979, the unit was brought into the planning of Operations Eagle Claw and Storm Cloud, which President Jimmy Carter had green-lighted to rescue the American hostages in the US embassy in Tehran. Due to malfunctioning helicopters, the mission was called off at the operation's desert landing site when a helicopter and a cargo plane collided, resulting in the death of eight servicemen. Detachment A members helped care for the wounded as the operation quickly withdrew back across the border. The unit itself and members of Detachment A who participated in the mission would be issued Letters of Commendation by the Joint Chiefs of Staff for the work they had done.

Although many of the personnel within Det A would continue serving in this new unit as it yet again evolved with the times, training another generation of Special Forces troops in urban warfare tradecraft, an unforeseen issue arose that would be terminal to their future. The unit was placed in the public spotlight when a *Newsweek* article exposed Detachment A's existence. Now in the public eye, it would be difficult to operate effectively in Berlin, as the Soviets could easily monitor their movements, and so the Pentagon ordered a review by Intelligence and Security Command (INSCOM), who ultimately made the decision to disband the unit and start fresh with a new one under another guise—the US Army Physical Security Support Element-Berlin (PSSE-B), officially acting as a military police unit based at Roosevelt Barracks, situated several miles from the original headquarters. Detachment A's deactivation began in May 1984, five years before the Berlin Wall would come down.

Such was the effect that their clandestine activities had on their Soviet counterparts in Berlin that the Russians believed the unit was actually eight hundred strong in number, when in reality it comprised no more than a hundred men at any one time. Their legacy is only now really coming to light as more veterans finally tell their stories. As Bob Charest attested of Detachment A's work, "This was a highly trained, one-of-a-kind unit. No one knew much about it during its existence. These were, in my opinion, the most highly trained men in Special Forces I have ever served with, and I spent almost twenty years in Special Forces."

CHAPTER TEN

Searching for a Grain of Truth

By the mid-1970s, both the Berlin Wall and the political leadership surrounding it had become dated, the former being far deadlier. By 1971 Walter Ulbricht had been eased out of his position and forced to resign on grounds of "ill health." The Soviets were frustrated by his refusal to follow their détente policy toward the West, including West Germany, and, faced with a flagging East German economy, they decided to act. With the backing of Soviet first secretary Leonid Brezhnev, Erich Honecker now took on the mantle of leadership, ruling with his small clique, including the minister of state security, Erich Mielke. Ulbricht retained the official title of head of state, but this new leadership was now closely aligned with Moscow. The ailing and somewhat bitter Ulbricht would suffer a stroke and pass away in August 1973. The Wall was his legacy, and by 1976 construction of a fourth-generation Wall began.

"*Grenzmauer* 75" would be state-of-the-art in design and construction, a world away from the prefab first version of 1961. The new iteration was speedily installed, comprising L-shaped reinforced concrete sections measuring 3.5 meters (twelve feet) in height and one meter (almost four feet) across, each section precision built to fit snugly alongside the next and topped with a horizontal steel bar that, when welded, provided a formidable barrier. A thirty-centimeter (one-foot)-diameter sewer pipe five centimeters (two inches) thick was cemented in place to act as the final deterrent. This new barrier ran a length of more than 106 kilometers (65 miles), at a cost of more than sixteen million Ostmarks. The "Death

Strip" was reinforced with more powerful searchlights, trip wires, automatic flares, and fields of spikes (pleasantly titled "Stalin's Grass"). New electronic sensors laced the fencing, too. It was quite impregnable, and escapes through it dropped significantly, to only single figures. With the intra-German border reinforced, too, the population was sealed in.

Honecker needed to maintain calm in the country and thus sought to improve living standards through "consumer socialism" with a greater focus on new housing, loosening controls on culture and the arts, and improving the consumer spending power of East Germans. In the background heavy industry was still a priority, with concerns about its environmental impact either fabricated for the world's press or ignored. East Germany may well have bragged it had the highest standard of living in the Eastern Bloc, but its industrial practices devastated parts of the country. And ominously, the official repression of dissent continued, as well as the use of lethal force to maintain the security of the border. Though the state had now been formally accepted by the United Nations and was improving relations with the West in general, the trade-off was to allow residence, and more freedom to cover stories, for the international press. A constant battle waged between those reporters willing to stray off the official trail set by the regime's censors trying to prevent them seeing for themselves what was going on in the country.

Mark Wood had studied languages at university, specializing in German, and had lived in both West and East Germany on student exchanges in the 1970s. Planning a career in the media, he began life in the editorial department of Reuters in London and happened to be in the right place at the right time when the call came for a replacement to take on the East German post in the late seventies. It was not a sought-after position, unless, like Mark, you had a fascination with what made the GDR tick and could rough it. "I loved my 'tour of duty' in East Berlin," he said. "I was a young, aspiring reporter who had bagged the Reuters East Berlin correspondent post—residing close to Checkpoint Charlie from 1978 to 1981 (Schönhauser Allee 27, right on the corner of Wörther Straße)—before moving up the career ladder and taking more senior roles within the company, first in Moscow and then at their West German headquarters in Bonn. I would be Reuters editor in chief by 1989, when the Wall finally fell. A few years later I was shown my Stasi file, which was comprised of twenty-eight volumes!"

Timothy Garton Ash was still in his teens when he first went into East Berlin in 1973, and would return as a journalist in the late 1970s. "There was the excitement of getting across the Wall," he recalled. "But of course, quite rapidly, one got much deeper into East German society, and then it became much more interesting." Garton Ash had a dual fascination with Germany, and with Berlin itself: how the country that had produced the genius of Goethe's writing could also descend into the moral horror of the Holocaust.

Hans-Ulrich "Uli" Jörges had now moved on from his unhappy childhood in his family's new home of Hessen, and had graduated with a degree in journalism, beginning his career in Bonn before moving in 1979 to work for Reuters in Berlin, where he would befriend both Englishmen. "By the time I managed to get to Berlin, it [the Wall] was in its stages of the final version being constructed that was so modern and cold, with the inner and outer walls, dog runs, guard towers, and trip wires, but seeing it close up didn't touch me. What did affect me was one could still see houses on the other side where the Wall was part of a house. The Wall was cutting it into two. In sections of the city it was like a graveyard, the place was devoid of life—and that did touch me deeply!"

Mark Wood, embedded in East Berlin, still has distinct memories of the city during that pivotal time. "In the seventies, my overall impression of the city was on the one hand utterly depressing, and on the other, a place of pure decrepit drabness. Walking through East Berlin, one was surrounded by unpainted, bullet-pockmarked buildings, all of which were in poor general repair. The winters were not only renowned for being unforgivably cold, but I also recall the all-pervading smell of briquette dust. The only heating fuel available to us East Berliners were the industrial brown coal briquettes, and I would use copious amounts (my Reuters salary helped) in the old pre–World War Two stove I had in my kitchen (one of only two in the whole building that worked). It still had old pieces of Soviet shrapnel in the tiles. Quite often, a balcony of a nearby neighbor within the block would simply fall off the building through decay and disrepair. At that point the authorities would round up a group of 'experts' to inspect one's own balcony, which usually involved all of them jumping up and down on it in unison to make sure it was 'safe.'

"East Berliners' clothing was drab; restaurant interiors, such as existed, were likewise drab. To those marooned in the austerity of the GDR with no access to the delights of the West, only one wine was available and then only sometimes, joyfully labeled 'Bull's Blood' and shipped in from their Communist ally, Hungary. There were regular shortages of everything but the staples, and what could be bought was invariably of poor quality. If an East German saw a queue, they would join it immediately, and only then check what might be on offer. It was no wonder that shopping and entertainment for the very few who had access, like me, was all done in the west."

For Uli Jörges, the thrill of finding the story was mixed with the energy of youth and living for the moment every day. "There is a special relationship between journalists that cuts across nationalities, language, and culture because you are all in it together, trying to get to the truth of a story amid tough times. We all worked and covered stories in East Germany for Reuters. For Mark and me, it was tricky to get information from the local SED [Socialist Unity Party] press officers, and it made it more fun going up against them to try to find the story we thought was there, that they were hiding."

For Wood, East Berlin was by its very nature in 1978, to a foreign correspondent's eyes, never dull. Granted, he didn't lead the cut-and-thrust life of one of his esteemed Reuters predecessors, the thriller writer Frederick Forsyth, who had not only lived in the same apartment Wood later had but claimed he had rather colorfully managed to circumnavigate his actual day job of reporting to instead enjoy various sexual and undercover escapades in Her Majesty's service with MI6. "My flat was the only one in the block with a working bathroom. Needless to say, that did not stop the Stasi from bugging it. In fact, I was later told by an ex-Stasi operative in the 1990s that the flat had fourteen listening devices placed in the bedroom alone, as well as my phone being tapped. Two doors down my corridor was a Stasi-owned room, which was the 'listening center' for the whole building—I never knew.

"Across the street, at living-room level, was a second Stasi position, taking photographs. Bizarrely, I still managed to effect good relations with my East German neighbors, even Kurt the military border guard, who every morning would greet me as he marched off down the street—in full uniform and jackboots—to stand sentry near the Brandenburg Gate. He was a local, but the majority, if not all, of the guards posted at Checkpoint Charlie were not of the city. They were recruited from Saxony, to the south, as the region was seen by the regime as ultra-loyal to the GDR. The problem was their guttural German dialect was almost impossible to understand if spoken quickly or, worse still, if they were barking out orders to unsuspecting tourists."

Wood and his friends knew their phones were tapped, and he was personally aware of being monitored. His daily routine would have him cross through Checkpoint Charlie into the western zone, mainly to coordinate coverage with Uli Jörges, or report on West Berlin stories, occassionally meet our guys in the military to trade gossip, or simply do some shopping. Uli Jörges was aware of the East German intelligence service's surveillance in West Berlin as well as East. "The Stasi obviously bugged my phone in our West Berlin Reuters office, and we knew they had mapped out our homes and wherever we stayed. My boss at the time would place his own hair follicles on his dresser in his bedroom to see if they would remove them when opening it when checking through his apartment—and they did! Very James Bond. You lived with secret services. We had the Reuters offices in West Berlin bugged not just by the Stasi but by the French, the Americans, and the British. I don't know whether the West Germans did it as well—probably."

The only way foreign correspondents could cover stories linked to the state's activities was via regular attendance at the GDR's chamber of governance—the "People's Chamber," or *Volkskammer*. Established in 1949, it was looked upon as the highest organ of state power. In reality, as in most of the member states of the Warsaw Pact, it was a talking shop, there to merely rubber-stamp every decision already decided upon by the politburo of the Socialist Unity Party. Since Ulbricht's SED had taken power, elections to the *Volkskammer* had been designed to ensure that a maximum number of SED candidates were returned to office. Reporting events, policy-making decisions, debates, and speeches in the chamber was one of the surest ways to develop narcolepsy. "After a week in the drabness and austerity of East Berlin, trekking through its bleak streets to follow up news stories and attend Soviet and GDR press junkets," recalled Wood, "to then have the unimpeached freedom to walk through into West Berlin with all its color, bustle, noise, good food, and freedom was a breath of fresh air. It was like taking a well-earned hot shower after a long day spent down in the coal mine—in my imagination, anyway."

Berlin's predicament and what might or might not happen to the Wall was an everyday conversation for anyone connected to reporting on the ground, but to some the future didn't seem so bleak. Uli Jörges recalled, "When I worked for Reuters's German service in Berlin from 1979 to 1982, I was shocked to find that I was the single West German journalist in the office who still believed that reunification would happen someday. First of all because I wanted it. Secondly, because the situation in Berlin simply did not appear tenable. In many arguments—whether in the office or in our local bar that the team would retreat to of a Friday evening—I would sum it up thus: 'Historically this cannot be the final model for Berlin. Border guards? Dogs? Minefields? And a wall surrounding a city of four million people? Forever?!' But saying that, I still could not imagine a peaceful revolution in the GDR—even in my lifetime. I thought bloodshed must occur for this to happen.

"I enjoyed living in Berlin, because I worked on both sides of the Wall and not only experienced the dance between Western capitalism and Eastern socialism but also got to examine firsthand fragments of German history from the war. *Hauptstadt* [the official name for East Berlin] was a living museum, and the people were walking exhibits. On a political level, when reporting, it was also extremely interesting to see almost every East German dissident I knew attending receptions in the Chinese embassy in East Berlin. The Chinese liked to play their mind games, not only with the Russians but also with the East Germans. Under Mao Zedong, they had always believed they carried on the torch of true revolution, which they always argued had died once Stalin had passed away. They saw Ulbricht as incompetent, and Khrushchev as a traitor to the cause. So their parties were a stick to poke fun at their weaknesses by displaying their opponents openly to ridicule them. I lapped it up!"

Despite the little everyday battles that foreign correspondents based in East Berlin such as Mark Wood would engage in with the various Stasi watchers on their tails, the serious side of reporting still had to be done. This could lead to trouble at times. "I was blockaded in my building for a few days by bored Stasi agents trying to intimidate me for my report on dissidents," Wood recalled, "but only once did I fear for my safety. This was when I was driving through country lanes to the north of the capital on my way to talk to the most illustrious dissident, Professor Robert Havemann, who was under house arrest. On this occasion an unmarked Stasi vehicle ran me off the road, and without further ado two men dragged me out of the car, threw me to the ground, ransacked the belongings in my boot [trunk], and threw my briefcase across the street. A few punches to the midriff and kicks to the legs as I lay prone were enough to scare the shit out of me. The warning to stay away from the area was taken with the grace intended and I soon sped back to the flat."

Mark's boss quickly disabused him of his desire to issue a formal complaint to the authorities. Despite détente with the USSR, taking the Stasi on head-to-head in the 1970s was never a good idea, no matter how embarrassed and bruised one might feel. He let the matter drop, but still had a yearning to pull the bull's tail. "Timothy Garton Ash was—and remains to this day—a close friend. He was a professional colleague of mine in Berlin and a fellow traveler in looking for the funny side of trying to do one's job in the face of GDR monitoring and paranoia. Knowing our phone was bugged, we would never cease to try and pull our watchers into a surreal world of subterfuge—all completely invented and preplanned as we talked on the phone."

One such ruse involved Wood claiming authorship of a comic-style Wild West story—*The Bloody Frontier*—that he had picked up at the bookshop in Tegel Airport on the way back from a trip out to London. Garton Ash called him one day—as arranged—to congratulate him on his newly published work, for which Wood thanked him and accepted his offer of a coffee at the local café they frequented, two blocks away from Checkpoint Charlie. "Tim traveled over from West Berlin for lunch, we chatted for a few hours, and then on my return to the apartment, as suspected, I noticed the said book was now gone from the shelf where I had left it. My Stasi file entry, I later discovered in the 1990s, flagged it as 'classic capitalist propaganda.' It was never returned."

Garton Ash also recalled another ruse he perfected on the Stasi monitors. "I wrote pieces for the *Spectator* under the pseudonym 'Edward Marston.' And Mark and I would have these conversations in which he'd say, 'Did you see that terrible piece by Edward Marston? The awful Cold Warrior,' etcetera. We had a bit of fun. There was a lot of variety." He would go on to record his story of time spent under Stasi surveillance in the international bestselling book *The File*, and recalled a more personal message from their watchers one evening over a late-night drink. "Mark and I would share many after-hours sessions of wine, discussion, and trying to bait our would-be Stasi followers. One infamous dinner went on into the early hours of the morning, and by 3 a.m. we were still going strong, though a little more uproariously. Mark's phone suddenly rang into life and he staggered across the room to pick it up. A humorless and tired voice barked down the line, 'Will you fucking go to bed!' It was the Stasi listener in the building who clearly wanted to get off to his bed and stop recording our conversation."

Although it was very exciting for both British journalists to be on the political front line, with its echoes of John le Carré, there was a serious message to get out, as Garton Ash summarizes: "Both of us had got deep enough into East German society to see just how serious and bad it was for the people who lived there."

In another book, *Und willst du nicht mein Bruder sein . . .* ("And if You Don't Want to Be My Brother . . . : The GDR Today"), he describes how ubiquitous the Stasi was, and the fear it engendered throughout society. "I was going to see a theatrical performance in Schwerin," he recalled, "because I happened to have some good friends who were actors. Just before we went into the bar afterward with the other actors, one of them said, 'Watch out—[the actor playing] Dr. Faust works in the Stasi.' . . . So Dr. Faust worked for the Stasi. It was ubiquitous." His opinion of anything changing for the country—certainly in the foreseeable future—mirrored what he was seeing with his own eyes. "We never saw the regime, or the Wall, falling; on the contrary—everyone was getting used to it being around for a long time. And the late 1970s and early 1980s, when I was writing my own analysis of East German life, it was quite a refreshing point of view. Unlike West German journalists who were closely monitored, and also many of whom were what I called 'anti-anti-Communists,' due to the predominant rhetoric being so anti-Communist [that] they were trying to put the other side. I just traveled around and talked to people. It gave me a pretty good sense of how nasty it was. So that, as you know, was what resulted in my being banned from the country."

For Mark Wood, traversing through Checkpoint Charlie was a routine of his working life that hardly ever changed. "The authorities kept the same guard rotations in place, so one could get to know individuals, but still not on a friendly basis. Everything was formal, and at times ridiculously officious. To them, the term 'East Berlin' was frowned upon." Wood would often see border guards set up minor confrontations with unsuspecting tourists from the West who found themselves on the wrong side of their humor. "Where are you going?" he would watch them ask. "East Berlin," the tourist would reply. "*Hauptstadt!*" the offended guard would then bark out. There this unfortunate holiday-maker would now stay until he was prepared to acknowledge *Hauptstadt*, and he would only then be sent on his way. "I witnessed this comic scene dozens of times," Wood recounted, "but never once did I see a GDR guard smiling. Not even when I stumbled through the checkpoint well after midnight—I had been covering a story in West Berlin and my pass allowed me to travel freely anytime between the zones—and came across the main guard hut throwing a party, with Abba blasting out of a cassette player. Dumbstruck for several seconds, I was brought back to reality by a hard prod to my shoulder from a leather-gloved finger and an equally hard stare from its owner—the checkpoint watch commander. Looking me up and down, oblivious to "The Name of the Game" serenading his comrades, he leaned in close to my ear and ominously whispered, 'You did not see this event!'"

The one and only time Wood would find himself on friendly terms with a guard at Checkpoint Charlie was in the most surreal of circumstances. November 1981 was a particularly bitter cold winter. It was snowing heavily when Wood drove up to Checkpoint Charlie on his way to pick up his girlfriend, who was flying into Tegel Airport in West Berlin. The entrance to the checkpoint was blocked by an East German ambulance, its lights flashing.

To his surprise, as well as dismay, the commanding officer of the watch—whom he had formally greeted hundreds of times over the three years of his residency in East Berlin—walked toward him, ushering Wood to come across into his well-lit and snug sentry office, which sat alongside the side of the spotlighted road one would drive along, through the various tank traps and barriers. "Slightly apprehensive, I walked in to be met with a nervous smile and the offer of a lit cigarette. 'Lousy weather, eh?' This was the classic East German put-down of West Berlin, as it was mutually understood by all of us that that was where the bad weather was coming from. 'We have a problem, sir, which I need your help with most urgently.'" The officer gestured out of the window to the road ahead of the sentry office to where the ambulance was parked, amid the various demarcation lines warning of imminent trouble if one went any farther. The officer continued that a heavily pregnant Turkish woman was in the midst of a particularly painful labor in the back of the ambulance. She had come across to *Hauptstadt* for a day's sightseeing, and suddenly her water had broken, and she was right now giving birth. However, the *Vopo* continued, his worried frown increasing, a major problem was occurring. "He lit yet another cigarette," Wood recalled, "as he outlined the impending disaster between large exhalations of cheap GDR tobacco. The ambulance medic had just told him the baby's head had turned and she couldn't deliver it, and with heavy bleeding she needed urgent medical attention. He did not want this problem to deal with, and could I—a fluent German speaker—help him out by taking her across the border? 'What about signing forms?' I inquired.

The usual time for having one's passport checked, stamped, checked again, and counterstamped always proceeded at a snail's pace, usually up to half an hour. I was assured this would all be taken care of, if I would only go right now!

"I agreed and in no time the ambulance drivers had carried the screaming woman to the back of my car. I was waved through and for the first time ever saw every single one of the many barriers and booms in Checkpoint Charlie lifted so that I could drive straight through the various chicanes toward West Berlin. No stopping, no passport to check, and our speed well above the ten kph the signs clearly stated that *all* vehicles must not exceed. Then the scenario became darkly surreal. . . . When you drove into West Belin there were normally no police or soldiers, no checks. This time a strong beam of light hit my windshield. Over the Tannoy system [loudspeaker], a very loud and agitated GI warned us (in both English and then as we got closer in more panicked German) to slow down. I ground to a halt at the US Army sentry box as an officer and a West Berlin policeman blocked the road and opened my door. The US Army officer gawped at the heavily pregnant woman screaming her head off. 'I am not the husband' was rather uselessly the first thing I uttered."

What followed was the exact opposite of their departure from the *Haupstadt*. Both officials marched Wood to their hut to undergo a speedy interrogation. "In hindsight, I couldn't blame them. I mean, who is usually allowed to race through Checkpoint Charlie by the GDR? Was this a Stasi operation? Were we people smugglers? It seemed like an hour, but possibly was only fifteen minutes of heated discussion and papers being waved in faces; threats of 'freedom of the press' and 'my girlfriend will kill me if I don't pick her up from Tegel!' I think we all did agree eventually that 'this woman needs to get to a hospital.' The next thing I knew a West Berlin police car with its siren blaring was leading me to the nearest city hospital. The baby, a healthy boy, was born soon after. And I still managed to pick my beloved up from Tegel, and had one of the most bizarre experiences of my life in East Berlin to tell her about."

Uli Jörges recalled further adventures with Wood in the early 1980s, at an open-air concert by the British band Barclay James Harvest on the Platz der Republik near the Wall. "It was a weekend toward the end of August 1980, when the Leipzig fair was on and every Western journalist would attend to get the usual government press release, and possibly attempt to ask an awkward question to Erich Honecker. Both Mark Wood and I remained in Berlin not only to see the band, but because we knew there would be young people from East Berlin desperate to see them play and hear Western music, and from that there may well be a good story." Both journalists watched the East German youth congregating on *Unter den Linden*, trying to listen to the music and aware they were surrounded by personnel from the FDJ (Free German Youth) brigades, the Stasi, and the local police. The mood became tense, and a standoff occurred. "Many were arrested and taken to awaiting lorries [trucks] parked in nearby streets. But no matter what the authorities tried to paint it as, we knew it was a full-blown riot against the regime and what the music meant to them—a threat!" Fortunately, as the only Western journalists witnessing the event, Jörges and Wood knew they had a scoop—and there was nothing the East German authorities could do to prevent their reporting it.

A group of Stasi officers came across to where they were standing watching the events unfolding and demanded to see identification. "We showed them our documents, which proved that Mark was British and I was a West German. We said, 'We are journalists, we are here working,' and we could go freely about our business. By this time, it was late in the evening, and the operation to grab rioters off the street was still in full swing. We noticed a young guy looking at us from a short distance away after the Stasi had left, and we immediately befriended him and asked him a few questions about the night's events. We were spotted by the same group of Stasi in conversation, and it was looking ominous that they'd now apprehend this young East Berliner, simply for talking to some Western journalists. We couldn't bear for them to take him away and instinctively grabbed his arm and walked him quickly to the local railway station—Ostbahnhof—by this time it was now 11 p.m. Mark and I paid for his ticket, wished him well, and watched him get onto the train heading out, but then our hearts sank as the Stasi operatives quickly got on the same carriage and took him into custody. We found out later he was given a short prison sentence."

Music aside, to Garton Ash, such was the atmosphere of oppressive and all-pervading fear that the regime didn't actually have to resort to violence often. It was a model, he concluded, familiar from Orwell's *1984*, in being "the perfect dictatorship that doesn't need to use physical violence." He firmly believed that only the will of Mikhail Gorbachev made it inevitable that the Berlin Wall would not survive past 1989. "All this nonsense about violence and East Germany being bankrupt and therefore had to collapse—if you had had sufficient political will and ruthlessness from the center, there was nothing inevitable about it at all."

For Uli Jörges, the job, the chase for the story, and the comradeship with his fellow journalists were the benefits that outweighed witnessing the grimness of the East German rule up close. "It was a bit of a cat-and-mouse game they played. Overall, for a young journalist, it was a wonderful life. I enjoyed it very much. I mean, it was a privilege to live on both sides of the Wall. It was incredible. You had all eras of history in one city."

All three men would recoil at what the GDR stood for, and the suffering it perpetuated on its people. For the seventeen million East German citizens penned up in their country, with their everyday lives monitored, assessed, manipulated, and directed by as concealed and malevolent a force as the Stasi, it was a form of daily humiliation. Unlike in the time of Stalin, people were not being rounded up, tortured, and shot. The system perfected in the GDR was by the end of the 1970s far subtler and unobtrusive—to the point that the Stasi's political prison of Hohenschönhausen in northeast Berlin was relatively unknown in the country. Unless you were unfortunate enough to be sent there. Like many foreign journalists covering the GDR, it was the reporter's task to convey the truth of what he saw and to make sense of it for his readers. The journalists told the world of the gray and grimness of the regime from the relative safety of the foreign press.

For those in the Allied military, however, tasked with the job of "officially" spying on the Warsaw Pact forces around Berlin's hinterland, the job offered excitement, certainly, but it could prove deadly, too.

CHAPTER ELEVEN

Catch Me If You Can!

For three little-known groups of servicemen, the newly constructed Berlin Wall added another layer of complication in an already challenging existence. They derived from each of the Allied powers—America, France, and Britain—the names of their respective units were the US Military Liaison Mission (USMLM), La Mission Militaire Francaise de Liaison (MMFL), and the British Commanders'-in-Chief Mission to the Soviet Forces in Germany (BRIXMIS). Each moniker was purposefully bland so it wouldn't linger in the public consciousness. They were, however, names that would ultimately stick in the craw of their Cold War enemies, East Germany and the Soviet Union.

Officially, the men in each unit were liaison officers. In reality they were sanctioned spies gathering intelligence behind the Iron Curtain in increasingly hazardous fashion as each became a curious anomaly in the battle between East and West. In practice for those involved it meant high-speed off-road car chases, furtive photography, ingenious concealment, sangfroid in the face of the enemy, and a looming risk of injury or death. It was a world of frequent diplomatic cocktail parties on the surface level, but beneath it these men operated at railway sidings or in wooded copses and on Soviet training areas where they could record the movements of men and machinery. They were the eyes on the ground for their national intelligence services, with far more primitive technology than exists today.

On many occasions they made prompt departures across plowed fields or down country tracks after being spotted by East German or

133

Soviet guards. If they were arrested and held, they would produce their "magic ticket," a pass that ensured a Soviet officer would arrive to authorize their release. Being in the USMLM, MMFL, or BRIXMIS had the glamour associated with espionage of the era, and the three units scored some intelligence triumphs at a time when the world seemed it might tip into a third global war at a moment's notice.

The spy era in Berlin and in East Germany itself was rooted in the closing chapter of the Second World War. Britain, the United States, France, and the Soviet Union were victorious allies, while Germany was the vanquished foe. Germany's unconditional surrender was sought by the Allies from 1943, and after that a series of agreements was made between the Allies about how Europe would be shaped when hostilities finally ceased. One of those protocols established that liaison organizations from fellow Allied countries could operate at will in occupied zones. At first they were known as field information agencies, technical, or FIATs. In the chaos that followed the fall of Germany, each nation's FIAT was concerned with repatriation, the pursuit of war criminals, the search for missing persons, and the distribution of reparations, among other duties. However, the Russian Sector didn't welcome personnel from other nations and tried to invoke tiresome bureaucracy to stifle investigations.

As a result, in 1946 British Lieutenant General Sir Brian Robertson reminded his Soviet counterpart, Colonel General Mikhail Sergeevich Malinin, of the contents of a protocol signed two years earlier that provided for an exchange of military liaison missions, and sought to deploy it again. Signed in Berlin on September 16, 1946, the Robertson-Malinin Agreement limited the size of the reciprocal missions to eleven officers assisted by no more than twenty staff. It declared: "Each mission will have similar travelers' facilities. Passes of an identical nature in Russian and English will be prepared."

The satellite office of the British mission was sited in Potsdam, while the equivalent Soviet one was in Bad Salzuflen in the North Rhine–Westphalia region. The agreement permitted a perhaps surprising amount of flexibility, stating: "Generally speaking, there will be freedom of travel and circulation for the members of missions in each zone with the exception of restricted areas, in which respect each Commander in Chief will notify the mission and act on a reciprocal basis." Furthermore, the information gleaned by the BRIXMIS teams could be submitted with relative ease to authorities at home. "Each mission will have their own wireless station for communication with its Commander in Chief. In each case facilities will be provided for Couriers and Despatch riders to pass freely from the Mission HQ to the HQ of their own Commander in Chief. These couriers will enjoy the same immunity as diplomatic couriers." Missions were also made responsible for accredited visitors of their own country.

The name given to the outfit was the British Commander's-in-Chief Mission to the Soviet Forces of Occupation in Germany, ultimately shortened to BRIXMIS. The Soviet unit was called the Soviet Military Mission (SOXMIS). Similar agreements were then signed by the US and France in April 1947. All Allies had their main headquarters in their individual sector of West Berlin, with an outpost in Potsdam, some forty kilometers (twenty-five miles) from the city and an important Soviet garrison town, that housed its mission staff.

British, American, and French teams weren't limited to Berlin and its environs, lying almost two hundred kilometers (125 miles) inside the border that divided Germany, but rather they operated across the territory that became the German Democratic Republic. They used specially marked cars that indicated they had a form of diplomatic protection, and light planes—equipped with cameras armed with long lenses and permitted to fly over East Germany within the twenty statute-mile radius of the Berlin Control Zone (BCZ)—were also at their disposal. On the road there were elaborate cat-and-mouse games, with each national team determined to collect essential information from their patrols and the deployed forces of East Germany and the Soviet military doggedly trying to stop them. They always attempted to remain unobserved, making split-second maneuvers to shake off their East German shadows. For their part, the Stasi "narks" that pursued them were patient and professional. And in some cases, they could be deadly in their reactions in these encounters, as we shall see further into this chapter.

Strained from the outset, relations between Britain and the Soviet

Union declined in the months following the agreements. Crucially, the Western Allies refused to acknowledge the existence of East Germany after it was established in 1949, and as a result USMLM, MMFL, and BRIXMIS persisted in only recognizing the authority of the Soviet military hierarchy to which they were accredited. Thus, frustrated law enforcement officers from East Germany could assert no authority. Allied staff almost always observed constraints put in place on maps by the Soviets, called "Permanently Restricted Areas." The Russians also gave notice of temporarily restricted areas, which usually indicated a major exercise was imminent. Teams generally observed the restriction but headed straight for the area to find out why it had been put in place. However, when stout East German signs were installed, declaring that the missions were barred, they were duly ignored or even removed by mission members. Such signs became valued souvenirs of an Allied observer's stint.

Berlin's immediate hinterland was home to more than 135,000 Soviet military men, more than 1,500 tanks and 2,500 armored vehicles, at least 40 combat aircraft, and 40 helicopters. These were spread across three hundred sites and storage facilities, and the Allies needed to ensure they had solid and accurate information on the movement and disposition of these units and what they were armed with—whether on the ground or in flights within the agreed airspace constraints of the BCZ.

It wasn't just East German police that took an interest in the Allied teams' activities. There was also the Stasi, other uniformed East German law enforcement officers (like forest guards and even railway guards), as well as the regular armies of East Germany (the National People's Army) and the Soviets. All would be goaded into different degrees of action against the mission teams, from intimidation to violent detention, despite the cloak of quasi-diplomatic protection provided by the Robertson-Malinin Agreement.

Amid the frustrations involved, the Soviet authorities repeatedly resisted East German pressure to scrap these agreements. The single official retribution that the Soviets could use against the British, American, and French missions was to declare individual mission members as "persona non grata," which effectively nullified their passes and meant they could no longer go on patrol, although some continued to serve behind the scenes. The measure was also used in retaliation if a Soviet mission member had been expelled from the Federal Republic of Germany.

In August 1961, SAS (British Special Air Service) veteran Lieutenant Colonel Ian Wellsted was a duty officer at the BRIXMIS villa in Potsdam on the night the construction of the Berlin Wall began. Like everyone else there, he was aware of Khrushchev's threat to occupy the whole of Berlin. It was initially thought to be the start of a big exercise, and it was only at daybreak that he realized equipment from three Soviet Army divisions appeared to be being deployed around the city. Immediately Wellsted went to West Berlin and reported what he'd seen. Then he realized that it was the building of a barricade rather than preparations for an invasion that he'd witnessed. He grasped that "everything we saw, we were meant to see so that the message was unequivocal." Wellsted, awarded the OBE (Officer of the Order of the British Empire) in the 1961 New Year's Honors list, believed the presence of BRIXMIS at that point might have helped to avert a Third World War.

The same day, an RAF team from BRIXMIS took to the skies in one of their two-man de Havilland Canada DHC-1 Chipmunk planes, surveying Soviet activity within the BCZ. Squadron Leader "Dickie" Dyer and Group Captain Gordon Young, as photographer and pilot, witnessed the autobahns around Berlin crammed with Soviet military traffic. After capturing the first pictures of the emerging crisis from the air, the pair agreed that the wall construction was an East German exercise with the Soviets determined to prevent any trouble on the ground that could escalate to an all-out conflict.

By the mid-sixties, when Colonel John Cormack was part of BRIXMIS, the atmosphere was radically different from that of its early days. "Both the Soviets and the East Germans could be aggressive," he recalled. "The East Germans were much more difficult because of the uncertainty of their status. The whole country was filled with people who were delighted to inform [the authorities] about our movements."

*   *   *

While the political atmosphere in Europe changed over the years, the nuts and bolts of the BRIXMIS mission remained the same (though the USMLM and MMFL missions would evolve over time), being led by an officer from the army with an air force officer as his deputy. Ranked below them were operations officers who planned tours for servicemen, giving consideration to requests for information received from their respective national intelligence agencies in addition to monitoring known military installations, railway lines, autobahns, and ranges.

Steve Harrison, who was with BRIXMIS between 1986 and 1988, told how men would find the deepest, darkest woods to park up for the night. "People used to mark on their maps areas that were suitable for sleeping where you were unlikely to be disturbed." Previously some mission teams had stayed in hotels, including the luxurious Hotel Elephant in Weimar. This practice was banned in the mid-sixties when one officer left camera rolls under his pillow. He was on a flight back to Britain the same day, in response to this catastrophic breach of security. However, when a British team returned some years later, after the ban was relaxed, they discovered that the hotel manager had kept the film cassettes in his safe, waiting to orchestrate their safe return.

Although winter temperatures were freezing, typically only the driver slept inside the car at night, although no one slept during daylight hours. The men kept a "Bag: Crewman Relief" (a piece of equipment used by RAF aircrews that had an ingenious arrangement of double skin and cork inside, so they didn't have to park to urinate). Along with a well-stocked first aid kit, they carried whiskey to foster camaraderie with Soviet officers.

The cars, with distinctive yellow plates bearing the mission's national flag and its title in Cyrillic script, enjoyed quasi–diplomatic immunity. So when they were stopped, occupants inevitably chose to remain inside until an authorized Soviet officer appeared on the scene, especially as the vehicle was often surrounded by either East German or Soviet soldiers wielding Kalashnikovs. While they operated with lists of surveillance sites, all tours were permitted to use their own initiative if they encountered unusual military movements on the road, leaving bases to take part in maneuvers—or an invasion. They might record the silhouette of a new tank or the tail fin of a plane, or measure the barrel of a hitherto unseen gun poking out from under a tarpaulin. It was deemed vital to know where missiles were sited. Departures and arrivals of men and machinery at barracks were of perpetual interest. The deployment of radar and how it evolved were crucial. For decades, every piece of Soviet armor carried a visible identifying number, which helped to identify its parent unit.

Information collected via photographs, film, serial numbers, and even drawings of equipment observed by the tour and given a secret classification was sent back to respective Allied top brass for analysis. Eventually, the estimated capabilities of Soviet military hardware were sent to domestic designers tasked with making equipment to counter any new threat. Covert work like this contained some surprising facets. It was known that Soviet bases were not provided with toilet paper and men often resorted to using communications sheets or pages torn from manuals. So all Allied intelligence teams were equipped with rubber gloves and plastic bags so they could trawl through waste-disposal areas looking for redeemable information.

Not all those posted to Allied missions were Russian-speakers, but there were always a number installed at the mission to act as interpreters when necessary. At first there was no training program to prepare new recruits. They were expected to learn on the job, using the benefit of experience gathered by others. One of their priorities was to learn the names and shapes of armaments that belonged to Warsaw Pact countries. Some limited training in the photographing of factories was introduced in the mid-fifties. The first bespoke BRIXMIS training course started in Britain in 1973. In total, forty-nine courses took place, which were extended to American and French servicemen in addition to those from Britain. It is worth noting that the challenge of managing the specialized and covert nature of these activities demanded that chiefs of missions have prior experience with special forces operations; as a result, the last three chiefs of BRIXMIS were all officers with considerable experience in unconventional operations.

*   *   *

In 1958, after British and American activity in Lebanon during the civil unrest there, an angry East German mob attacked and damaged the Potsdam premises. It was symptomatic of a growing hostility toward Britain by the Soviet authorities and their East German pawns. Although the level of danger faced by the men in the field heightened, there was no question of reducing Allied activity. Another lakeside villa, known as the "Mission House," was duly found in Seestraße Potsdam for the British mission. Domestic staff were handpicked by the Stasi and dutifully reported back any information they could glean. As far as the British were concerned, this was entirely to be expected and part of "the rules of the game." Sometimes misinformation was fed to the staff, not least to give them greater purpose and so enhance their job security. (In the same vein, the British fully expected the building to be extensively bugged, and the 1990 confessions of a former Stasi man confirmed their suspicions were correct.)

Outside, the building was guarded by East German police from a sentry box, observing traffic. In the near distance a Stasi officer was usually lurking, to further monitor what occurred at the Villa. It wasn't the only opportunity for "narks" to start tailing a car, as its first stop was usually the West Berlin headquarters. All cars had to leave Berlin through the Soviet checkpoint on the Glienicker Bridge, also used for spy exchanges, so their initial movements were not especially secret from the Soviets and their East German allies.

If tours broke down or were detained, the crews' first action was to demand that the local Soviet *Komendant* be called to the scene. He was responsible for the liaison with the local civil authorities and for all dealings with the Allied missions. When the *Komendant* turned up, he would take the men's passes away for inspection. If detained, the tour might be released at the scene or it might be escorted away out of sight of Soviet military activity. Those not equipped with the necessary language skills had to follow the *Komendant* back to his offices so an interpreter could be found. Rod Saar, who was detained five times in the seventies when he was part of BRIXMIS, told how the Soviet *Komendant* would throw accusations at the crew—who for their part would then produce a copy of the Robertson-Malinin Agreement that legitimized their actions.

"This charade could go on for hours. In rare cases it went on for several days," said Saar, who revealed a trick regularly used to escape custody. It involved an admission of taking photographs of churches, birds, or similar objects and producing the supposed film.

"You always had in your pocket a totally unused film that you exposed [to daylight] in front of him. It was a matter of surprise." The drill was not to admit to anything and not to sign anything. "Once you put a signature on a piece of paper, they had your signature. What they might choose to do with that thereafter you may not know." As another BRIXMIS operative stated, "One tour officer said to me anyone who does sign with his own name was a fool, and in order to get out of a sticky spot, he did sign 'Sir M. Mouse.'" They would only release you once they had permission from the Soviet External Relations Branch, or SERB. Afterward, there were two further issues to contend with involving the British hierarchy. "In my time, you would get some fairly stony faces if you had been detained," explained Saar. "It was seen as a black mark. This changed in later years, particularly when the chiefs came from a special forces background." A lack of understanding about how the tours operated prevailed further up the chain of command in the British military hierarchy and particularly in the Foreign Office, he said. Secondly, the job in hand had to be abandoned, with the Allied mission car being dispatched or even accompanied back to Potsdam.

Mostly the car—or cars—following Allied mission crews kept their distance. During big exercises or times of national crisis—like the downing of US pilot Gary Powers in a spy plane in 1960 or the Cuban crisis in 1962—the tailing was ostentatious and felt more like harassment. Seasoned Allied operators soon learned to recognize number plates linked to the Stasi, who generally drove nicer cars that weren't available to ordinary citizens. Normal state police officers had less robust vehicles like Trabants, which, if they tried to drive Allied cars off the road, came off second best.

Often vehicle skirmishes occurred when teams tried to infiltrate a military column as it crossed the country. The Allied mission cars might get hemmed in by large military trucks and were sometimes forced to break out by heading off across fields. However, real damage could be caused when heavy vehicles, like Soviet-made Ural trucks, were used to force cars from the road, and life-threatening incidents happened on a regular basis. Sometimes on a busy exercise during training, a near miss could occur every fifteen or twenty minutes. For Captain Peter Williams of BRIXMIS, his second tour of Berlin in the summer of 1982 would find him becoming—along with the new chief of BRIXMIS and his driver—the target of a Stasi assassination attempt while they undertook one of their official reconnaissance missions.

"A normal tour by car would usually cover at least several hundred miles of driving around specific areas of interest whilst we also attempted to lose our Stasi trackers," Williams recalled. "On this particular trip we believed we had done so. I was acting as the new chief's tour NCO and we were heading west toward the area of the Inner German Border between East and West Germany. I had been told to 'take the brigadier out, give him a feel for what we get up to, and bring him back in one piece!'"

As the tour vehicle came to the village of Athenstedt, situated just inside the inner east-west border, an official warning sign told them they were about to enter an area closed to Allied missions. As their car turned into the village, Williams was surprised to find they had unwittingly stumbled upon a National People's Army early warning radar site—which he didn't know existed. Quickly, he invited the brigadier to stow away his camera and for their driver to put his foot down in order to get past the radar site.

"The Opel Senator quickly sped past the main gate, just as a Czechoslovak-made Tatra-148 ten-ton truck roared out across our path, hitting our car broadside. The noise was incredible as the truck plowed into us as we braced ourselves for the deadly roll that I knew would certainly kill us. The side of the Opel caved in as it was violently shunted off the road and into the upcoming ditch." A quirk of fate then saved their lives. They hit a fruit tree, which kept the car from rolling and instead wedged the Opel against the truck, which now came to a standstill. Shocked and dazed, the two British officers climbed out of the wreckage to be met by a small band of heavily armed air force personnel and plainclothes Stasi agents.

"Once our pulses had started to subside, I turned to the brigadier and suggested that what we needed to do was demand that the *Komendant* be summoned to the scene, and that we also needed to do what British soldiers always do in a tight corner: have a cuppa! As a result the subsequent Stasi report on the successful ambush contains several photographs of us making cups of coffee."

The armor plating welded to the chassis of the Opel had saved them from being crushed to death. Williams and the brigadier answered very few questions and instead called in for assistance (and a Soviet official to lodge a complaint), which duly arrived sometime later in the evening light. The Opel was driven onto the BRIXMIS recovery trailer, and all three men jumped into the mission Mercedes Geländewagen towing vehicle sent out to them, bidding a sardonic farewell to their would-be assassins.

They had been extremely lucky. Many years later, once the Wall had come down and the Stasi files were opened, Williams read a report about the incident. "It confirmed my belief that this indeed had been a preplanned and high-level sanctioned ambush operation. I read communication signals from the local Stasi radar station to its agents at Athenstedt of our whereabouts and when we would reach the village. If only I had checked our office wall map for the route through Athenstedt before setting off, I would have noted that the road past the radar site bore a sign warning 'Suicide Alley'! In 2011 I would meet the Tatra truck driver whose ramming had been intended to kill us. He confirmed that those involved in the ramming received two weeks' extra paid leave for their work that day. If they had succeeded in our assassination, then it would have been six weeks extra leave and a thousand marks! One might see the humor in this exchange until one realizes that people were killed in this way."

In March 1984 a French warrant officer, *Adjudant-Chef* Philippe Mariotti, was killed when a Ural truck, which the Frenchman had attempted to swerve to avoid, driven by an East German struck his car head-on. The incident was planned; the truck driver was a member of the Stasi. A report on the tragic episode by BRIXMIS observed: "This action was a deliberate statement of intent to crack down." Saar believed that while some rammings were planned, many were not and occurred as a result of evolving tensions when BRIXMIS work was carried out.

The following year almost to the day, Major Arthur (Nick) Nicholson, an American mission member who had been a graduate of the British training course, was shot dead by a Soviet sentry at a training area, an incident that will be detailed in the next chapter. For the British, the most severely injured casualty of authorized intelligence gathering was Sergeant Bob Thomas, who was critically hurt following a collision with a Ural vehicle near an East German installation. He lay trapped inside the wreckage for an hour after the 1976 incident.

Collaboration among the Americans, French, and British was close, and among them they made sure all necessary areas of East Germany were covered on any given day. The Allied garrisons in West Berlin would monitor East Berlin itself. Operations officers from each mission met for weekly meetings. However, all three had different ways of operating. The Americans used two-man teams, for example, reflecting one effect of having fewer passes.

Close relationships also developed between Russian and British commanders, rooted in mutual respect and the copious consumption of whiskey at regular social events designed to smooth the passage of BRIXMIS in Potsdam. By the end of his stint as chief, Brigadier David Wilson said: "I learned a lot about diplomacy, and I learned a lot about East-West relations. I found the Russians fascinating. They were much more like us than we would pretend. You can translate an English joke into Russian and a Russian joke into English, and both would still be funny at the end.

"On one occasion . . . a Soviet naval officer wished to see the Plötzensee prison in the Western zone of Berlin. He was the son of a Soviet officer who had been executed by the Third Reich. I can still feel the extraordinarily numbing chill on escorting him into the prison museum and seeing a copy of the Führer's cordial formal invitation to guests to witness the execution, with refreshments to follow. BRIXMIS was the only possible mechanism for arranging such a liaison visit, and despite the poignancy of the occasion, it was much appreciated by SERB, as well as by the officer himself. This sort of thing helped to keep our current account with the Soviets well in credit, ready for future 'cashing' on a rainy day."

There were plenty of intelligence triumphs scored by BRIXMIS that helped military leaders assess more accurately what was occurring on the ground at the time. In 1955, the first T-54 tanks and AK-47 rifles were photographed. In 1962, surface-to-air guided missiles were first spotted. A few years later, the first nuclear weapons storage sites known in Germany were located. Prior to the Czech crisis in 1968, liaison missions together counted 65 ambulances, 62 fuel tankers, 192 medium tanks, 22 antiaircraft guns, and some 1,100 support vehicles heading south toward the border. When there was no sign of their return, British analysts knew there was a move to effectively occupy Czechoslovakia. BRIXMIS intelligence eventually led NATO to the conclusion that the Soviet threat had been exaggerated. The risk of nuclear war receded.

Nigel Dunkley of the Royal Scots Dragoon Guards would serve in Berlin three times—once as a lieutenant, once as a captain, and once as a major—and would find himself posted to Berlin at the back end of 1977, with the regiment's Berlin armored squadron. "My initial impression of Berlin was one of excitement. I was amazed how many bullet holes there still were, particularly in East Berlin. It was equally thrilling to be roaring around Berlin with fully bombed-up ammunition. Everything was live, and our training meant we had only fifteen minutes to get our first tanks out of the barracks, day or night, if hostilities began. The British Infantry Brigade (BIB) had a squadron of Chieftain tanks—'the dear old dinosaur on tracks,' as we used to call it, a powerful gun; we were very heavily armored, and everything was good, except for the engine, which was too weak. It wasn't even seven hundred horsepower. When you think that the Germans, before the end of the Second World War, were stipulating nothing less than one thousand horsepower in their tanks—ours were underpowered!" The British had fourteen Chieftains to defend the British sector of West Berlin, based at Smuts Barracks on Wilhelmstraße in Spandau.

Training hard for any eventuality, the squadron had one of several options in case of a Soviet invasion. One was to take a troop of tanks down to Gatow airfield and set up a defensive perimeter in order to secure the field for families flying out. The second was to go and defend the two bridges on the main road, the Heerstraße, near the Olympic stadium—the Stößensee and the Freybrücke—whilst engineers set charges to blow them before the Soviets could get their tanks across. "Another one," Dunkley recalled, "was to dash down as fast as we could to the Brandenburg Gate. That was my favorite. We made a lot of noise!" The Brandenburg Gate area was seen as a key position by the East German NVA (*Nationale Volksarmee*) to capture West Berlin. Once the British armor was on its way, the Stasi would monitor and time their journey, take registration numbers, and take photographs.

Dunkley's introduction to BRIXMIS came during a visit to East Berlin, via a friend from his regiment. "I saw his gray beret in the distance on a visit and I didn't know that he was there. It was all rather sort of semi-covert and quite exciting to me. I then got a bit of a briefing by him, but there were a lot of things that he couldn't tell me, obviously, within the constraints of the Official Secrets Act. But he let me know that what he was doing was actually quite an exciting job." Dunkley's friend invited him for dinner at his quarters. "I saw a mud-splattered, half-wrecked-looking Range Rover, with only one number on yellow plates, front and rear, with Cyrillic script written on it, which said: 'Commanders'-in-Chief Mission to the Soviet Forces in Germany.'" At dinner, Dunkley learned about BRIXMIS and the duties it performed. "In my duties as an officer in the Scots Dragoon Guards, I thoroughly enjoyed flag tours, which involved driving in a huge, glossy-painted Opel Admiral. We were dressed in smart 'No. 2' service dress uniform and had the freedom to pass through Checkpoint Charlie and into East Berlin at will. We would locate and photograph Soviet and NVA barracks, counting tanks, armored vehicles, etc. With particularly being an armored organization, an armored squadron, we were interested in the Karlshorst Soviet Army Independent Motor Rifle Brigade, situated in the district of Karlshorst in East Berlin. This kind of mission had me hooked, and I wanted to come back to Berlin. I was prepared to go off and spend nearly two years of my life in a classroom learning Russian and the tradecraft that intelligence work required and saying good-bye to conventional soldiering."

BRIXMIS had special equipment and training, and on the surface, lots of liaising. They had a dining club in Potsdam where Soviet and British officers gathered with their wives. But that was just a thin veneer. Their role was to do as much intelligence work as they could on both the Soviet Army and the NVA of the East German forces. BRIXMIS spent an awful lot of time pushing the boundaries of what was acceptable reconnaissance without taking too many risks of retaliation, their rule being "don't take undue risks if the gain is not worth it," especially if the relevant information had already been recorded by the Allies. "On the other hand," noted Dunkley matter-of-factly, "if it's something new that we haven't seen before—and of course, BRIXMIS personnel came from the army and RAF—then the risk that you take could be lethal, could be fatal, but might be worth the risk. It's up to you."

On their missions, the tour personnel had no commanding officer, with all decision-making at the sole discretion of the men in the vehicles. "You've got a highly trained observer in the front—we had some extremely competent NCOs—and warrant officers sitting in the front seat," Dunkley recalled. "They were calling the equipment as we saw it. And we were photographing it, sitting in the shadows in the back." The drivers were regarded as the most important members of the three-man teams for BRIXMIS. "There were air force drivers and there were RCT [Royal Corps of Transport] drivers who were absolutely outstanding. I would not be talking to you right now—and I'm not exaggerating when I say that—without the quick thinking and skill and ability of some of those drivers that we had."

The main vehicles were the Opel Senator, the Range Rover, and the Mercedes G-Wagon. The Senator was anything but standard-issue—armor-plated, with a 180-liter (about 50-gallon) fuel tank in the back—and had been converted to be fast, powerful, off-road, four-wheel drive, with a low profile and very quiet engine. The Range Rovers were quite slow and heavy and not reliable enough due to so much extra equipment and armor plating. The Mercedes was considered by many to be the top of the line, as Dunkley described: "We completely doctored them so that they had a sort of single dentist's chair in the back and a hatch on the top, and we removed the spare wheel and mounted it on the back door, so that it would look like a Soviet UAZ 469 jeep. The Americans and the French used them as well."

The vehicles had to be very durable, as they sustained lots of damage. Drivers made them climb over low stone walls and grind their way over terrain rough enough to basically wreck any other vehicle. The extra armor plating was fitted underneath to stop the chassis cracking, and to make the car semi-bulletproof. "There were sometimes bullets that did come into the back of vehicles," Dunkley recalled, "which was an unpleasant experience. But what really I didn't like very much, particularly after you'd been on tour patrol for a couple of days, on tour for a day or two, is that you'd hear the fuel getting down a bit, sloshing around, in a half-empty fuel tank—and it was right behind your back. If you leaned back into your seat, you could feel the fuel tank with your spine, which was actually pretty unpleasant."

BRIXMIS members had to take the three-week Special Duties Course at the Intelligence Center in Ashford, Kent, which the Americans of USMLM attended, too. Here, they learned how to master different types of cameras, including 1,000mm lenses with doublers that could accurately pick out details a mile away, such as a license plate. They also were taught to use standard 180mm zoom lenses and pocket cameras for close-up shots. Video equipment was used, too.

By the 1980s units were issued image intensifiers, which could be attached to cameras, and image-intensifying night-vision goggles. "We had a special switch on the vehicle," Dunkley recalled, "which you could hit—the 'James Bond' switch, as some drivers used to call it— which meant that it cut every single light on the vehicle. You could open a door or put the brakes on, for example, and nothing would show."

A key job took place at night: going into East Germany to recover thrown-away documentation and paperwork from Soviet and NVA units. For that, BRIXMIS personnel had a right-angled, six-inch flashlight with an infrared lens on it. Living off the land on lengthy missions was the order of the day, and the teams also had equipment for brewing up water to make drinks and heat rations.

The basic tour was termed the "local tour," which involved monitoring the nearest Soviet unit, the 35th Motor Rifle Division, and also border guards of the East German forces. "This was our primary mission, and it took basically only twenty-four hours," Dunkley recalled. "If it was really busy, then you wouldn't sleep." A longer tour could last two or three days, and the intelligence that was brought back might include the teams filming or photographing a complete division on maneuvers, which could involve several thousand vehicles. There was always a danger of running out of film. "I think the longest one that I ever did was four days or five days," said Dunkley, "by which time you are very tired, because it's a twenty-four-hour job and the information you've collected risks becoming out of date."

The Soviets and their East German allies of course tried their best to hinder the Allied teams' movements. In the city's hinterland, signs were placed everywhere on training areas and garrisons, stating: "Entry prohibited for members of the military liaison missions." In other words, the *foreign* liaison missions. Likewise, there would be *"Sperrgebiet"* ["Prohibited Area"] signs everywhere on East German army training areas, all of which were ignored, as this was against the original agreement from 1945 governing how the Four Powers would cooperate with one another. What was different, however, was the maps that were issued by the Soviets, which Allied teams then had to copy and translate onto their own maps. These PRAs—"Permanently Restricted Area" maps—pinpointed where the Soviets and NVA protected their main training areas, their nuclear weapons storage sites, their bunker sites, and so forth. "These," Dunkley notes, "you disregarded at your own peril. And if you were a naughty boy and were caught literally behind those particular signs, saying that you're going into a permanently restricted area, then you could expect to perhaps get away with it once, maybe even twice—but after that, you might be declared 'persona non grata.' This did happen to a couple of friends of mine, who were no longer allowed over the Glienicker Bridge [the 'Bridge of Spies'] into East Germany." This sanction meant the person in question was no longer operational for the task for which he had been trained for over two years. But again, the operator in question had to weigh up "risk versus gain."

On a routine tour, the first thing Allied mission tourers would do was check into East Germany, at the Glienicker Bridge in Potsdam, and hand over their Soviet passes for verification. While this went on, Soviet guards and East German police would be observing the team and communicating ahead with their respective units that a mission was coming their way. There would follow a cat-and-mouse game of the Stasi trying their best to tail the team whilst the mission driver did his very best to shake them off. The job of observing what they wanted could not begin until they were free of surveillance themselves.

Major Dunkley, like nearly all of his colleagues, had several near-death vehicle "incidents." "One stands out for me," he said, "from March 1984. It was against the 35th Motor Rifle Division. I saw that an ambush had been set up. They let me through the check-in front door into this ambush area. *I'm in trouble,* I thought. *This is going to be exciting, but if they have put an ambush in place, then there must be something unusual happening and there must be a really, very good reason to stop us seeing it. So what do I do?* We could press on as fast as we could before they could react. Or turn back, have a cup of tea, and come back a different way more covertly later on. Of course I felt some fear, but your training is so good that you learn how to control it and how to live with it. The next thing I knew was that we were looking at some very interesting equipment being put onto a train. It was a place where there had been an almost fatal incident involving an American officer. In my particular case, I've got seconds to photograph what's going on, and then to hightail out of it."

Dunkley spotted armored vehicles roaring toward his position from several sides. The Soviets intended to box the BRIXMIS car in and crush it—the passengers inside would stand no chance of survival. "So I executed the well-known cavalry order: 'Run away!' . . . It was instinct and training from our driver, Corporal Peter Lock, who charged our car head-on toward the Soviet heavy armored vehicle, which was also charging toward us. At the last minute, he dabbed the brakes and swerved in underneath the glacis plate, knowing that this charging rhino couldn't alter course as fast as we did, and we escaped just with some scraped paint. That's the closest I probably came to serious injury or possible death." A few weeks later, *Adjudant-Chef* Mariotti was killed at Halle in a further head-on altercation.

Encounters with ordinary East Germans could be very mixed for BRIXMIS vehicles. "We'd been operating for years with these big cars with yellow number plates with just a single digit on them," Dunkley explained. "Lots of East Germans, particularly those near training areas, airfields, and headquarters recognized us quite regularly. Some of them were good Boy Scouts and would immediately roar off and go and find the nearest policeman and make a telephone call or go and knock on the doors of the Soviet Military Police. But the majority of them were curious, friendly, and interested in what they could get out of us, be that cigarettes or *Playboy* magazines. We also carried seven hundred and fifty East German Ostmarks, which is about a month's worth of pay, with which we could bribe a farmer to tow us out of a mud hole with his tractor."

Colonel Lawrence Kelley of the US Marine Corps served with USMLM in the 1980s and vividly recalled the dangers as well as the black humor one could witness when driving through the East German countryside. Ordinary citizens of the GDR state were very aware of the consequences to themselves, their future careers, and their happiness should they meet and talk with any Allied mission personnel. The East German military—particularly those doing their compulsory military service— were strictly ordered not to fraternize, but they did as long as nobody else was watching. The city of Dresden is in the Elbe River valley, and it was known to many Germans and Allies alike as the "Valley of the Clueless"—*Tal der Ahnungslosen*—because the population there couldn't receive West German television. Kelley said, "During the Cold War the West German government went to great lengths to inform and influence the East German populace, and the media played a prominent role in the effort. By the early 1980s West German television's broadcast coverage extended to virtually the entire territory of the GDR, save for the corner of the country near Dresden. Yet despite the gratis coverage, actually watching the programming was anything but 'cost-free.'

"While the top echelons of the SED enjoyed unimpeded access to *Westfernsehen* [West German television] and could even have special antennae built to enhance reception, the East German government outlawed the viewing of such 'propaganda' by the populace at large. Yet it did so in vain. Despite the significant risks of punishment, East Germans high and low indulged themselves discreetly with the highlights of various Bundesliga soccer matches. Regrettably, though, sometimes the message that the information-hungry population took away from the broadcasts represented a dual-edged sword, as one tour in early 1985 made abundantly clear to me."

By the early 1980s, the Soviets had started to bring online their new main battle tank (MBT), the T-80. Both USMLM and BRIXMIS tours had already succeeded in getting interior photographs of the T-64A and T-64B tanks, which had yielded valuable technical data and insights. With its revolutionary turbine engine, the radical T-80 design represented a quantum leap in capability over the previous model T-62. Consequently, the Soviets took extensive measures to hide both the delivery and operations of the new weapons system. While the missions detected the initial deliveries almost immediately (more than 2,500 would be deployed into East Germany by 1986), making good visual sightings, much less obtaining good photographs, proved difficult. As Kelley stated, "Over time, we made many partial sightings and even conducted focused operations designed to ambush the tank, but mission success came only in December of 1984, when the French Mission caught and photographed a small column of T-80s moving near the Königsbrück Training Area. Yet even after that point, collection remained difficult, and while our sightings of the T-80 increased, our information on it long remained fragmentary.

"On a cold winter's morning in early 1985, SSG Ron Blake and I headed for Area B in part to look for the tank. We knew that the Weimar regiments of the Soviet 79th Guards Tank Division had it and took up an observation post in a field east of their training area, near a road that defined the PRA [Permanently Restricted Area] border. From there we could easily hear the characteristic whine of the tanks' turbine engines, but seeing the vehicles proved impossible. Fog limited our visibility to a few hundred meters, but we waited anyway, hoping against hope that one of the tanks might emerge along a nearby trail.

"Instead, much to our chagrin, a scruffy shepherd with his flock appeared in our rearview mirror, heading to his home village. He approached the vehicle, recognized it immediately, smiled broadly, and wanted to chat. I did not especially relish that idea, for while East German locals sometimes provided information of value, current circumstances made the situation dicey. Should 'Narks' or 'Sovs' appear and give chase, the last thing that we needed was to be stuck in the midst of a hundred sheep! Nonetheless, I rolled down the window and began speaking with the shepherd to see what he knew, all the time watching for signs of trouble. He was gregarious, but his sociability notwithstanding, after five minutes it became clear that he had nothing to offer. I let the discussion wane, hoping to encourage him to leave, but, to my dismay, he then turned to the tour NCO and asked: '*Und wo kommst Du her?*' ['And where do you come from?']. Whereupon Ron, in his finest Texas-accented German, replied, '*Ich komme aus Dallas!*' At this unexpected remark the shepherd's eyes lit up like beacons, and he enthusiastically exclaimed, '*Dallas*—Tuesday night! *Dynasty*—Thursday night!' So much for the ban on *Westfernsehen!*"

For the Allied top brass back in West Berlin and in their respective capitals, the information fed back from the liaison teams was invaluable, as Major General Robert Corbett confirmed. "The liaison missions were always originally designed as a reassurance mechanism. Their work meant each knew what the other side was doing and would therefore not be subject to being taken by surprise or cause unnecessary confrontations. That was the original idea. But we learned so much about the Warsaw Pact, particularly about Soviet equipment, and along with the French [MMFL] and Americans [USMLM], the missions were our eyes and ears. I sat with the chief of BRIXMIS quite frequently to talk about what was going on on the other side. It was always part of my duty to keep a finger on what *might* happen, and if it were to happen, what we were going to do about it. In other words, an understanding of the potential capabilities of the opposition was absolutely crucial.

"The information that was provided to me by the BRIXMIS tourers and their command element became especially important and valuable to my staff and to me personally. It helped us immeasurably in planning for and managing, in conjunction with my French and American counterparts, the volatile and complex situation facing us in Berlin from the summer of 1989 onwards. The Allied missions were enduringly brilliant in their ability to provide information that underpinned many crucial decisions made during the Cold War."

CHAPTER TWELVE

Death of a Soldier

Amid the overtures of high-level negotiations between the reelected President Ronald Reagan and General Secretary Mikhail Gorbachev by the early spring of 1985, there were accurate indications of a thaw in US-Soviet relations that could be perceived within the Allied military in Europe and in Washington, Paris, and London. For the first time since the Soviets' 1979 invasion of Afghanistan, the United States Military Liaison Mission (USMLM) received permission to attend the annual Soviet Army-Navy Day reception in Potsdam in force rather than with the usual token representation. The move preceded more planned meetings that year at a high-ranking level between the two sides. As Major Arthur D. Nicholson Jr. departed the safety of the Potsdam compound of USMLM with Staff Sergeant Jessie G. Schatz driving their vehicle, they headed out as planned to drive one hundred miles northwest of Berlin. It was a sunny Sunday morning in March, and no operational grounds existed for anxiety toward dealings with the Soviets, the prospects for gathering valuable data seemed good. They were a qualified, extremely experienced crew on a routine tour reconnoitering standard targets during an off-day that should have encountered nothing more menacing than boredom. Instead, tragedy struck that would destabilize international relations.

Major Nicholson was shot and killed that afternoon outside tank sheds located on Ludwigslust Sub-Caliber Range 475, in a move that stunned the West, brought shock and revulsion down on the Kremlin, and created a crisis between the superpowers. After approaching the facility covertly, Nicholson had dismounted from his car to check for the possible presence of Soviet armored vehicles—per the brief he had received in Potsdam. Major Nicholson had not been assigned this target per se, though he had been authorized to visit it as a backup. His principal task was to check and police upriver crossing sites (and their associated bivouac areas) along the Elbe south of Ludwigslust, where GSFG (Group of Soviet Forces in Germany) had just conducted a major exercise. All ground tour personnel routinely performed such tasks; doing so properly was expected to take and should have taken all of Nicholson's available time. Nonetheless, before departing Berlin he had requested and received permission from the ground ops officer to cover Ludwigslust Soviet Training Area 475, time permitting. The reason: He suspected that the Soviets might have deployed a new tank, the T-80, there.

The facility in question served the independent tank regiment of 2nd Guards Tank Army—one of five key formations to be used in any planned attack toward the West. The tour personnel at USMLM knew it to be guarded under normal circumstances, and there had been the occasional flare-up of aggression from the troops stationed there, but nothing Nicholson believed would endanger his life. The Americans entered the area with considerable caution, stopping in the forest to watch and listen at intervals as an armored convoy was returning to base. Sergeant Schatz, who had just visited the site a few days prior, pointed out an area that had been recently occupied, but the Soviets had since departed. The men then approached the sheds, photographed the signboards displayed nearby, and positioned the vehicle to permit the tour NCO to pull security while the tour officer checked for Soviet armor.

Unbeknownst to either man, and despite Staff Sergeant Schatz's best efforts at observation, a Soviet sentry—Junior Sergeant Aleksandr Ryabtsev—remained undetected, concealed in the adjacent woods. According to information obtained later, he had been walking his post on the near side of the sheds as the Americans approached. Hearing the vehicle, the Soviet NCO made his way through the woods on the flank of the range, to a position about fifty meters behind the Ameri-

can personnel's position. Too late to shout a warning, Sergeant Schatz
noticed the Soviet, just as he opened fire—the first bullet whizzing over
Schatz's head; it was not a warning, but a miss. Nicholson sprinted back
to the woods, for the safety of the car. The second or third shot fired by
Junior Sergeant Ryabtsev found its mark, striking Major Nicholson in
his upper abdomen and slightly below his heart. The American groaned,
fell to the ground, called out to Schatz, and promptly lost consciousness. In the meantime, Staff Sergeant Schatz slammed the hatch shut,
started the car, and frantically threw it into reverse in an effort to reach
his fallen officer.

Horror struck at how rapidly events had spiraled out of control,
Staff Sergeant Schatz sprang from the vehicle to administer first aid, but
the Soviet NCO sentry gestured to him to stay in his vehicle and not
to come any farther forward. Desperately using sign language, Schatz
then communicated his intent to the Soviet and took a step toward his
fallen officer. The sentry, who had held Schatz at gunpoint the entire
time, then shouldered his AK-74, ominously took aim at Schatz's head,
and grimly motioned him back into the vehicle. Seeing the futility of
further action and the hopelessness of the situation, Sergeant Schatz
complied. He secured and covered the tour equipment, checked that
the doors were locked, and waited. Shock set in quickly as he looked
on at the motionless body of Major Nicholson—mere feet away. The
Soviets would later claim that Sergeant Ryabtsev had issued a challenge
in English, Russian, and German, fired a warning shot into the air, then
shot to disable Major Nicholson. Sergeant Schatz, a native German
speaker, heard no challenge in any language, and there had been no
warning shot, and no shot to disable, either, in his opinion. Just three
shots that were intended to kill.

The Soviet sentry reported his action by telephone immediately,
specifically mentioning "*missiya*" ("mission"), and a contingent of
armed troops appeared within minutes. Over the next three hours,
many Soviet officers and soldiers arrived to secure the area, collect data,
and investigate the situation; considerable confusion reigned. Yet no
one rendered even rudimentary first aid to Nicholson. Finally, at 1650
(one hour, five minutes after the shooting), an unidentified individual

in a blue jogging suit took Nicholson's pulse, waited a few seconds to be doubly sure, and then pronounced him dead. The protracted failure to provide or permit any medical attention at all ensured that the wound he had received had been fatal. It would be this culpable negligence that would be the final straw of repeated aggressive incidents toward Allied missions (one estimate had them numbered at least four to six times a year). It froze American-Soviet relations, as President Reagan's administration castigated Moscow. Although it wasn't known at the time how serious Nicholson's injuries were, just as serious was the repeated firing on Allied personnel by Soviet troops. To many within USMLM, there seemed to be an unwritten order from the Soviet high command, passed down to junior officers and their troops, that such action was deemed permissible.

Just after six o'clock that evening, two hours after the incident, the Soviets informed USMLM at Potsdam of the incident with the tour and requested they attend the scene, without actually providing the Americans the exact location—believing they had acquired the information through illicit activity in the first place—even at this time, there was mistrust and paranoia. By 7:30 p.m., two officers (Colonel Lajoie and Lieutenant Colonel Kelley), driven by Staff Sergeant Everett, had departed Potsdam to attend the scene and bring back the men, but they didn't know what they would find. Two hours later, having driven at high speed through the darkness, the group were met and escorted the final few kilometers of their journey, to what they believed to be the place where the incident had taken place. They happened upon a group of approximately fifty Soviet officers, with at least one probable KGB officer, whom both LaJoie and Kelley had met at various representational functions. Under the glare of headlights the Soviet group stood aimlessly around as if waiting for something to happen—Lajoie and Kelley got out of the car and approached them. Colonel Lajoie was directing his questions at various officers, hoping for a concise answer as to what exactly had occurred, when an unidentified colonel reticently revealed that Major Nicholson had been shot and killed. It was then that the senior-ranking Soviet officer—General Krivosheyev—appeared and the atmosphere heated up considerably. The leaders at USMLM had a dim view already of the Soviet commander's abilities and temperament—he was known for his limited powers of intellect.

Instead of expressing remorse, or even offering a detailed explanation as to how the major had died, Krivosheyev exploded at Colonel Lajoie, declaring that his actions would sabotage relations between the commands and placing all responsibility for the fallout squarely on his shoulders. Continuing the surreal and aggressive interview, the Soviets then ordered Lajoie to witness an inventory of the dead American officer's belongings, ordered Sergeant Schatz to undergo interrogation, and demanded to thoroughly inspect the American's vehicle. Further, they stated that Nicholson's body would undergo an autopsy at a Soviet medical facility the following morning, which an American observer could witness. The atmosphere turned very ugly as the American officers refused and stood their ground despite more threats. Lajoie insisted Sergeant Schatz be accorded the rights guaranteed under US law during the questioning, which the Soviets turned down, citing that they themselves were the ones who had jurisdiction, leading to a prolonged and fiercely contested debate which raged on for hours. Eventually, with no real progress made, Lajoie agreed that the Soviets could interrogate Schatz, but the sergeant had the right to refuse to answer any questions that he considered inappropriate. Despite many attempts to elicit the answers they required, the Soviets could not entice Schatz to condemn himself or Nicholson for their actions that had led to the tragedy.

By midnight, Colonel Lajoie had struck an agreement with his opposite number that the Americans could depart and take both their vehicles, and that Lieutenant Colonel Kelley would remain with Nicholson's body as the Soviets removed it from the site and took it back to Potsdam, where forensic specialists planned to perform an autopsy as part of the legal investigation. As they drove back, Lajoie took steps to contact USAREUR (United States Army Europe), though this was long before the era of cell phones, so contacting Berlin directly from a service area near Ludwigslust would have been nearly impossible. Instead, he called USMLM in Potsdam House and had the duty officer relay his instructions to an officer at their HQ in West Berlin, who had been placed on alert. That officer drafted a flash initial operational report to be sent electronically to Heidelberg. Other, more detailed communications followed later.

Very early that Monday morning, March 25, Colonel Lajoie, accompanied by Nicholson's close friends, their wives, a chaplain, and a doctor from the Berlin MEDDAC (Medical Department Activity) broke the dreadful news to Major Nicholson's wife and daughter. Delays occurred, as the party returned to Potsdam at approximately 0300 hours. The examination of Nicholson's body could only begin with the onset of normal working hours, but still the Soviets attempted to gain the upper hand. Major (Dr.) M. A. Morgenstern, the American military physician designated to officially observe the forensic proceedings, spent four hours being delayed at the Glienicker Bridge—at gunpoint—before the Soviets would authorize him to cross. Once he arrived at the morgue, he was deprived of his tape recorder. Having been informed of the wishes of Nicholson's family and of the new orders of the chief of mission, he succeeded in preventing the autopsy, despite several attempts by the Soviets to circumvent his own position and win US acquiescence via pressure. In accordance with the new guidance, the US agreed only to a visual inspection of the body and uniform, though it would also permit X-rays, if GSFG insisted. Despite all of this, both American officers held sway over the body and the effects of Nicholson, and a certain dignity for him was retained. It was time to bring him home.

The US party escorted Major Nicholson on his final crossing over the Glienicker Bridge at 1715, as the world's media glare intensified. As the group reached the American side of the bridge, Colonel Lajoie draped Nicholson's body with the Stars and Stripes, the Berlin Brigade Honor Guard rendered a final salute to the fallen officer, and the short motorcade sped off toward the Berlin MEDDAC, where medical personnel prepared it for the flight to Frankfurt. To the accompaniment of the Berlin Brigade Band's subdued rendition of "Abide with Me" an honor guard at Tempelhof Air Base placed the casket on a waiting aircraft bound for Frankfurt, where it would be formally received and further transported to the facilities of the 7th Medical Command, where USAREUR physicians performed the autopsy that Nicholson's wife had hoped to avoid. As with the ceremonies on the bridge, the media recorded and dispatched emotional scenes as the last American serviceman to die in Germany during the Cold War was flown home to be laid to rest in Arlington Cemetery, Virginia. Now the inquest could begin and blame be apportioned.

A colonel and his assistant were dispatched to Berlin from 1st Per-Com, a USAREUR-subordinate unit based near Heidelberg who interviewed all USMLM personnel connected to the incident. It was clear to all involved (save for the Soviets) and to those in BRIXMIS and MMFL communities that this had been a rash and unjustified act. The chief of BRIXMIS termed it "barbaric" in his protest letter to GSFG. General Otis officially remonstrated with his opposite number, General Mikhail Zaitsev—commander of Group of Soviet Forces in Germany—that Nicholson had been illegally killed, and more to the point it had been officially sanctioned from the very top.

On March 28, the Berlin community paid tribute to Nicholson in a moving multinational service at the American Community Chapel. Feelings remained emotional, irrational, and very high among the Berlin Brigade, and especially among some who felt they might be in a position to do something about it. As Staff Sergeant James Stejskal from Detachment A recalled, "We worked alongside US Military Liaison on various operations and reconnaissance trips into the GDR by providing reports on what we were seeing when on recon, watching what the Russians and East Germans were doing, where specific units were moving to, photographs of senior ranking officers, etc.

"One of the guys in my unit was actually in the vicinity when Major Nicholson was killed, and said he'd placed himself in a tough position, perhaps he had taken a risk not worth taking, but the Russians were protecting their security when Major Nicholson was shot and killed. Our commanding officer took some of these photographs to senior staff of the Berlin Brigade to discuss which one they could successfully target. In the meeting he just dropped this information onto the table, and said, 'If necessary, we are prepared to do what is required of us.' This offer of retribution—however well thought and planned out, did not go down well at all. In fact the senior command was aghast. 'You are willing to start World War Three over the death of one guy?' Well possibly not World War Three, but we were willing to get some retribution." Needless to say, the offer was turned down.

Major Arthur Nicholson was a brave man, but was he caught in the wrong place at the wrong time? He had created the situation in which he found himself by attempting a very risky action at a site known to be guarded and, at times, volatile. His assigned tasking lay elsewhere, but he had a strong desire to "detect" a new variant of tank at that location, the possible presence of which a few intelligence reports of unknown credibility and a previous shooting incident had suggested. Many Allied tour members had faced similar dilemmas over the years, and as previously commented, they had to weigh up if the target was worth the risk. Nicholson was buried with full military honors at Arlington National Cemetery on March 30, posthumously awarded the Purple Heart and the Legion of Merit. In an unprecedented move, President Ronald Reagan signed the papers to promote him posthumously to the rank of honorary lieutenant colonel. Three years later, amid the thawing of relations between the superpowers as Gorbachev met with Reagan at summits in Geneva and Reykjavik, an official apology for his death was finally issued by Soviet defense minister Dmitry Yazov. President Reagan had consistently brought up the subject of his killing at every opportunity with the Soviets.

Months and years after the incident, the Soviets had steadfastly stuck by their mantra: "Nicholson's death was tragic, regrettable, and atypical of relations between GSFG and USMLM. But the entire blame for it lies with the American side." This policy infuriated then secretary of defense Caspar Weinberger, who declared that the Nicholson incident would never be closed until or unless Moscow issued an apology and paid compensation to the family for its loss. Of course, Moscow categorically refused. Whatever Weinberger's motivation, his statement, which President Reagan then transformed into national policy, represented a shrewd political ploy. It was clear to all who had dealt with the Soviets that Moscow would never acquiesce to such a demand. That meant that Weinberger's demands represented a club with which to beat them in perpetuity, scoring political points but never closing the incident.

As Colonel Lawrence Kelley summarized, "This posture handcuffed us both locally [the chain of command had placed 'temporary' restrictions on what USMLM was permitted to do] and nationally. In the interim, Gorbachev, who had ascended to power only two weeks before the shooting, began implementing dramatic policy reforms and transformations. Over time, he encountered serious internal resistance from hard-liners, which the US noticed and monitored closely. However, for lack of an apology, or compensation, Washington could only render limited assistance to him. Thus, we found ourselves in a self-created bind. We could continue to lambaste the Soviets publicly but could not provide full-fledged assistance to a man on the brink of internally transforming the USSR. The world had reached a historical turning point, and the US needed to act.

"In late 1987, Weinberger resigned as SecDef over the Iran Contra Affair, and Frank Carlucci succeeded him. Carlucci was an experienced and intelligent top-level government figure who clearly recognized the issue. . . . In 1988 he approached the president and requested the authority to press for an apology once more, this time with General Dmitry Yazov. . . . The president approved his proposal, and Carlucci met with Yazov in Bern during the preliminaries to the June 1988 Moscow Summit. He told Yazov that together they needed to resolve this issue in order to put US-Soviet relations back on track. Yazov said that he understood but did not know the details of the situation, since the shooting had occurred long before his tenure. He promised to have something for Carlucci at their next meeting.

"The next time they met, Carlucci pushed Yazov for his response, but Yazov still had nothing to offer. Carlucci then took him and an interpreter into an adjacent office and proceeded to write a statement on the shooting that, he believed, would suffice. The interpreter translated it, and Yazov said that he could live with it. Back in Washington, Carlucci informed the president and other top administration figures of his discussion with Yazov and telephoned Karen Nicholson. He then discarded Weinberger's call for compensation and declared the incident closed. No publicity of the 'apology' occurred until after the summit, but ultimately Carlucci's press spokesperson made an appropriate announcement, releasing the text to which Yazov had agreed: 'I express my regret over the incident and am sorry this occurred. This does not promote improved relations. Secretary Carlucci and I have agreed we will do all we can to prevent these kinds of incidents in the future.' Carlucci told me that he felt he could accept this text, taken in context with other actions and statements made privately by Yazov, as an apology. For the Soviets' part, Moscow never publicly acknowledged this statement but, tellingly, also never denied that Yazov had made it."

Whether the Soviets truly rendered an apology for Nicholson's death is a matter of interpretation. What was clear was that by 1988 both the USA and the Soviets had to move on from an impasse. There were "bigger fish to fry." The final irony would be that six months after Nicholson was inducted into US Military Intelligence's hall of fame, in June 1991, the Soviet Union itself collapsed.

PART IV

THE STRUGGLE TO BE FREE

For West Berlin's children, the full horror of what the Wall did to their city was not as apparent as it was to their parents. The Wall held a morbid excitement for them.

"It is difficult to portray how life was so hard and dreary. The ache to get away from the Stasi secret police snoops, from the grey meat, from the clothes that itched and the air that stung your eyes was palpable."

—Hans-Peter Spitzner
(see Chapter 17)

CHAPTER THIRTEEN

The Singing Jew of Checkpoint Charlie

The 1980s would see a new generation of East Germans, which had been raised under this regime, begin to want more of what they could see the Western capitalists had. To prevent this discontent spreading throughout the country, the only option was to insulate the country completely, with severe restrictions on travel abroad. However, the Soviets could not stop Western influence infiltrating through their borders. Whether it was East German citizens coming back from a permitted trip abroad, or their relations visiting from other countries, or foreign artists performing, or simply listening to an illegal radio set or watching television shows from West Germany—it was a game of cat and mouse for many Germans, whether you were trying to escape the system, sneak under their radar to offer support to others, or trying to protect the regime itself, which you believed in.

Estrongo Nachama was someone you would have been unlikely to meet in Hitler's Berlin just after hostilities ended. Not only had the Nazis exterminated millions of Jews throughout Eastern Europe, they had also by 1945 managed to deport the Berlin community of 56,696 Jews, too, thus ending their presence in the city, which reached back to the time of Frederick the Great. This is the journey one man would take through war, genocide, and redemption—traveling thousands of miles, enduring hardship, suffering, and anguish—to decide he would rebuild his life and his religious community in the heart of the defeated Third Reich. Even if the war-torn world he had miraculously survived now plunged itself into a new Cold War, his home would be right in the center of it. His devotion to the Jewish community in both East and West Berlin across the decades before and during the Berlin Wall's existence earned him worldwide fame, as he nurtured and grew a community from hundreds into thousands.

Nachama had been born the son of a grain merchant in the northern Greek city of Salonika. His family's Jewish ancestry was Sephardic—which meant they had fled from Spain toward the end of the fifteenth century as the diaspora then settled throughout the Mediterranean and in the Ottoman Empire. Nachama's family line was academic and religious, with many of his ancestors important rabbinic and Talmudic scholars. After attending Jewish elementary school and a French gymnasium, and discovering what an extraordinary baritone voice he possessed, Estrongo Nachama joined the family business and became the cantor of the synagogue in Salonika.

By the beginning of 1941, Greece had repelled one invasion by Italy, but could do nothing to prevent the later German assault in April, which went on to conquer the country, occupy Athens, and then finally capture Crete. Nachama traveled with the retreating Greek forces as his home city of Salonika fell on April 9, and as with nearly all Jewish families who suddenly had new Nazi rulers, Nachama, his parents, and two sisters would eventually be rounded up and transported to a concentration camp, Auschwitz, in the spring of 1943. All but Nachama were gassed, and he would spend the next two years of living hell surviving on his wits, charm, and his extraordinary singing voice.

Prisoner 116155, as was tattooed on Nachama's wrist, entertained the camp guards, inspired and revived his fellow prisoners with his unique and powerful baritone, his popular rendition of "'O Sole Mio" gaining him the nickname "the singer of Auschwitz." As the Soviets advanced through Poland, the Jews at Auschwitz, including Nachama, were moved to camps in the west, such as Sachsenhausen. Heavy labor work and his irrepressible optimism seemingly gave him the mental and physical strength to survive the infamous "Death March" of prisoners of the Sachsenhausen concentration camp. In May 1945, with the war in Europe over, he was freed by nearby Red Army units from his captors, in a small Brandenburg town called Nauen. From there, he was drawn toward nearby Berlin, originally with the intent of catching a train back to Greece. But the march from Sachsenhausen had weakened him to the point he was stricken with typhoid, and only nursed back to health by a Christian Berlin family whom he befriended. At this point, by 1947, just as the Allies were slowly sliding into a Cold War, Nachama decided to put his roots down in the city. He had come to know the Jewish community of Berlin, whose leaders had learned of the young man's extraordinary singing voice and offered him the position as the community's cantor. He would soon meet his future wife, Lily, who had survived the Holocaust in hiding.

By the time of the Berlin Airlift in 1948, Nachama's voice was being heard celebrating Sabbath over the RIAS airwaves in the American sector, with his fame soon spreading as the program was taken up by other German radio stations. Before long, it became known even among non-Jewish Berliners, as he became a regular part of US garrison life, administering worship to Jewish soldiers. Despite the ongoing tensions between the Soviets and East Germans on one side and the allied powers on the other, the Jewish cantor seemed to float between the two halves of the city pre-1961, primarily due to his Greek citizenship. Though his son Andreas recalled that the experience was still disturbing for him as a young boy. "When you were going to East Berlin, let's say through the Brandenburg Gate, you had to stop there and you were controlled, and your car, they were looking into it, whether you had any goods with you. They asked if you were armed or not and things like that."

Andreas became a rabbi, a published author, and a scholar of the German genocide of Jews between 1933 and 1945, and his relationship with his musical father was close, and never dull. Born in 1951, as the Cold War exerted its grip on the city, he stills remembers vividly how isolated West Berlin felt back then. "I was living here in Berlin with my parents and the Cold War was somehow very present because you could hear it every day in the air as Soviet MiG fighter planes broke the sound barrier above the city."

What was left of Berlin's Jewish community was not divided as the city had now become. Though Jews worshiped in various synagogues across both East and West Berlin, there was still just one community. The workers' uprising in East Berlin on June 17, 1953, changed all of that. With its brutal suppression by the Soviets, East Berlin became a harsher place to live, work, and worship, and subsequently there evolved an eastern and a western Jewish community. Estrongo Nachama quickly bestrode both camps, his Greek passport again enabling him to travel safely between the two, though he was primarily working for the western community.

When the Wall was erected suddenly on August 13, 1961, the family was in Italy, to holiday in Venice. They watched in horror on Italian television as the evening news brought pictures of the barriers going up, and the anguish of Berliners. Somehow, they managed to drive back to West Berlin through East Germany.

The Jewish community in East Berlin developed differently from the one in the west of the city. Those staying in the east were mainly old people, with the younger ones going over to the west. The eastern community was also smaller, as very few new members could actually get into that part of the city.

Cantor Nachama was one of the few Jews from West Berlin to be authorized to travel into East Berlin after 1961, and as a young boy, Andreas wanted to travel with him, but his lack of a foreign passport prevented him traveling through Checkpoint Charlie. "My father would declare, 'If you want me to come and sing, you have to get a permit for my son to come, too.' And I always got it," Nachama recalled. "He would take me on the S-Bahn to Friedrichstraße, where there was a special entrance for permit holders. And we'd travel through together. It was a great adventure."

Though his main role was to administer religious care to the community, it did not prevent Nachama from taking across supplies, whether monetary or otherwise, to help those he thought needed it. As Andreas recounted, "Every time he went through Checkpoint Charlie, he had to declare the amount of money that he was carrying, the Deutschmark and the DDR-Mark. I would fill out his forms for him as the form had to match what he was carrying otherwise there would be problems. Sometimes he was searched, but mostly he could pass through. There were good and some bad guards—and he knew which ones he liked to deal with, i.e., they were less strict.

"Once he forgot to declare what money he was carrying—quite a lot of west and east Marks, and one of the custom controls was very sharp. He [Nachama] was sitting on a bench in their customs room. Fearful of being caught with excess currency, he took out the money from his pocket and put it between the seating cushion and the back cushion. The customs guard asked him, 'You don't have any money with you?'

"'No, I don't have any money,' he replied, and they performed a body check, ordered him to undress and looked through everything. But in fact he had no money with, or on him. So he passed through the checkpoint without any trouble.

"Two or three weeks later they were sitting there again, waiting to get his stamp into his papers. He spotted a friendly border guard, whom he knew, so he put his hand back between the cushions where he had hidden the money, felt for the package, and quickly stowed it away. When he was back safely in the west, he opened it and was shocked to find ten times the amount he had originally left. It seemed as if everyone was using the same place, too. He gave it to the Red Cross." He didn't just transfer money—coffee, bananas, and citrus fruits were favorites of his East Berlin community. He often brought prayer books for the synagogue in East Berlin. But it wasn't really noticed because they were the same books he usually carried, often reprints. A border guard would have had to look very closely at the paper to see it had not turned yellow and to realize that these were new books.

Cantor Nachama rarely performed services in East Berlin as this would have happened at the same time he would have been doing them in West Berlin. In East Berlin, he mainly administered funerals, not just for East Berlin Jews, but also for those from West Berlin who wanted to be buried back in the east, where their spouse's or the family grave was. He also gave concerts, singing with the East Berlin Radio Choir and also the Magdeburger Dom Choir. He performed many memorial services for the victims of the Shoah, and the service was an old Berlin ritual he knew by heart. The funerals were two to three times a week, and he tried to arrange them so as to conduct two appointments in one trip, to save time. The guards never suspected him despite this level of traveling, as there were others who crossed the border more often.

Professional musicians, for example, who worked in the orchestra in East Berlin, traveled every day, sometimes more than once. Surprisingly, Nachama never came on the radar of the Stasi, though he was aware that he could be observed. In his Stasi file, opened in the 1990s, it said: "Hasn't got anything in his mind but singing."

Andreas Nachama would often travel into East Berlin, though via a different route, as his West Berlin I.D. card granted him a different route, via Friedrichstraße, than his father's via Checkpoint Charlie. "Getting through Checkpoint Charlie could be very different, at certain times of the day and week, especially when there was a lot of traffic," he recalled. "Once, his [Nachama's] car had a mechanical problem and wouldn't start, so it was towed to the border and then he actually had to push it through by hand over the border because there was no service to tow it across. He then called me from Checkpoint Charlie, pushed the car to the side of the road until I arrived with my old Volkswagen to tow his car away. The guards on both sides all laughed. They did help, as far as they could, push the car, because they knew and liked him."

For his sixtieth birthday in 1978, RIAS had a half-hour program celebrating Estrongo's life and the contribution he had made to Jewish life in the city. He was now chief cantor; he led the choir, and had even managed to have a walk-on part in the Oscar-winning musical *Cabaret*, starring Liza Minnelli and Michael York. The presenter of the RIAS program asked him why the community in West Berlin had six thousand members whereas the one in the east had only four hundred? How do you explain that there are so few and here so many? The question could have potentially caused him problems, as the authorities might have wondered, why did he need to travel to East Berlin so often then? But his reply was typical of the way he had survived the war; he brazened it out. "Well," he said, "in East Berlin, I am only doing the funerals, in West Berlin, I am doing the prayer service."

Cantor Estrongo Nachama died on January 13, 2000, aged eighty-one years old. He was still teaching music students the day before he died. His journey from war-torn Greece, to the concentration camps of the Nazis, to witnessing the start and the end of the Cold War, had made for a life full of optimism, compassion, religious tolerance, and love for his people. He was one of the key figures who rebuilt the Jewish community in the heart of Hitler's Reich. "My father was pleased that by the end of 1989 the Jewish community was reunited," remembered 'Andreas. "And travels to East Berlin were not restricted to Checkpoint Charlie anymore, and many routes could be taken. He enjoyed these practicalities. He certainly did not shed a tear for the old regime." Many elderly German Jews who survived the Shoah decided to have their bones buried in Israel. But Cantor Nachama is buried in Berlin.

CHAPTER FOURTEEN

Going Underground

It had been a fairly uneventful shift for the military policemen stationed at Checkpoint Charlie in the early hours of the morning on January 9, 1972. Apart from the usual diplomatic, civilian, and military traffic passing through to and from East Berlin, the main focus was keeping warm on duty in the predawn of a bitterly cold January morning. The icy wind often swept across the vast expanse of the wasteland between the two border controls, buffeting the American flag flying at the checkpoint and the high-pitched singing of the telegraph wires that stretched along Friedrichstraße. It was a night to be tucked up in bed. As the harsh lights of the Wall illuminated the small military checkpoint hut a hundred yards away, two figures slowly emerged from the frozen ground a few yards farther on from the base of the Wall. It was a bizarre sight as they quickly reached down into the hole to grapple with a third miner as he struggled to extricate himself from the small hole his fellow tunnelers had just climbed out of. They then proceeded to hug one another wildly.

Taking in the clean, fresh air of freedom, the three East German men blinked at the bright lights ahead and studied the buildings on the western side—as if for the very first time. Of course, it was indeed their first experience standing as free men in the American sector, by Zimmerstraße and Friedrichstraße. Their story of escape is remarkable in that it was made so close to Checkpoint Charlie, where so many border guards were situated for preventing illegal crossings. The problem for the East German authorities was they expected to actually see their "border violators" in the flesh before they stopped and arrested them. Tunneling under the Wall just wasn't expected. For Peter Schöpf and brothers Peter and Manfred Höer, their three-week operation was following the tradition of a long line of their fellow East Germans who had chosen a subterranean route in their bids for freedom.

Years before the Berlin Wall was constructed, the city had seen various underground schemes hatched and put into operation as both sides in the Cold War attempted to monitor and undermine one another. In our modern world, with rolling twenty-four-hour news on television and streamed online, and instant communication via mobile phones, our secret services have an easier time monitoring the opposition. Satellite technology allows them to spy on, analyze, and if need be strike at potential enemies thousands of miles away from the safety of an office or living room. During the 1950s, however, as the Cold War increased in temperature, the Allied intelligence agencies of the CIA in Washington and MI6 in London had no such technology at their disposal. Surveillance by personnel on the front line or secret listening devices were the primary weapons, and Operation Gold (MI6 labeled it Operation Stopwatch) would prove to be one of the greatest tunneling operations devised within Berlin's boundaries, many years before the Wall was constructed.

Berlin was by this period the focal point of a communication network that stretched from West Berlin through France and on to London, and behind the Iron Curtain from East Berlin to deep within the Soviet Union. Worryingly for Moscow, on the Eastern side of the curtain, the level of sophistication was reflected in land lines strung up along telegraph poles for hundreds of miles or buried underground in pipes. Nothing radical had changed since the end of the Second World War. The Allied espionage agencies mutually agreed on a daring plan to tap this flow of vital information at its source, constructing a sophisticated tunnel at the beginning of 1954, from a warehouse on a US Air Force radar site in the Neukölln district of the American-run sector of the city.

Headed up by Bill Harvey from the CIA and Captain Peter Lunn, head of MI6 in Berlin, with the actual tunneling led by Williamson of the

US Army Corps of Engineers, Operation Gold would be a tremendous feat of both engineering and accuracy. Beginning in December 1953, over the next twelve months a tunnel 1,476 feet long stretched from the US base into the Soviet Sector, to locate and tap into a series of cables measuring only nineteen inches in length. More than three thousand tons of earth would be removed to construct a tunnel shored up with metal plate and housing a sophisticated monitoring system and a miniature railway line, the whole thing lined with explosives should the need arise to retreat quickly upon detection. Surveillance began in December 1955 once the wiretapping equipment had been installed by British technicians. Unlike the work of the operation's forebears at Bletchley Park who had broken the Enigma Code, the intelligence gathering of Operation Gold involved the less sophisticated methods of listening in on a mountain of random phone calls between Russian dignitaries, military commanders, secret police, and other Soviet officials coming through East Berlin. The recordings were then sent back to London for transcription. During its life span, Operation Gold delivered to the Allies more than sixty-seven thousand recorded hours of material to analyze and confirm what was going on in the Eastern Bloc. But the whole operation had been compromised from the very beginning. The Soviets knew of Gold before it was even active.

MI6 had gestated the "Cambridge Spy Ring," who gradually broke cover from the mid-1950s onward, causing untold damage to the security of the West as well as stressing relations between the Americans and British. George Blake was different. He had embedded himself deep inside MI6 as a trusted linguist and case officer in Berlin, having been turned by the KGB during his captivity during the Korean War in 1950–53. He had discovered Gold's existence before it went live, and had informed Moscow, who weighed up Blake's own value to them against thwarting the wiretap operation in its infancy. They allowed it to go live, feeding Gold information while maintaining their star asset in London. Within eighteen months, the Allies had built up a treasure trove of fifty thousand reels of tape, containing among other items more than 40,000 hours of translated conversations and 1,750 intelligence reports. From this haul of information the Allies were thus able to build an accurate picture of the Warsaw Pact's order of battle, their actual strength, and the quality of their command. They even knew what condition the railway system in East Germany was in, as well as the Soviets' key people heading up their nuclear projects. But though the Russians had been forced to supply genuine material in order to maintain Blake's position in London, he would go on to cause untold damage to countless CIA and MI6 operations across the globe, resulting in hundreds of agents being captured and killed before his discovery and capture in 1961.

On April 21, 1956, eleven months after Operation Gold had commenced, the tunnel on the eastern side of the border was "accidentally discovered" by a unit of Soviet and East German soldiers, who broke into the tunnel with a media posse happening to be there to record the Soviets' pronouncements about a "breach of the norms of international law." Far from becoming a scandal that would be hard to explain away without embarrassment, the Allies and the Soviets themselves were surprised to see the world's press instead celebrate the ingenuity and daring of the whole plan. It had possessed both.

By the time of the Berlin Wall's construction in August 1961, the authorities had blocked all underground sewer and canal networks that had been used as escape routes for more than six hundred East Germans. By the end of 1961 would-be escapers were forced to attempt other methods, such as digging their way to freedom, with more than seventy tunnels being excavated at various points along the Wall over the next three decades. They were started by individuals as well as groups, dug to various depths, and covered short or very long distances in length, depending on where the tunnel was to break to the surface beyond the Death Strip.

Of the three hundred people who succeeded in digging their way to freedom, there would be onetime escapees who would build new lives in the west, such as the student physicist Reinhard Alfred Furrer from Austria, who would escape in 1964 and go on to become one of the first Germans into space in 1982. Then there were "professional escapers" such as Hasso Herschel from Dresden. A witness as a teenager to the 1953 East German uprising, he would be expelled from school at eighteen, and drift from job to job to finance further studies in West Berlin.

He was then arrested by the Stasi for selling his belongings to support himself, and was interrogated, jailed, and on occasion severely beaten while in prison serving a six-year sentence. He fled to the west himself in October 1961 to escape national service and would spend the next decade digging several tunnels from the west back into the east to free his family, friends, and fellow East Germans. He had made a promise to his friends beforehand that whoever succeeded in fleeing to the west, would then help the others achieve the same goal. Like all tunnelers, Herschel ran many risks to life and freedom: either betrayal by informers to a police force with "shoot to kill" orders, or drowning and crushing from flooding or cave-ins. Hasso was involved in the "mass-breakout" tunneling operation in September 1962 with Tunnel 29. This operation yielded twenty-nine East Germans successfully crawling their way to freedom to Bernauer Straße, including Hasso's sister—Anita Moeller, who fled with her husband and daughter. She recalls, "We went into the house, down to the basement, and then had to get into a hole in the floor. First, I was worried, because I'm claustrophobic. I'm afraid of dark and narrow places . . . but once I was inside the tunnel, there was no time left for my fears." Further breakouts would occur in the Wedding district due to the soil being mainly clay—perfect for tunneling. This district, especially in the Bernauer Straße area, which was so close to the Death Strip, would see fifteen tunnels dug alone.

Much like the Second World War operation in 1943 at the German POW camp Stalag Luft III, which involved more than two hundred Allied prisoners of war attempting to break out and was later made famous by the Hollywood film *The Great Escape*, two years later a small band of West Berlin university students would dig their way into the city's record books. In October 1964, after six months of round-the-clock digging in small teams, Tunnel 57 would become the biggest mass escape during the life of the Berlin Wall. With their jump-off point at a disused bakery on Bernauer Straße, twelve men managed to dig a vertical shaft more than 36 feet deep, and from there a tunnel to the west more than 450 feet long (the length of a football field) to an outhouse located in the courtyard of a building at Strelitzer Straße 55. They worked weeklong shifts amid great secrecy to hide their plans from their friends and family, as well as to ensure all earth taken from the tunnel was hidden and their equipment was undiscovered. The tunnelers' dedication was matched by the bravery of the close friends, relations, and sweethearts who agreed to go with them and flee to the west. Before they completed a successful mission, disaster struck when their plans were discovered by Stasi operatives who had been alerted by suspicious border guards nearby.

On the second day of the escape, with escapees in constant fear of being discovered or betrayed, desperately wriggling their way through the dark, claustrophobic tunnel to freedom, the authorities struck in a bungled attempt to capture the fugitives. Two Stasi agents returned to the bakery with border guards, including Sergeant Egon Schultz. Quickly realizing their cover had been blown, the escape sentries guarding the entrance to the bakery to welcome arrivals with their code word, "Tokyo," retreated to the darkness of the courtyard to warn their comrades the game was up and then attempt escape themselves. In the chaos and confusion of flight, an exchange of fire resulted as the Stasi men and border guards quickly gained access to the darkened courtyard. The fugitives decided to make a stand to buy more time for their comrades crawling to freedom, unaware of what was going on above. Advancing into the darkness, Sergeant Schultz was hit in the shoulder by a bullet fired by one of the escapees and fell to the ground in shock. As he attempted to get to his feet, he was felled from behind by a second, fatal shot. He died on the way to the *Krankenhaus der Volkspolizei* ("People's Police Hospital"). Only decades later, once the GDR had collapsed and the Stasi files of the incident were analyzed, was it accurately reported that the second shot had actually been fired by a fellow border guard. At the time, however, the international furor was immense.

The East German authorities reacted quickly to condemn the murderous "Western agents," demand their extradition back to the GDR, and subsequently ensure that Sergeant Schultz's funeral was high profile in the Communist and worldwide media. His coffin was held almost in state, at the Friedrich Engels Barracks in East Berlin, before being driven amid solemn ceremony the 230 kilometers (about 140 miles) to his hometown of Rostock near the Baltic coast. Tens of thousands of East German civilians adhered to a strict government edict to line the country roads and town streets along the route to pay their last respects in a show of socialist solidarity. Schultz was buried in the Neuer Friedhof Cemetery in Rostock, where Erich Honecker gave the oration, laced with political barbs toward the Allies: "We condemn a system which has made murder a political weapon. We condemn its henchman who will not escape punishment!" Schultz's old school, where he had been a teacher before joining up, was given the honorary name *Egon Schultz Oberschule* ("Egon Schultz Secondary School"). Eventually, over time, more than a hundred collectives, schools, and institutions would be named in his honor. In response to being labeled murderers by the state, the sorrowful diggers from Tunnel 57, now free in West Berlin, sent balloons over the wall with a letter stating their motives: "The real murderer is the system that addressed the massive flight of its citizens not by removing the cause of the problem, but by building a wall and giving the order for Germans to shoot Germans."

Manfred Höer's experiences growing up in the East German state were similar to many of his countrymen's and those of the East Berliners with whom he grew up in the 1960s. Although not standing out as a revolutionary wishing to fight the system like Hasso Heschel, and only eight years of age when the Wall was built in 1961, by his early teens Höer was aware enough of what the state didn't provide for its citizens when compared to governments in the West. "They tried to create a picture of the West as being the enemy and the East would be our guardian angel. And the more they said it and the older you became you saw behind this façade. Of course, you also watched the news in the West, and the *Aktuelle Kamera* [a GDR TV news program, like news programs on the BBC, or NBC, CNN, etc.]. And if you had any intelligence, you could deduce that the authorities were lying to us."

His elderly parents were close to retirement, his grandfather lived in West Berlin, and his eldest sister had married and moved to the Federal Republic in 1960, locating five years later to West Berlin with her husband for his job. "For those who didn't work at the MfS [Stasi]—these people could buy things at the Intershop, they basically didn't suffer any shortages—for the common person that was unobtainable. Everything that came from the West was seen by us as the *Holy Grail*. When my sister came over to visit, she would bring gifts, including toys, but we didn't play with them, as they were put on a shelf and admired for being from the West. Other gifts like a biscuit tin or a pack of 'Maggisoup' [Maggi is a popular brand for soups], the empty packages were put on display, and when you had a celebration with guests, others would see them, and be impressed one had connections to the West." By fourteen, Manfred had left school and was working in a factory kitchen as an assistant cook before starting a new career with the city's main electricity supplier, Berliner Elektrizitätswerke Aktien Gesellschaft (Bewag), servicing heating systems. Little did he know that this career change would bring him the biggest opportunity of his young life.

With his father taking early retirement in 1970, the family made a fateful decision to move from their home in Weinbergsweg near the border. Taking advantage of the GDR's policy of allowing elderly citizens to travel freely to the west in order to place the burden of their care on the FRG finances, Manfred's parents moved across the city, leaving him and his younger sister in the east. Six months later, his troubles began. "I was summoned to the community police ABV [*Abschnittsbevollmächtigter* or "section representative"] where an officer said: 'Listen Mr. Höer, you work close to the border and your parents have now moved to the west. Do you also want to go over to the west?' I replied, 'No, I am doing well here.' Of course, you couldn't tell them that you wanted to leave, too. But during the course of the conversation he made it very clear to me that within the next year I would be withdrawn from the border and relocated due to the risk of me escaping." Höer was quickly rehoused in a one-bedroom apartment in the Friedrichshain district, back then still showing many signs of the terrible damage from the Second World War. His friend Peter Schöpf would frequently bunk in with him, and he began work with the Ministry of the Interior in late 1971. Höer had by now also fallen in love with a girl from the west (Inge), who had been introduced by his sister when she had visited. Their desire to get

The luck of the Irish. Just some of the Irish Guardsmen under Lieutenant Corbett's command tasked with protecting the vital supply train headed for West Berlin in October 1961.

Lieutenant Robert Corbett of the Irish Guards would come through a baptism of fire at the East/West German border to deliver his convoy of supplies to the beleaguered city of Berlin. He would go on to play a more significant role twenty-eight years later.

Socialist Unity Party leader Walter Ulbricht longed to isolate West Berlin and establish East German sovereignty over the whole city before the "brain drain" of his country's workforce became a tidal wave to the west.

4

Sergeant Adolf Knackstedt of US Military Intelligence in civilian clothing, undertaking another undercover reconnaissance mission in Berlin in the late 1950s.

By the autumn of 1961, Checkpoint Charlie found itself as the focal point of East/West confrontations along the border as troops from both sides faced off across yards of no-man's-land.

5

Conrad Schumann vaulting the wire. If one image could sum up the futility of the reasoning behind building the Berlin Wall, it is this one.

6

The arrival of Vice President Lyndon B. Johnson and the hero of the 1948 Berlin Airlift General Lucius Clay on August 20, 1961, did what the American government hoped it would—show the Berliners they were not forgotten by the Allies.

Crossing the border at the point of a bayonet. When Allan Lightner, the senior US diplomat in West Berlin, took his wife to the theater in East Berlin on October 22, 1961, he didn't know it would spark an international incident.

A key eyewitness to what the Soviet tanks were intending to do at the infamous standoff at Checkpoint Charlie was then-Lieutenant Verner Pike of the US Military Police (*right*) standing with his driver, Private First Class Jacobs.

10

The senseless killing of East German teenager Peter Fechter near Checkpoint Charlie in August 1962 brought international condemnation on the Communist regime.

June 1963: The triumphant arrival of President John F. Kennedy finally gave West Berliners the chance to acclaim their savior in the flesh, as well as cement America's commitment to protect the city.

11

12

The Secret Army. The men of Detachment A were the ace up the Berlin Brigade's sleeve should the city be overrun by Warsaw Pact forces.

13

Mark Wood's primary role as a Reuters correspondent in East Berlin in the 1970s was to cover the state's economic progress, as well as daily life in the country under the watchful eye of the Stasi.

14

A lucky escape. Captain Peter Williams of BRIXMIS sips his cup of coffee standing next to the wreckage of his vehicle, which minutes earlier had been rammed off the road by a Stasi hit team.

15

Rocking the wall. Hundreds of thousands of East German music fans shocked the state authorities by flocking to witness Bruce Springsteen's memorable concert in East Berlin in July 1988.

Mikhail Gorbachev's official visit to celebrate East Germany's fortieth anniversary in October 1989 marked the death knell for the ailing authority of Erich Honecker. The younger generation, led by Honecker's deputy Egon Krenz, would seize the opportunity to oust him days later.

Peter Spitzner with his daughter Peggy celebrate their remarkable escape through Checkpoint Charlie in West Berlin in September 1989.

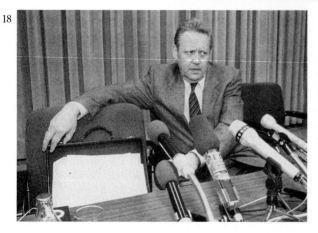

Under the spotlight. SED spokesman Günther Schabowski's disorganized press conference on November 9, 1989, began the sudden collapse of the authority of the East German regime. The Berlin Wall would open hours later.

By the morning of November 10, the diesel fumes of East German Trabants choked up Checkpoint Charlie as hundreds of vehicles trundled their way to explore West Berlin.

The following days would see once prohibited areas that enclosed iconic sites, such as the Brandenburg Gate, open to the public. East and West Germans danced on the Wall as the international press covered events.

Major General Robert Corbett, along with his fellow Allied commandants in the French and American sectors would act decisively and with great diplomacy to ensure there were no outbreaks of violence on either side after November 9.

22

For Lieutenant Torsten Belger, a third-year student at the NVA's training academy in Sietow near the Czechoslovakian border, the events in Berlin would come as a rude awakening to what a perilous position East Germany was in.

The final chapter. Sergeant Michael Rafferty of the 287th US Military Police stands with his British and French counterparts at Checkpoint Charlie prior to its closure in June 1990.

23

Farewell. The Allied hut that had stood on the same spot for decades is finally removed amidst much fanfare, formally ending the Cold War on June 22, 1990. The event was watched by diplomats, the military, Berliners, and the world's press.

24

married and his need to escape the rigidity of life under the socialists drove him to look for a way out, which would soon show itself.

Manfred's job as a boiler man for the Bewag took him on various jobs to repair and maintain heating systems in the nearby building that housed the administration of the Bewag. It was here that an opportunity arose. In early December he was tasked to repair a radiator on the third floor of the Bewag building that overlooked the border with Checkpoint Charlie, in sight a hundred meters (a little more than three hundred feet) away. Having been given the key by the porter, Manfred had freedom to look around as the building was empty of staff. Realizing that the porter's lodge held tools and materials to gain entry to the building's cellar complex, Höer took a set of pliers and a portion of sealant wax that would replace the official seal he would need to break to gain access for his first reconnoiter. Upon entering the cellar, he realized almost immediately that it was like a gateway to freedom, being barely a few dozen yards away from the actual Wall itself. He turned on his heels, resealed the lock with wax, hung the key back in the key cupboard, and returned home to reveal his initial plan to his astonished friend, nicknamed Schöppi, who readily agreed to join him in his endeavor.

First, Schöppi would need to start work for the Bewag in order to gain entry to the building to assist him. "In the east that was no problem. You didn't need to adhere to a notice period. Every company was content to get staff. You could hand in your notice from one day to another. Even from a police point of view, that did not raise any suspicion. It was just to get an ID card, if there had been an inspection, because it was the border area." Schöppi quickly got his and was placed at the branch at Kopenhagener Straße, yet it also enabled him to access the site where Manfred was working. Both returned on Christmas Eve to scope the cellar out for the best place to begin tunneling. They were in a critical window of time as staff would return just after New Year's. It would not be plain sailing.

The tools they would use were very basic: a small shovel, a chisel, and a hunting knife. "The first wall we discovered," Höer recalled, "I thought, *It must be it*. We worked with a brace, which then got stuck and Schöppi looked at the other door and said, 'We could save ourselves the trouble. Look over here.'" So they moved to another part of the basement. "There we got a shock. The whole wall here was full of pipes encased in concrete boxes. But [we discovered] there was one section without cables, where we could start the tunnel, as the earth was soft once the brickwork was broken down. And when we had kicked the bricks out of the way and dug for a meter, there was the base of a lamppost and then we knew that must be the road." It was the beginning, the barbed-wire barriers at the perimeter of the Death Strip before one came to the Wall just over twenty meters farther on. Even with the concern of the work lying ahead of them, the arrival of East German border guards, who came to check on the building over the festive period and had been alerted by the noise the pair were making, gave them both a severe shock. Having covered up their work, resealing the cellar door with the wax sealant, they quickly retreated to the main boiler room, to speak to the inquisitive guards. Manfred and Schöppi bluffed their way through the questions. "We said: 'We are the boiler men, we have to heat the system up. Although no one is here over Christmas, we have to make sure nothing freezes, because it could break and cause damage.' They had a look at it and we had cleverly prepared things to heat up the boiler. They looked at the back, where the hall was, our shower room, the sealed door and the staff room where we had breakfast and rested, when the boiler was heated.'" The noises the guards had been alerted to they explained away as the coal being carried into the boiler room to prepare the heating system.

Though both men dug with intensity over those first two days—taking one-hour shifts in the tunnel as it grew in length—the distance achieved was still only four meters (thirteen feet) in length. It dawned on them that they still had another 75 percent of the route to go. To dig so far together, in such a small window of time, might prove too great a task. They needed help if this was going to succeed. So Manfred recruited his brother, Peter. He agreed he would dig with the pair after New Year's Eve, but as far as a life in the west, he wasn't keen to leave his wife and family. All three agreed no one should be told of their plot, as betrayal might well follow. They would take shifts at digging and keep up the pretense to friends and family until they had succeeded.

As the tunnel became longer, the amount of fresh air lessened, forcing the men to shorten their shifts from hourly to thirty minutes maximum as they dug away at the soft clay soil, but progress was being made. "We also got a metal container the size of a shoe box. We put two holes on each side and put a string through them, so that you could pull it into the tunnel, and when the box was full, the other person could pull it out and empty it. It was time-consuming, when you can only make progress with a shoe box. The longer the tunnel became, the longer it took." They would dig until 3 a.m., sometimes 3:30 a.m., and then stop, shower, and get changed back into their boiler suits in order to maintain the building's heating system in case any skeleton staff coming in wondered what was going on and came prying.

On New Year's Eve they were alone again, and they took time off for a short while to go up to a higher floor and watch the fireworks lighting up the West Berlin sky—wondering whether their plan would succeed and they would reach their goal. Past midnight and into 1972 their only surprise was the night porter coming to wish Manfred a happy New Year before going home to his bed. After New Year's Day they were forced to put down their tools as Manfred found himself on a day shift.

The men by now had gotten into a routine which was working well for them, but the strain of keeping up the charade to others and the fear of a spell in a Stasi prison were weighing heavily on Manfred's mind, to the point he thought he would break down. "I was a nervous wreck, as we never slept in those three weeks. Whenever there was knocking or ringing at the door you thought: *Oh no, now they have discovered it and they got us.* I thought we should give up, because it was taking too long, it was cold, and my clothes were wet from digging the sand out. But then Schöppi and Peter would encourage me and say: 'We don't give up. Either they get us, or we get out.'" Determined to succeed, they continued until by January 9 they believed they had reached the base of the Wall itself, which energized all of them, but obstacles still presented themselves. "We wanted to crawl through underneath the Wall. It was built on three bricks; and underneath those were another three thick electrical cables servicing the street above, so we had to dig even further below it, to get underneath it and then back up again." Even though they were now beyond the Wall, and the Death Strip itself, they were still in great danger as the pathway on the West Berlin side was still inside the GDR. Elated at how close they all were—crawling one behind the other in a claustrophobic, dark tunnel, they had all decided they would fight their way to freedom should anyone now try and arrest them. Peter broke through the frost-covered ground cover, creating a hole of three centimeters (a little more than an inch) in diameter with a thin pole, checked that the lack of bright light confirmed they were now in the west, and carved out a much wider exit for the group. "We walked along the length of the wall within its shadow, toward Checkpoint Charlie. There was a call box for the police, a '*Rufsäule*' [special pillar-mounted telephone for certain services]. 'Yes, the police, what do you want?' We said we were three East Berliners, who just escaped via a tunnel at Checkpoint Charlie. Is it possible that they could come and get us? He said: 'What? Can you say that again!?'"

It may not have had the numbers of Tunnel 29 or Tunnel 57, but the ingenuity and daring to tunnel under the Death Strip with just a small shovel and a knife, using a tin box to remove the earth was indeed a great escape.

CHAPTER FIFTEEN

Chimes of Freedom

C an one song spark a revolution? Can one man speak for a silent and imprisoned population? One could argue that the former is open to many interpretations, so probably not. However, the latter could easily be true, as seen by many young Berliners who were lucky enough to witness "the Boss" coming to East Berlin in the summer of 1988.

As the eighties unfolded, the pressure on the East German government to be less repressive of its population became ever more acute. Rising tensions, especially among the younger generation, were conspicuous even to the elderly cabal that ruled. In part that was due to reforms being introduced by President Mikhail Gorbachev in Soviet Russia. His twin policies of *glasnost*, or "openness," and *perestroika*, which entailed restructuring a cumbersome economy, now made East Germany seem a dinosaur, even through the prism of Communism. Young East Germans were feeling increasingly suffocated by a regime that aimed to control how they thought, where they went, and what they watched or read. With West German media beamed into many East German homes, it was proving impossible to keep the population ignorant of what was on offer to the youth of the capitalist West, the consumer goods that mattered to every teenager—clothes and music. If the youth of the GDR were not permitted to travel to the West to taste the life they could see on illegal television programs, then perhaps the government could bring a little of it to them, as long as they were in control.

The authorities decided that permitting a major rock concert in the summer of 1988 might well diffuse a difficult situation. Some in the politburo worried a new concert could cause a repeat of the violence seen at David Bowie's concert near the Wall in June of the previous year. They were overruled. In fact, the musician this time was Bruce Springsteen, a giant of American rock and a global superstar with a definite blue-collar following who empathized with the lyrics of his songs. From albums such as *Born to Run* and *The River* in the 1970s and early '80s, through his groundbreaking *Born in the U.S.A.*, which had catapulted him in 1984 into an all-conquering stadium act, Springsteen and his E Street Band were a huge name for any mayor to attract to play in their city. East Berlin was no exception.

For one young West Berliner, Andreas Austilat, the promise of someone of Springsteen's stature playing his city was too good an opportunity to pass up, even if it meant crossing into the grim half of Berlin. Like any young person, Austilat loved rock and pop music, and living in the west allowed him to buy and play any music he wanted to, and to attend concerts, unlike the limitations East Berliners endured in the GDR. "By the time of being at university," he said, "I had already got into the local punk scene and managed to travel through the border again to Potsdam to check out what music was there. Thus, by the summer of 1988, [West] Berlin had already had David Bowie play live, right by the Wall the year before, which had been a huge moment for the city, on both sides. It had really stirred the population, especially when he sang 'Heroes.' Pink Floyd and Michael Jackson also performed that summer before tens of thousands of fans, and East Germans had flocked toward the border crossings to hear them, which had caused mayhem for the security forces. Bryan Adams was playing that June, with Bruce slated to play the following month."

The venue was a disused cycling track in Weißensee, ten kilometers (six miles) northeast of the Brandenburg Gate. And the euphoria induced by a four-hour set played to a crowd numbering some three hundred thousand was seared into the collective memory of a generation. Gaining permission to stage the event itself seemed a major triumph at the time. It had by no means been a given. At the Bowie concert (with Eurythmics and Genesis) the authorities, fearing such youth gatherings, had ordered the crowd's dispersal, with *Volkspolizei* using truncheons and electric stun guns for broaching so-called "sensitive" areas. Mass arrests followed. In fact the concertgoers' only crime had been to crowd the boundary that divided Berlin to soak up all they could of the occasion, although they did respond to a heavy police presence with provocative chanting. Mantras like "*die Mauer muss weg*" ("the Wall must go") and "*wir wollen Freiheit*" ("we want freedom") surely sent a shiver down the spines of the constraining politicians who governed the Germans.

Although they couldn't see the stars' performance, fans could certainly hear the music. East German bureaucrats had asked counterparts in the west to ensure the speakers did not face the Berlin Wall and an inspection was duly carried out. But as soon as West German officials were gone, unknown concert staff swiveled the speakers in the direction of the GDR once more. Afterward, a Stasi report complained that the country had been double-crossed by the western authorities but that a wind traveling from east to west had mitigated much of the effect. At the very least, it all illustrated there was a huge appetite in East Germany for the kind of large-scale gigs that now occurred regularly around the globe since the heady days of Bob Geldof's all-day concert to raise money for famine relief in Africa, Live Aid. That event had signaled to many governments and politicians the power of popular music to reach a global audience, and how if promoted correctly it could shed light on causes, people, and perhaps even countries.

The Tunnel of Love Express tour wasn't in the tradition of Bruce's previous tours of visiting numerous cities and venues across many months. It was announced as a short series of shows at selected European venues, and as such tickets would be extremely hard to come by. Springsteen was slated to play a West Berlin date on July 22 at the Waldbühne, which had a capacity of twenty thousand seats. It instantly sold out. Having frantically tried all his contacts to buy tickets, and failed, one of Austilat's friends then said they might get lucky, as Springsteen had announced he'd perform at the Radrennbahn cycle-racing track in Weißensee, East Berlin, three days before the Waldbühne show. The East Berlin gig could hold possibly 150,000 to 160,000 people, so they would have a better chance of obtaining tickets.

"Christian's cousin, Sven, lived in East Berlin, and they regularly kept in touch. We drove across with him a few times to go to gigs and to meet with his family for weekends, and typically we would also bring over presents of food and drink. Sven was indirectly introduced to me through my girlfriend. We often did things together, spending time around Berlin's hinterland, which was exotic for us. We said to Sven that we wanted to see Bruce Springsteen as we didn't get any tickets for his West Berlin show. Sven said he could deliver, though how he managed to get tickets, I still don't know. I assume his father, who worked in broadcasting, had some contacts. We once were at his home and he was watching *Tagesschau* [*the* West German News program, like BBC News, at 9 p.m.], and we made jokes because the GDR authorities frowned on this kind of thing. I said to his father, 'You watch *Tagesschau*?'

"'Always,' he replied casually.

"In any case, with three weeks to go to the gig, Sven announced he had scored seven tickets, at twenty Marks apiece. We even paid those one to one and it was still a bargain. Only issue there was eight of us going, so we hoped we'd be able to score one more at the event—Sven was hopeful, but I wasn't."

But how had East Berlin managed to persuade a rock icon of Springsteen's stature to play in the first place? The official youth wing of the Communist Party, the *Freie Deutsche Jugend* ("Free German Youth") or FDJ, took up the mantle. It decided to offer an invitation to Springsteen to play in East Germany, hoping that, if it was successful, the nation's youth would remain faithful to Communism. By happy coincidence Springsteen was keen to include a date behind the "Iron Curtain" on his tour and had been making his own overtures to come to play in front of the proletariat. He had wanted to perform in East Germany after visiting in 1981, when he and E Street's Steve Van Zandt had crossed through into East Berlin via Checkpoint Charlie for an afternoon's sightseeing as tourists. Both men had been shocked at how much seeing such a repressive society close up had affected them. As Springsteen described in his autobiography, *Born to Run*, "It was a different society; you could feel the boot, the Stasi in the streets, and you knew the oppression was real." It was a place that could benefit, he felt, from the rapture that rock could bring. Now that time had arrived.

Although Springsteen's acceptance was a major coup for the FDJ, its organizers were still by no means certain the concert would take place. Springsteen had impressive working-class credentials. But they knew the older Communist Party officials—with the power to pull the plug on their plan—might still need some persuasion. Having heard a rumor that Springsteen once donated a printing press to Nicaragua and its left-wing rulers, the FDJ decided to attach a political element to the concert, crucially without informing the Springsteen camp. Although much of the proceeds of the twenty-Ostmark ticket would pay for staging the event, anything left over would go to the Karl Marx Hospital in Managua, an East German–Nicaraguan venture. The Sandinistas were the avowed enemy of the Reagan administration.

Excitement mounted until Springsteen and his twenty-five-strong entourage arrived in East Berlin on July 18, 1988, via Checkpoint Charlie, the day before the concert, and drove down Friedrichstraße. Springsteen's longtime manager and confidant Jon Landau recalled the disparity in the accommodations in East Germany, "When we arrived a few of us were assigned to the Grand Hotel, which was owned by the Japanese at the time. But the crew and even some of the band were required to stay at an East German hotel because they were desperate for Western currency." "The Grand" was the GDR's luxury flagship hotel, intentionally constructed and placed in the heart of East Berlin in order to attract high-paying Western tourists, celebrities, and politicians. It had been heralded by the SED as a symbol of their ability to compete with the big-name chains of hotels throughout West Germany. Erich Honecker himself had opened it the previous year. As Landau said, the management insisted on payment in Western currencies, not the Ostmark.

Springsteen was not the only rock star to have played in the country, although Bob Dylan's highly anticipated appearance at Treptower Park in 1987 was a disappointment after he played a limited number of songs and refused to engage with the crowd. The following year Depeche Mode, Joe Cocker, and Bryan Adams would play there, too, all before

Springsteen's arrival. The difference between those concerts and the one to be staged by Springsteen turned out to be in its scale and message.

However, there was a behind-the-scenes hitch that nearly skewered the entire event. When Springsteen and Landau arrived, they learned for the first time about the link with Nicaragua, via official posters advertising it—and were deeply upset about being used by East Germany for propaganda. While Springsteen was happy to pin his political colors to a mast of his choosing, he felt ambushed by this FDJ-orchestrated move. At the time none of the Americans would have understood the political sensitivities that the youth workers were trying to service. For their part, the ambitious young East Germans had no idea that Springsteen had recently turned down a $12 million offer from American car manufacturer Chrysler, who wanted to use "Born in the U.S.A." in an advertising campaign but—the inappropriateness of the song lyrics aside—the rock star had firm ideas about his personal branding. The same had happened when President Ronald Reagan's campaign team had wished to have the song play at his reelection rallies across the country.

Jon Landau was quick to spot the problem. "I was sitting in the lobby of the Grand Hotel the day before the concert," he recalled, "when I was approached by a member of the FDJ who thanked Bruce and myself for doing this concert on behalf of the anti–Nicaraguan war organizations. I calmly went and found our East German contact and asked him to show me the ticket. When he did, the word 'Nicaragua' jumped off the printed ticket. I quickly decided that our tour director George Travis and the East Germans' top person needed to go to the field and take down any merchandise, signs, posters, etc., that referenced Nicaragua. We made that demand and that was it—we were looking to do a show, not get involved in some major scene. And the East Germans were cooperative in removing the materials." Though the concert organizers could remove the posters and any other pamphlets relating to supporting the Sandinistas, even the printed tickets had the same message, but Landau was content to allow the show to continue anyway. They had made their point and won the battle. "They knew they had tried to take advantage of us and had been called on it."

Springsteen had his own message to send, too, and began by telling fans gathered at his hotel via the press: "The people have a right to hear good music and that's why I'm here." It turned out that more people wanted to listen to that music than anyone could have anticipated. Not only were there authorized tickets in circulation, but also many thousands of counterfeit ones. And it wasn't just East German fans that were keen on getting them, but those in West Berlin, too.

As the day of the concert unfolded, traffic in that part of the city close to Weißensee soon built up. As the crowds thronged on foot toward the venue, ticket collectors abandoned their posts in the face of an onslaught. Andreas Austilat and his friends were among the masses excitedly heading into East Berlin. "We went there by car and got relatively close to the area of the event. Which I thought was unbelievable because back then, if we would have gone to the Olympiastadion, it would have been impossible to get a parking space. There were simply too many cars. We got relatively close, where we managed to park, and then we walked the final kilometer to the venue. My friend Andreas, who had traveled with us without a ticket for the show, managed to buy one from a tout [scalper] for ten Marks east and ten Marks west. As we got closer, there was a stream of people, it was a giant mass of tens of thousands, as far as the eye could see. Two very large lorry [truck] trailers were parked at the entrance, with concert stewards from the FDJ and possibly plainclothes police, too, monitoring the crowds."

The procedure was that fans were supposed to hold up their tickets for the official stewards to verify they were legitimate, but it quickly became apparent to Austilat when they arrived that the organizers had completely lost control, as thousands of fans were waved through whether they held up a ticket or not. "Fences and gates were broken down by the tide of people which must have numbered in the hundreds of thousands by now. It felt as if the whole city had turned out for him. The police and stewards had pretty much given up by now, and we simply walked into the racetrack without any checks. Andreas, walking alongside me, moaned, 'Why did I actually buy a ticket just now, as I could get in for free, no one is checking my ticket!' I gave up trying to locate any food or drink as the stalls had closed long before due to the demand and the little supplies they had, and toilet facilities were at a minimum, too. It was getting more chaotic by the minute. My main memory of the venue was it was like a dust bowl, not a grassy green racetrack. That long, hot summer had burned up the grass, and now the masses were trampling it into the hot earth."

Like many people there that day, Austilat's main concern was how he would see and find his friends whom had agreed to meet once inside the stadium. "We had agreed to meet at the transmission mast from the East German TV. But there was no way we could get there, as it was heavily protected with fencing which was stronger than the perimeter fencing the crowd had easily swatted aside. By some miracle, as we made our way toward the front of the crowd, our friends appeared just in front of where we were standing looking for them. It was the biggest thrill of the day, as we never thought we would find them in a sea of fans." The friends took in the scene of humanity around them and marveled at the stage the East Germans had managed to erect. "There were towers of scaffolding flanking the stage, with towers of loudspeakers attached, and a huge lighting rig above. We loved the fact they had also erected a giant television screen, which would help those far back."

Those holding properly purchased tickets rued the expenditure while others celebrated their foresight in turning up speculatively. Although estimates vary wildly, it's thought there were at least three hundred thousand people in the audience that day and possibly even more. For any concert, that's an exceptional number. But in East Germany, allowing such a mass of uncontrolled people to gather in one place felt extraordinarily laissez-faire of the regime, as if one of the ties that bound the population had been shed. Austilat was surprisingly skeptical about the level of control the regime had over the concert, and in fact felt the exact opposite about what he saw in terms of a heavy police presence. "They must have been all incognito, because I saw little police. There were a lot of FDJ people there, as it was their event they had organized and promoted as such, but very little police. What I also found very touching were all the self-made flags flying on poles and the posters held up to the stage that read 'Born to Run.' I thought, *Wow, that is really subversive,* because you always looked at the context, that you could also interpret it in a different way. Especially the American flags, which usually didn't belong to the cityscape. All self-made because you couldn't buy it as it was the case with us. In the West at that time, for other concerts, you could also buy T-shirts at stalls, a vast offer of gimmicks. That didn't exist at all at this gig. It was a real 'back to basics' kind of event—the music and what it represented made it special."

Before he went on to play, Springsteen asked his German chauffeur, Georg Kerwinski, to translate a message the rock icon wanted to say on stage. Without thinking too much about it, Kerwinski obliged. The show got under way with Bruce and the E Street Band pumping out the classic "Badlands" to get the crowd going straight from the gun, but possibly also to lay a marker for the type of message his lyrics could convey. The chorus was sung back to him by the crowd uproariously, with the final line especially significant:

> We'll keep pushin' till it's understood
> And these badlands start treating us good

As well as the new songs from the *Tunnel of Love* album, more classics for the plight of the working class followed: "Born in the U.S.A.," "War," and of course, "Born to Run." As Kerwinski watched mesmerized on the sidelines, and Springsteen played into the second hour of the gig, he realized to his horror that mentioning "walls," as he knew Springsteen was planning to do in his short speech, could backfire badly on everyone involved. The East German government was always raw when it came to referencing the Berlin Wall, genuinely feeling that the nuances of its purpose were misconstrued in the West. A panicked Kerwinski went to his boss, the West German promoter of the event—Marcel Avram—and alerted him to this possible public relations disaster if the message he had written down was read out on stage. Jon Landau now became involved and attracted Springsteen's attention from the side of the stage, gesturing him to return down the stairs center stage that he had sprung from to start the show. While the E Street Band thundered on above their heads, Kerwinski struggled to make himself understood, but finally scribbled a message to Springsteen: "Scrap the word *Mauer* [or "walls"] and replace it with the word 'barriers.'" It was a subtle distinction, the significance of which only a German familiar with East German sensitivities could discern.

Springsteen gave the thumbs-up and sprang back to the stage to continue. Another surprise that had been foisted on them at the last minute was that the whole show would be broadcast live throughout East Germany by state television. Perhaps stopping the music for a brief message felt the most opportune moment for any star with a message to say on such a platform. With "Born in the U.S.A." still ringing around the stadium, Springsteen paused to broadcast his chosen words. "It's nice to be in East Berlin," he began, in Americanized German. "I want to tell you that I'm not here for or against any government, I have come to play rock 'n' roll for the East Berliners, in the hope that one day all barriers will be torn down." Notably, he and the E Street Band now kicked off with the chords of a Bob Dylan song, aptly called "The Chimes of Freedom." The first verse ends like this:

> As majestic bells of bolts struck shadows in the sounds
> Seeming to be the chimes of freedom flashing.

Although the authorities would cut out his words in the television broadcast, at the stadium, the crowd went wild, though possibly just because he was speaking, or because that cranked up the music again. For those who did hear his words, it may well have been what they had wanted to hear someone say all their lives. It was all the more bizarre as all East Germans had been brought up during the nuclear arms race believing that all Americans wanted to kill them. That "truth" issued by the East German government was now called into question. Some waved their illegal hand-stitched American flags. Dozens of people fainted in the crush near the stage, their bodies passed on raised hands to the back of the stadium where first aid could be administered.

Andreas Austilat and friends, like many in the audience that day, were slightly confused as to the messaging coming from the stage. "We hadn't understood much of it at the time due to the noise of the crowd and because he spoke such strange German. I didn't understand what

Springsteen said about 'barriers and walls,' one couldn't understand much as it was drowned out in all the cheering, and so we didn't think much about it at the time of the concert. Afterwards I heard that it would have been cut short if he had said something wrong. How would you have cut it short? You could have pulled the plug. But I want to see that person who pulls the plug where there are three hundred thousand people in front of a stage. That person must be mad. I can't imagine that. I would not have thought of the East Berlin police being capable of dealing with a riot of this size, as the West Berlin police were battle-hardened with all the demonstrations that took place since the Wall went up."

Despite the size of the crowd, the lack of official control, and the fact it was a rock 'n' roll event, Springsteen's concert was a very peaceful affair. "There were no fights, and no drunks," recalled Austilat, "but no wonder, really, as there wasn't anything to drink! Bruce Springsteen was extremely impressive because the fact that someone gives a four-hour concert, I have never experienced that before. I had the impression that Springsteen, too, had never seen such a mass of people."

Backstage, in a TV interview, Springsteen elaborated on his experiences in East Germany. "[The concert] was something I had thought about for a long time. . . . [East Germany] felt a little less gray to me this time than it did when I was here in '81. Even with the people on the street, there's a little more life, a little more color. I've been enjoying East Berlin very much so far." Landau, too, was pleased, and relieved that the concert had gone so well. "I thought it was a very powerful day and have been told over the years by many German friends that it added fuel to the fire for freedom. It was not necessarily one of our best musically, but it was certainly one of the most inspirational things we have ever done, both for the audience and for all of us."

The concert became the touchstone of a generation. Those who didn't attend almost certainly watched it on television. Andreas Austilat still believes the concert represented not just a moment for rock 'n' roll, but one that certainly affected his view on the whole city of Berlin and what he thought of the eastern half. "Regarding our friends, although we were usually seen as the 'rich relatives from the west,'" he said, "here we met on an equal footing, as this time they could offer us something that we didn't have tickets to see: Bruce Springsteen. Then there was the concert itself—a major, historic event for the whole city—which, to be with our East Berlin friends, was a beautiful thing to share." The euphoria was tinged with some melancholy for the young fans as the reality of the "divided city" hit home. "We had to be back in West Berlin by 2 a.m., and I think that it was rather disappointing because they wanted to go with us somewhere afterwards and so we went to the city center, but it was already around midnight and it was dead with nothing open or happening. In West Berlin the nightlife would be in full swing, and we all knew it. Sadly, the evening broke up as the euphoria of the gig ebbed away with the night."

Like Woodstock, held in New York State over three days in 1969, it was far more than merely a rock concert but represented the optimism and expectation for a better future among young people. It undoubtedly emboldened those who were enduring rather than enjoying life behind the Iron Curtain. But while the concert may have contributed to the fall of the Wall, it wasn't the only spark to light the flame. There was growing resentment at the way senior citizens from East Germany were permitted to enter the west at will, while young people were caged. A ban on the widely distributed Russian magazine *Sputnik* after the concert fed the bitterness further still. *Sputnik* reflected the new thinking in Russia, which general secretary of the SED and leader of the GDR Erich Honecker, in particular, fiercely opposed.

CHAPTER SIXTEEN

At the Edge of Control

Major Peter Bochman, a former platoon leader in the East German border guard, served at Checkpoint Charlie for many years. Unlike the Allies, the East Germans rarely rotated their staff from one area to another—personnel could work at the same station for lengthy spells. Bochman helped develop many of the Wall's security features and originated a facial recognition system designed to help guards test authenticity of a passport photo. Trainee border guards were required to pass his flash-card examination, comparing and contrasting two different photos to determine whether or not both were the same person.

"My first posting with the *Grenztruppen* was based in the south of East Germany, in Bad Schandau, in Saxon Switzerland, near Dresden, working on the border of the GDR to the Czech Republic. In the early 1970s I transferred to East Berlin as the (new) visitor regulations, in the wake of the Basic Agreement [the Basic Treaty, when the sovereign states recognized each other for the first time] in 1972, opened up new border crossings, so there was a need for well-trained people. There was no time restriction, or limitation of your service in a specific posting—one simply went where one was ordered." There were several border crossings in the GDR that had a special resonance for the East German border guards. The most important to the regime was the transit control of Marienborn on the Inner German border, which monitored traffic between West Berlin and West Germany. Then the border controls at Schönefeld Airport to the southeast of Berlin were vital to protect from infiltration. Friedrichstraße station in the heart of the city obviously was of a high-profile significance due to the Allied positions opposite it. And then there was the world-famous border crossing at Friedrich/ Zimmerstraße (Checkpoint Charlie), where Peter Bochman found himself stationed.

"Checkpoint Charlie was important because of its historical situation in Berlin but also because of its history altogether. And of course because of its traffic categories, which were there. There was the military, the four, who were allowed free access through it: the Soviets, the Americans, the British, and the French. There was also the regime's East European cousins: the Poles, the Czechs, and the Slovaks. And then it was generally a control point for foreigners. GDR citizens could also travel through, but these were exceptions to the rule—it was mainly for military and civilian government people." As international recognition grew for East Germany, so many foreign tourists started to travel through it, too, giving the major crossing points such as Checkpoint Charlie a strong international flavor. "One also had to monitor all the daily business traffic, which was in the financial interest of both sides, and the day tourists on foot, bicycle, car, and coach."

The other extraordinary and unique aspect of working at Checkpoint Charlie for the East German guards was their encounter with other political groups who found themselves protesting on the western side. On the West Berlin side, "We always called it in the 'Vorfeld,'" recalled Bochman, "even though relations with the Allied border guards were peaceful and cooperative. Every day, more or less, there were camera crews from all over the world, who were covering these stories. It was just at the epicenter of German events, whether you were watching from the west or eastern side, it was the beating heart of the Cold War which drew international focus." To be chosen for a posting to this iconic border control was seen by Bochman's comrades as something—a "blue ribbon" post. However, for those actually working a shift there, it was a very pressurized and stressful environment. "There was no advanced training, or a qualification for the work there. You learned from the ebb and flow of the traffic and the people around you. I was lacking foreign language skills, but I had comrades within the unit who helped me to translate until eventually I could manage without trouble."

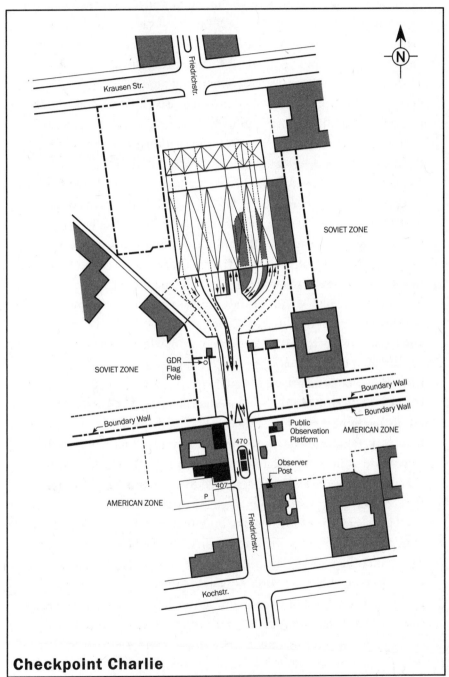

Checkpoint Charlie

© MDL Design

In order to process the levels of human traffic coming through on a day-to-day basis an atmosphere of calm was always sought by the East German border guards at Checkpoint Charlie. "If the travelers could pass through without any issues," Bochman recalled, "then we could function properly and not have too many holdups or long queues developing." Diplomats and the Allied armed forces had to be able to travel through without hindrance, though disputes had arisen as far back as the famous tank standoff in 1961. International recognition for the GDR came at the price of upholding the key pillars of the Four Power Agreement. "Of course, we would have civilians who could be stubborn, or cause a fuss, such as not displaying their identity cards properly, whether intentionally, or by accident as they were not listening to our instructions. They would see the military—who were in uniform—not needing to show identification as their uniforms told us who, or what, they were. Everything was still registered and monitored. Rarely did anyone ever get through whom we didn't already have under surveillance."

The border control at Friedrichstraße ran an efficient service by falling back on their strict selection policy of who would be processed first. From a queue of waiting travelers first would come the military, then the diplomats, or those of equal rank, across all foreign nationalities, who were processed altogether when entering. However, once both groups had gone through the first checkpoint, they would then combine to form just one more queue for final checking. The common civilians were divided into two groups of "*Abfertigung.*" One group included tourists, businessmen, and privileged tourists traveling through by foot or by car. The other group was day-trippers traveling in coaches.

Working for the Ministry of the Interior meant that ultimately Bochman and his comrades worked for, or with, the Soviet forces in the country. "When it was the anniversary of the Russian Revolution, for example, then we always had a bouquet of flowers, or two, given to us to use as props for photo opportunities for Russian soldiers traveling through the checkpoint. If a Russian officer drove to the center of air traffic security (control), or to the Soviet war memorial near the Brandenburg Gate, we would stop them, hand over the bouquet, and a picture was taken. On any other day of the week, the barrier was simply opened, and closed with a brisk nod of acknowledgment. Other than that, there was no contact, as very few Russians spoke German, and those that did were working for the KGB, whom we certainly didn't wish to mix with. But I could say the same of the British, French, and Americans and for the American military and Secret Service, who worked in their area in the same way."

As access improved, so the popularity of visiting East Berlin grew and grew, placing a strain on the border guards' ability to maintain this efficient service. From the early 1970s to 1986 East Germans had been allowed to travel to the west, but few had the money (60 DM was a month's wages to many), a car to travel, or the actual patience to bear the endless bureaucracy of the state, which was designed to keep the applicant in years of limbo, not knowing until the last minute whether the application had been successful. The policy of granting their citizens freedom of travel only for "urgent family business" was relaxed in 1986 and sparked a flood of more applicants. Border crossings rose from 66,000 in 1985 to well over 550,000 the following year. Within eighteen months this would shoot up to 2.2 million. "Staffing did prove to be a problem into the 1980s," Bochman said, "primarily because the bureaucracy within the GDR mushroomed at all levels. Every single person brought a mountain of paperwork as they went through our inspection process to enter the country [*Abfertigungsprozess*]. Who were they? What were they wearing? Where were they going? Whom were they going to see? How many hours did they intend spending in the GDR? What were they bringing back across the border? All of this meant the passport control posts had to record more and more information, and also fill in cards—remember, we had no computer system; it was all achieved by hand and a complex filing system. Naturally, offices all suffer from staff shortages when people are on leave or are sick, and so did we. Especially at the weekends, when fewer men were on call."

During an average week, Monday to Friday, Bochman's unit would process dozens of cars, vans, and coaches. On the weekend, on average, they would process at least fifty vehicles. "It was generally occurring at a specific time of day rather than spread out across hours—so there would be 'surges' where you were rushed off your feet. For example in an hour, one could process eleven buses with foreign tourists on a day's excursion, wishing to take advantage of the east-west exchange rates and shop for bargains; then businesspeople; and finally military and diplomats. This was where the problems for staffing occurred: first thing in the morning, after working hours, and then during the evening of a weekend."

Passport control was by its very nature an intense complex system, which would commence as soon as the traveler was walking up to the checkpoint, having passed through the first security cordon. It was here that Bochman's training would come into play. "I would start to size up their ethnic appearance, and gauge their nationality, too, before we actually then began processing them through. Once I had checked them off and had the relevant forms completed, then they would go to our customs control for money transactions (if required) and undergo a luggage inspection. All done whilst under surveillance. At larger crossings there would be a bank for financial exchanges, a medical clinic, and a veterinary checkpoint, too. But not at Checkpoint Charlie."

CHAPTER SEVENTEEN

The Last Escape

The summer of 1989 in the GDR was very much like any other for the majority of people outside the cities. In East Berlin, Leipzig, and Dresden, peace protests were breaking out, but no one envisaged that radical reform would take place, or that their everyday way of life would radically alter. Events in the Soviet Union seemed on a different planet to the average East German citizen, as the new policies heralded by General Secretary Mikhail Gorbachev began the slow thaw in East-West relations. Gorbachev was a product of the anti-Stalinist reforms Nikita Khrushchev had brought into his own government in the late 1950s. Without the opportunities opened then to someone from his background in Stavropol in the North Caucasus, Gorbachev's progress to the Soviet leadership might never have happened. He now saw his mission as bringing social and economic reform to the Soviet Union before it was too late and its Cold War rival—the USA—was over the horizon. In 1985 he had remarkably kick-started social and economic reforms—*perestroika*—within the Soviet Union to accelerate economic growth. The following year, he ushered in *glasnost*—a term for a more open society that tolerated debate in politics and culture. Change was coming from the East, and within five years of Gorbachev's rule, its influence would be felt in Poland, Hungary, and East Germany.

Away from the geopolitical realm, the issue the GDR regime faced was that much of its population still wished to leave the country. Though the borders were rigidly enforced, there were still methods of gaining one's freedom—whether by escape or by legitimate means. If one was

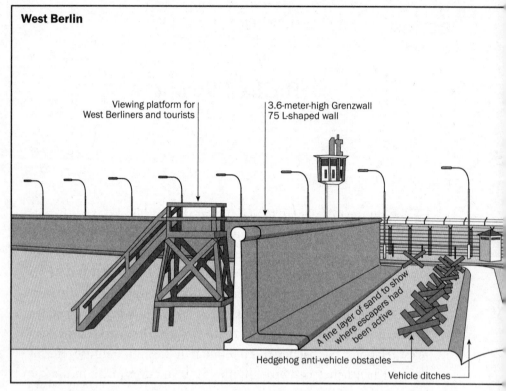

West Berlin

Viewing platform for
West Berliners and tourists

3.6-meter-high Grenzwall
75 L-shaped wall

A fine layer of sand to show
where escapers had
been active

Hedgehog anti-vehicle obstacles

Vehicle ditches

The Death Strip, 1989

aged, the government was more than willing to allow you to leave and so have the burden of your care into old age become the responsibility of the West German government. Many took up this offer. For those in prison for political or social crimes, the West German government could buy their freedom. By 1989, almost eighty-eight thousand East Germans had ended up in prison due to being caught escaping, or simply considered politically "unreliable" in the eyes of the East German authorities. West Germany bought the freedom of more than thirty thousand of these prisoners, at a cost of 250,000 marks each (approximately 100,000 euros in 2019 values). This barter of people in exchange for goods had begun under Konrad Adenauer in 1963, when the first eight prisoners were bused across to the west. Since then, the

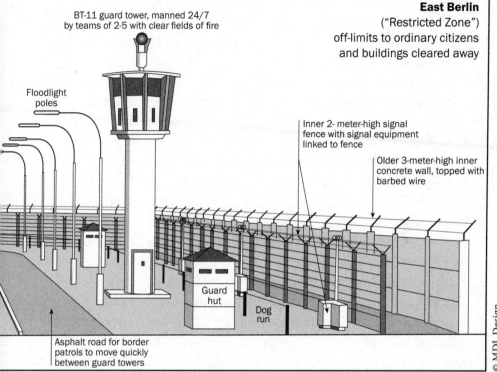

BT-11 guard tower, manned 24/7
by teams of 2-5 with clear fields of fire

East Berlin
("Restricted Zone")
off-limits to ordinary citizens
and buildings cleared away

Floodlight
poles

Inner 2- meter-high signal
fence with signal equipment
linked to fence

Older 3-meter-high inner
concrete wall, topped with
barbed wire

Guard
hut

Dog
run

© MDL Design

Asphalt road for border
patrols to move quickly
between guard towers

Stasi had implemented an industrial process of human trafficking to bolster the economy.

For those East Germans who had grown up in the state, the veil was slowly lifted as to what they had to sacrifice by living in the country. Only then would an urge come from within to find a better life and flee the place. One such case involved Hans-Peter Spitzner, the last East German citizen to risk everything in order to escape the GDR in the summer of 1989 through Checkpoint Charlie. This is his story.

"As a child," he recalled, "you didn't think about the many things in life. The family was at the center and you did what your parents asked of you. As a teenager I was in the FDJ and also trained in textile engineering." Spitzner wasn't completely ignorant of what the socialist system he lived in was capable of in terms of dealing with dissent. "I knew the events of the 'Prague Spring' of 1968 and how the Soviets crushed it. The Russian soldiers who marched into Czechoslovakia had camped in the forests behind our house in Reichenbach. I experienced that at close quarters. I was fourteen years old back then."

As he grew up to attend university, Spitzner still believed in the system he lived under and the regime that governed his life. Teenagers like Peter were integrated into the Pioneers, later the Free German Youth, and the GST—*Gesellschaft für Sport und Technik* ("Society for Sport and Technic")—where they received a pre-military education, preparing the East German youth for national service and indoctrinating them sufficiently for the coming class war struggle with the West. "Up until then I was an obedient sheep, receiving the gold badge for Good Knowledge three times. We repeated party slogans our teachers taught us—even if they themselves didn't believe it."

Spitzner's journey to becoming an enemy of the state began when he applied to university. "You were allowed two applications, and my first one was rejected. I was then invited to see the Party secretary of the company that was linked to the vocational school which I attended. He told me: 'Yes, we can get you a place to study, but you have to join the SED.'" It was a pivotal moment as, shocked and upset, Peter started to doubt that system for the first time. "I wanted to have a career that I built myself and not to rely on friends in high places. I sensed the hostility from the Party secretary and many of the teaching staff at my college." Although he wasn't aware of the consequences, these early thoughts of disobedience signaled that Peter had crossed the Rubicon of saying no, and he had signed the sentence for his own destruction.

In his second application, Peter won a place for textile engineering, which would ultimately lead to teaching the subject, starting his higher education career in a town in Saxony. It would be here that his problems with the state really began, as he quickly saw for himself the parsimonious state of supply in the country. "One had to fight for everything—and there were constant queues." Added to this was the realization that he would have to bend to the authorities' political will. "As a teacher you had to submit yourself to brainwashing. At work, every Monday, we had to attend a compulsory Party course, whether one was a member or not. The speaker would make several announcements which painted the system in bright shiny colors, but our reality looked very different. No one dissented."

At the college Peter taught a general syllabus, alongside the doctrine the regime wished the college to integrate into everyday classes for the students. A lesson in a textile engineering class focusing on cotton manufacture around the globe would promote the Soviet Union's cotton as better than Egypt's. "One can only keep up this pretense for so long and then the questioning of what one is doing in such a role, teaching innocent children, soon dominates one's thinking." As older students came to the point where they would need to choose a branch of the military for their national service, Spitzner did his best to tone down the desirability of extending this into an actual long-term career. But the Berlin Wall dominated the thoughts of everyone who came into contact with it.

"When I visited friends in East Berlin, we would, of course, take a look at the 'Anti-Fascist Barrier,' the 'Death Strip,' and study the faceless border guards who protected us from the 'Class Enemy,' as well as watching the East German population themselves—this is what we had always been told it was for. The Wall was permeable, but only in one direction, namely from west to east. There was also the one-day visa agreement [*Passierscheinabkommen*]. There were different regulations that West Berliners could go to the east for one day, but had to be back in the west by midnight. But for us, there was nothing, we were trapped in this cage.

Spitzner's feelings about the GDR started to express themselves openly, and from then on he became marginalized in the eyes of the college's headmistress, who was a Party loyalist. He was a marked man who was never seen on any awards list and never received any honors, unless it was as part of a collective effort. It became clear to him that ultimately his career path to becoming a senior lecturer was now compromised. But preuniversity he had learned another profession—as a weaver, which paid more (almost twice as much) than being a teacher. Those who worked in the industrial and production jobs earned more money—possibly a by-product of keeping the workers contented (to a degree) after the 1953 uprising. Peter decided to indirectly boycott the upcoming elections for union representatives, spoiling his ballot paper, which he then publicly acknowledged when the results were announced to a packed staff room. His name was now passed to the Stasi.

Peter lived in a two-bedroom apartment in Karl-Marx-Stadt (now Chemnitz). It was a warm summer's morning in 1989 as he lay in bed asleep. His wife and daughter were visiting her parents' house. There was a loud rapping at the front door, which shocked him into action. Believing it was a neighbor locked out, he quickly went to the door and opened it only slightly as he was still naked. The door was violently pushed back as four men burst in. "One of them showed me a small, narrow, foldaway ID card of state security. And another held an official paper up close to my face, 'House search.'" The Stasi operative added that they had a civil citizen as a witness to Spitzner's transgression, and he was ordered to dress, and in the meantime the men—all in civil clothing, no one had a uniform—turned his flat upside down, ransacking anything they found of interest. Every cushion was lifted, every book, coffee cup, and vase was closely examined; they even looked behind the curtains.

In shock, Peter dressed mechanically, with one of them guarding him in case he tried to hide anything in his clothing. "After an extensive search of my house, all they could find objectionable was a Bible. Other than that, nothing. I wasn't working in the underground resistance, nor in any protest movement, so there wasn't anything to incriminate me with. I was a one-man protest movement. Hardly revolutionary." They then took him away to the state security prison at the Kasberg, a typical Stasi-run, nondescript building with a gray and sad interior. He was pushed into it by two men. "There was a long hallway, and I had to wait silently, before they then led me to a small room. There I had to remain seated with a bright lamp shining into my eyes. It wasn't cold, but I was shivering, squirming on a very uncomfortable chair facing a wooden desk. A Stasi officer came in unannounced with a jam jar containing something I recognized as a piece of cloth. He opened the lid and ordered me to take out the piece of fabric, hold it for a time, and then return it to the jar. At the time I didn't know why, but I now know why it was needed, and they would use it to track me if required." The Stasi had multiple methods and means with which to track and capture people, and scent profiling was one of them. Tens of thousands of suspects like Peter had their individual scent secretly recorded by the authorities, to be analyzed, filed, and used to create a case against them if the investigation warranted it.

After an eternity of fifteen minutes, a Stasi officer came in for the interrogation and sat himself down behind the desk opposite Spitzner, and the questioning began. What was his attitude toward the State and the Party? Did he have contacts with the West? His reluctance to promote a long-term career in the NVA [National People's Army], and his protest vote during the union meeting were recorded on typed-up notes in front of the officer—obviously supplied by the school management. "The remoteness of the investigator's questions, his robotic, clipped voice, and the mechanical way he went about recording my answers were chilling, as was his unapologetic refusal to allow me a drink, or go to the toilet, after hours of interrogation." The session lasted for hours, until he was led out to a normal office full of staff, where he was fingerprinted, and his mug shot was taken from different angles. Once this was all accomplished, they accompanied him to the street, where he was ordered to sign their nondisclosure agreement and then go on back to school. Peter blinked in the bright sunlight and gasped at what he thought was a fortunate release, but he knew deep down that he was now in the grip of the octopus.

Spitzner belonged to a vocational school attached to a large textile company, which like many others ran a children's summer camp— theirs was at Lake Zechlin—for seven- to fourteen-year-olds. In 1980 he had been invited by his school to be a camp leader for a fortnight at the eight-week camp. It was well equipped, with its own kitchen, a housekeeping manager, a doctor, a nurse, and a lifeguard for the lake activities. Peter would run a solidarity bazaar, collecting money for purposes no one knew. Each morning the camp would perform a flag ceremony complete with a salute and a heartfelt tribute to the GDR. Peter did his best to divert the children's focus away from anything connected to politics, and instead toward having fun and appreciating the sacrifices their parents had made to send them here.

Fast-forward to August 1989, Peter was again at the camp, lying on the lakeside beach reading the FDJ's newspaper, *Junge Welt* ("Young World"). "One article detailed the worsening economic situation in East Berlin and the GDR as a whole and laying the blame on the West." As Peter read on, it denounced how the Allies were allowed access to East Berlin unhindered. And at the border from west to east they just had to show their documents without being questioned by the guards. Added to this was the exchange rate advantage of their currency spending power in the GDR, which meant many travelers could purchase rare and expensive items in the east. The message was clear: This practice was destabilizing the economy East Germans were working so hard to build, and if there were not enough carpets for the country, it was the fault of these selfish capitalists. "Reading this article made me think about how the car boots [trunks] of these Western travelers were never checked by the border guards."

Spitzner's wife—Ingrid—had traveled to Austria to visit her mother, leaving his seven-year-old daughter with him at the camp. As he mulled over the article, a plan developed in his mind. "If I did think about an escape attempt hiding in a car boot, it would only involve myself and my small child." He knew secrecy was essential—not to even confide to his daughter what they would be doing.

As he drove home from the campsite, he planned how it could be done. "We can't tunnel out, not together, we'd be captured for sure. A plane is out of the question. But a rolled-up carpet is no bigger, or as heavy, as an adult, and certainly more than a child. If we managed to get ourselves into a car boot of a foreigner, then we might get through." The opportunity was slowly outweighing the risk in his mind as he traveled back to Chemnitz. As the car turned into his street, he had made his mind up—they would do it!

What do you prepare when you want to leave the country? Peter would only take what he and Peggy could reasonably carry, and no more. To do otherwise would compromise what they had to do. The second consideration was what did he need to bring in order to build a life in the West? He quickly packed his paperwork proving his qualifications, their official insurance cards—important for a pension—and finally, their social security papers. Looking around the flat, he spontaneously grabbed two Meißen porcelain jars—which had been a present from an aunt. Not for sentimental reasons, but purely to barter once they reached East Berlin, in order to perhaps assist their escape. He then went to his local bank and, on the pretense of wishing to buy a car, withdrew the bulk of his savings. Touchingly, he had already found the family's prized tins of pineapple and tangerines, saved for special occasions—and as a treat for Peggy they had eaten them prior to undertaking this dangerous journey.

On August 16, they set off in the car, and as Peter drove, he began to explain to Peggy what their real intentions were. " 'You know that mom is in the West, yes?' To a child whose geography lessons at school had the whole of Western Europe blacked out on the map, this place was a fairy tale, but she did sort of understand what I was getting at as I continued gently, 'Then, we're going to visit her there, and so have to hide.' By telling her it was a game of hide-and-seek, which she often played at kindergarten, I could convey to her it wouldn't be anything scary to hide in a car boot. If we were to get to the point of sneaking through the Berlin border crossing, she would need to remain calm and not be afraid.

Peggy was excited more than afraid—she was only a seven-year-old girl after all—but she was struggling with the worry about being carsick on such a long car drive. Peter was not worried about being caught with their travel documents and important family papers, which could signal to any border guard that something was amiss. They were on their way, and he knew they needed them—the opportunity outweighed the risk. "Possibly my naïveté as to our chances of success enabled me to make this attempt. I didn't realize for instance that Allied troops visiting East Berlin were forbidden to take any passengers, or transport goods for them. Every member of the military was instructed: 'If someone in the East approaches you, stating he wishes to go to the West, you must refuse. You are forbidden to do so.' Well, I knew we would have to try it anyway. Maybe, just maybe, we will find someone."

He had often traveled to East Berlin for short breaks and so knew the layout of the city, and where best to approach Westerners. In their smart military uniforms they always stood out amid the drab and austere surroundings. In the center of Berlin, at Alexanderplatz, the area around the Rotes Rathaus, the Nicolai church, the Neptune Fountain, there were always many Allied service people to be seen, most of whom were in cars, or on buses. The sheer number of them offered Peter some hope that it would be possible to get a ride. He parked the car in nearby Karl-Marx-Allee, where it was free to leave it. From there he and Peggy could easily walk to Alexanderplatz, where the tourists were.

For accommodation, Peter knew of a hostel near the Friedrichstadt-Palast, but they found shelter from an unlikely source—the church. "On our first day in the city, Peggy and I were sitting in a café having a quick bite to eat as I pondered our first move. . . . A tap on my shoulder snapped me out of my thoughts, and I spun around to see a familiar face—a pastor whom I knew from Chemnitz. Smiling and quizzical, he asked, 'What are you doing here in Berlin?' I made up our official reason—a family excursion—to which he inquired, 'But, where are you staying?' I started to make up some excuse and he butted in offering his own place as accommodation."

They arrived on a quiet, tree-lined street and were led to a beautiful nineteenth-century-style parish house, with several bedrooms upstairs and a large kitchen and dining room on the ground floor, either side of an impressive hallway. Once Peggy had been put to bed, Peter sat up with the pastor to talk and gauge whether he could trust him. "I carefully steered our conversation toward politics and noticed that he, too, was critical of the regime. Feeling secure, to a degree, I announced, 'I want to go to the West with my daughter—we need to get out of the GDR.' It felt as if a burden was off my shoulders, as I hadn't expressed this desire openly outside of my own house. To my great relief he smiled, sat back in his kitchen chair, and said the place was ours for as long as we needed it." Peter thanked him but knew time was not on his side. His wife's travel permit from the GDR would run out in five days' time. Peggy and he needed to make their move very soon, within the next three days.

*　　*　　*

Their first attempt saw them approach what Peter assumed to be a Western bus. The tour group had excitedly disembarked, leaving only the driver standing beside the door, enjoying a cigarette. Peter had seen that the luggage section was near to where he was, and gesturing to him, he asked in broken English if Peggy and he could travel inside the half-empty compartment. Peggy stayed close to her father, as any child would in such strange surroundings. The driver studied them, glanced at the area behind, and drew one last drag on his cigarette before dropping it to the floor, exhaling, and with a sad smile gesturing a finger drawing across his throat. Peter nodded, and quickly moved on. A second attempt that afternoon met with the same fate. "I tried the same tactic for the next three days but still without success. I had by then also started to approach individuals, mindful of the various security cameras and *Vopos* on alert. In my heart, I had started to give up hope of this tactic working. With a young child in tow, my options were limited as one couldn't simply walk around the center of East Berlin for several hours trying to catch strangers' attention. It would stand out eventually. To stave off interest, and keep Peggy's spirits up, we would take breaks for ice cream, or sit in a café and people watch, or play 'I Spy.' I don't think she wanted to engage very much with what I was doing. And of course, she would have not been able to."

It was now the final day of trying to escape before suspicion would follow them and Peter's wife would need to return home to the GDR. They said good-bye to the priest, thanked him, and then drove again into the city to try a final time. The morning was one of fruitless inquiries with desperation slowly rising within Peter's belly. By mid-afternoon they were resting, with Peggy eating some lunch sitting on a bench. The child was tired by now. In his head he was resigned to defeat and working out how best to head home. "But still, an inner voice told me, 'Stay, just for one final try, it might work.' I walked toward a line of parked cars, and a particular vehicle, a black Toyota Camry, caught my eye. It had an American license plate, but of particular interest was its impressive rear boot."

Fear and panic drove him forward; he had nothing left to lose. "If this attempt didn't succeed, we were going home, as I didn't want to drive home to Chemnitz in the dark." He approached the car and could see through the rear window that a man was still sitting in the driver's seat. Peter smiled reassuringly, seeing that the man looked worried as he gestured for him to roll his window down. "His face looked like the dozen or so other faces that had stared back at me in this place over the past three days. But, surprisingly, he opened his window, greeted me. His name was Erik Yaw, and he was a sergeant in the US Army." Sergeant Yaw listened carefully to Spitzner's proposal of wishing to get to the West with Peggy, who was now asleep in a car near the sergeant's. At first, the American soldier didn't react, but just stared at the East German while he mulled over what he'd listened to. Then he got out of his car and walked to Peter's vehicle, to look into the window and catch sight of Peggy. "He noticed her with a smile which transformed into a light laugh. A positive signal!"

He then walked back to his own car and sat back in his seat. The next ten minutes the pair conversed in broken English as Yaw asked several questions as to why Peter was here, why he wanted to escape to the West, and more importantly, how they would get through the border crossing in his car. Spitzner outlined the plan. They would need to drive out of the center of the city—toward Treptower Park—in order for Peggy and him to then get into Yaw's trunk, before returning to drive through the border controls. Spitzner noticed how the American was wrestling with his thoughts as to what he should do now. Peter was dreading the reaction of "It's too dangerous, sorry." And then like a thunderbolt to his brain came the magical words: "Okay, I'll do it!"

"The game was now a reality. He had to trust me, and I him. We both had a lot at stake if this went wrong." They agreed to drive to Treptower Park, where Allied personnel were allowed by the GDR to visit. Peter set off with Peggy in his own car, which Yaw followed. Peter constantly checked in his rearview mirror to ensure the soldier didn't lose them, amid the constant fear that Yaw would suddenly change his mind and veer off back toward Checkpoint Charlie. But that didn't happen. Yaw drove behind obediently and then drew alongside Spitzner's car once they had reached Treptower's parking area. Peter wasn't coming back for the Trabant, so he had no need to make it conspicuous.

Acting as casually as it was possible to do in the circumstances, they loaded their few belongings into the American's Toyota. The main issue now had to be addressed. How would Peggy handle being inside a stranger's car trunk, in the hot summertime, lying in the dark and traveling through the border controls in silence? "She seemed to take it all in her stride and eagerly got herself into the car boot. Forty meters away, I spotted an East German couple strolling toward us with their children in buggies and so quickly closed the boot on Peggy, speaking softly to reassure her. Once the couple had passed by, none the wiser, I opened the boot again to a cheerful daughter and got in myself between her and the two bags wedged in at the side. It was a black car, attracting heat on a hot day, and we'd be squashed, but we had to do it."

The journey began, and as Peter's mind focused on what he needed to do in order to succeed, the immediate concerns of being in the trunk seemed to evaporate from his mind. He had reassured himself he would be able to monitor his journey, as he knew the route well, but after the third turn he became completely disoriented. How long Yaw had been driving, and where they were, had simply gone, to be replaced by a growing fear that they would be discovered. All the while the music from the car speakers was "Hotel California" by the Eagles. That fear became stronger and stronger as time progressed and he believed they were nearing Checkpoint Charlie. So many thoughts flowed through his mind: *If we do get caught, what will happen to us?* Prison for him and a state-run home for Peggy. Perhaps Ingrid would be imprisoned, too, once she returned home from Austria? Mixed with this sometimes irrational fear was adrenaline surging through his body. But they had found someone at last to help with their escape, and there was no going back, they had to continue. Sergeant Yaw drove and drove as Peter and Peggy sweated in their dark hole. "All the while, Peggy tried to wave her hands to fan cool air onto my face! It was still a game to her, thank goodness. Then we arrived at Checkpoint Charlie, and there he had to switch off the music.

"There was a very small hole in the boot for air, and that you could see, partially see—though only up into the air. I merely saw the streetlights—as the border crossing was illuminated day and night—but nothing more. Then suddenly, my world collapsed, as Erik started reversing the car! *That's it,* I thought, *we've been pulled over as they know something odd is in this vehicle. We'll be dragged out of here and into prison!"* The reason for the reversal, however, must have been more mundane. It seemed that Yaw had actually driven into the wrong lane of the checkpoint. Perhaps because he was American; maybe there were different lanes for different nationalities. And after he had reversed out of the lane they had been in, he then drove forward and came to another halt and switched off the engine. All Peter could hear now was the frenzied beating of his heart as it threatened to burst out of his chest. He focused on breathing slowly to calm himself and to not panic Peggy.

He assumed they were now at the border control, as he could make out Erik talking in English to various voices standing around the car and moving in and out of Peter's range of hearing. "I understood he now had to show his identity card. Then, a special and joyous moment: Through the muffled car interior, the music resumed! It reduced the tension. The car started its ignition and we drove on! The border areas were rather wide. It was not that there was simply a barrier; Erik had to drive into a labyrinth of chicane-style zones. I looked up out of the peephole in the boot roof one more time. I could now suddenly see lamps, which looked different from the East German lamps. The car continued on without stopping for what seemed hundreds of meters, as my hopes, my dreams of escape, seemed to be becoming a reality." Peter tried not to squeeze Peggy's sweaty hand too tightly in his excitement. After twenty minutes, which seemed like an hour, the car stopped, the engine was switched off. He heard the driver's door open and footsteps get nearer to the trunk. "Suddenly the light flooded in as Peggy and I both shielded our eyes in surprise. A dark figure towered over the boot. 'It's okay now, we're across the border, you can get out of the boot.'"

Peter quickly alighted and helped his daughter out. They stretched their legs as they found themselves in the courtyard of a high-rise building. By the front of the car, Sergeant Yaw was in discussion with a military officer to allow them to stay in his flat. "Both Peggy and I drank water and took a shower to clean up from the heat of the car boot. I had forgotten to bring clothes for Peggy due to traveling light, but the American managed to gather up some clothes for her and the following day we went out for the first time in the West for lunch—it was surreal. That first evening, we were taken to the refugee center at Marienfelde, where we were registered, given a small room to stay in and a bag of food."

Peter now had two days left to get word to Ingrid before she would return to the East. She was in Berchtesgaden—made famous by Adolf Hitler—spending a few days with her mother in a guesthouse. The panic set in again as he realized he had to reach her before it was too late, and he did not even know the number of the place she was staying, only the name of the woman who ran the boardinghouse—Frau Pfaffinger—and the village. Searching the phone directory, he found that the name Pfaffinger appeared twice. With the first call, from a local phone booth—this was still the time before mobile phones—he struck lucky. Ingrid and her mother were staying there, he was told, but they had gone on a day trip to Innsbruck. "Please pass on this important message for me. Her husband has traveled through to West Berlin with their daughter, and she must not return to the GDR." He spoke slowly and loudly in order to be understood, while Peggy occupied herself by people watching. He prayed the message would get through in time.

The next morning, Erik picked the pair of them up again and drove to the same telephone booth, and Peter called the guesthouse again. Ingrid came to the phone, and the momentousness of what they had achieved hit home for all concerned.

Spitzner was still in awe of why Eric Yaw had helped them in the first place. Even today, he believes "it was an inner sense of duty to help a fellow human being who wanted a better life, and he knew what would have happened to us, too, if we had been caught." Peter asked Eric what he would like in return for helping them both so much.

"Nothing," came back the reply. "I don't want anything for that. I did it, because I could empathize with you, Peter." Spitzner still wished to thank him, properly, with something that was precious, so Eric would know it was from the heart. Smiling at him, he held up the Meißen pot as a gift, which Erik accepted; it was now a symbol of a bond between them. The pair agreed Eric would pick Peter and Peggy up again the next day. But the family's journey to start a new life in the West would still have a few hurdles to overcome.

That night, back in their accommodation in Marienfelde, just as Peggy was drifting off to sleep, and Peter was heading the same way, there was a loud knock at the front door. Immediately, he was swept back to the feeling of impending arrest by the Stasi—only this time, these people wore a different uniform. Opening the door, he stared into two gun barrels of American military policemen, with their ubiquitous green helmets with a white stripe.

"They barked at me in broken German, 'Are you Spitzner?' I nodded. 'Then get dressed and come with us!' Spitzner would eventually be told that the reason for his arrest was that he had obviously escaped illegally through the Wall. Erik had assisted him, and this in itself was an illegal act, too. Not wishing to wait until Peter might say something, Yaw had informed his superior of his actions.

Now, here he was walking along to be taken for questioning. The American officer who undertook the interrogation used far less subtle methods than the Stasi official who had reduced him to a quivering wreck months before, but at least he did speak in fluent German. "His line of questioning wasn't systematic to break my will, it was harsh and ferocious to scare the hell out of me. Why had I come to the West!? With whom, and how!? What had I paid, where and to whom!? What job did I have in the GDR!? Was I a member of the SED!?'" Over and over again they went through Peter's story, as if the officer was trying to catch the East German refugee out in some way. Did he think Peter was actually a spy for the Stasi?

After a few hours of this, and his testimony not budging one inch, the officer was seemingly convinced that it matched what Erik Yaw had testified to in his own questioning. The American interrogator now became noticeably friendlier and offered Peter advice as to his next steps in West Berlin. Their paperwork for the West was processed quickly through the various departments of the Americans, the British, and the French—all of whom had to stamp their approval. He and Peggy then were given their health checks, which were passed easily. Only then did they receive their West German passports. They had both left the GDR.

Peter's wife wanted to come to West Berlin immediately. "I was thankful she wasn't angry with me for the escape, and for putting Peggy's safety in danger. On the contrary she was understanding and pleased. She financed her flight from Munich to West Berlin by returning a set of expensive headphones she had bought for me as a treat, and her mother provided the rest for the flight. Luckily now Ingrid's mother and father were in the West on holidays visiting relatives, but they had decided to return to their homes in the East, so they believed—tearfully—that they wouldn't see her again for many years. It was a heartbreaking decision for them." Ingrid finally flew into West Berlin. To surprise her, Peter was on the platform when her train pulled into the S-Bahn station Marienfelde. "The doors of the train opened, and as hundreds of passengers disembarked, my beautiful wife stood opposite to me with her pieces of luggage. I hadn't seen her so emotional, and we fell into each other's arms. As a passenger walked by, she muttered, 'It must be love.' They didn't know the half of it!"

The family settled in Idar-Oberstein, Rheinland-Pfalz. On the map, it was similar to where they had lived in Chemnitz, lovely countryside with rolling hills. "So, we flew from Berlin to Frankfurt and continued the journey by train to Idar-Oberstein. At the station we were picked up by someone from the Workers' Welfare Association and brought to an accommodation. There we spent the first few weeks." Sergeant Yaw visited the family once they had settled in Idar-Oberstein. "He asked me to come down to the car as he had something to give me. In the refugee camp, he had always brought us Coca-Cola and crisps [potato chips], from the PX shop at Andrews Barracks, so I assumed this was another delivery. How wrong could I have been?" Carefully taking out the package from the back of his car, Yaw smiled and, with great reverence, handed Peter the gift. "It was the Meißner vase I had given to him that day at the Marienfelde camp. 'I simply kept it for you,' he said, 'so that no one in the camp would steal it from you.'" With tears filling his eyes, Peter gestured to hand it back, but the American soldier shook his head. "I don't want anything for that. I simply kept it safe for you, it's yours to keep," he said, and pushed it back into Peter's arms. "From that day, Erik and I were brothers," Peter said. "His family is my family."

On the night of November 9, 1989, Ingrid and Peter Spitzner were with friends from the nearby town of Kirchweiler enjoying dinner. Once SED press spokesman Günther Schabowski had finished his news conference, the couples couldn't take their eyes away from the television as the events quickly unfolded. "We ended up eating our dinner in the living room watching the coverage as first the crossings opened and the crowds then started tearing down the Wall itself. Peggy came up from the cellar, where she'd been watching a movie with our friend's children, to see us all hugging, weeping, and laughing. I thought now no one has to risk his or her life anymore. Now no one needs to be afraid anymore. If people really want to go to the West—just to travel, it was mainly all about traveling—then they don't have to leave everything behind, to be regarded as a criminal by the state."

Peter and his daughter were the last fugitives to flee the GDR via Checkpoint Charlie. They live happily as free Germans.

PART V

THE WALL FALLS

With the opening of the checkpoints on November 9, 1989, the world's media were quick to send their teams to report the seismic events of the Wall actually falling.

"Those who are late will be punished by life itself."

—General Secretary Mikhail Gorbachev,
East Berlin, October 1989

CHAPTER EIGHTEEN

A Family in Berlin

A s the decade of the 1980s came to a close, to the outside world there didn't seem to be any particular signals that the fabric of the East German state was coming apart from within. With Erich Honecker looking firmly in control, the world's media was instead focusing more on what was going on in China at the beginning of 1989. The outpouring of public demands for democratic reform in the capital, Beijing, would quickly lead to mass repression and bloodshed. The Iron Curtain and the Berlin Wall were still facts of life for East Europeans, with no sign of them being removed anytime soon. Events that summer and autumn would prove otherwise.

The three men who commanded the American, British, and French garrisons in 1989 would find themselves unwittingly in the crosshairs of history. They had all begun their military service during the first decade of the Cold War and had enjoyed such successful careers that taking on such a high-profile position on the front line of the division between East and West simply matched their experience. They were fearless, expected high standards of their subordinates, and reveled in the command of troops. As luck would have it, they were exactly the right men, in the right place, at the right time.

By the start of 1989 the young British lieutenant who had looked out of the Reichstag on the Wall being built in 1961 had now returned as the garrison's commandant—only now he was a major general. Robert Corbett had rapidly risen through the ranks since those early days in Berlin, with a series of promotions from commanding officer of the Irish Guards to chief of staff to British forces in the Falkland Islands after the war, and on to leading the 5th Airborne Brigade. The offer to go to West Berlin had come out of the blue, with his final interview for the post headed by Sir Geoffrey Howe, then British Foreign Secretary. "I said to him," Corbett recalled, "as I had to others, 'What chance is there of change? Is this going to remain the situation, or do you think it could change?'"

"'No,' he replied, 'General, the Wall I suppose might become a little bit more porous, but essentially there will be no *effective* change in our lifetime.' I remember making some speeches when I got there—you know, one had to sort of say a few things—saying that I hoped that the situation would become easier and that there would be some relaxation of the travel restrictions and the difficulty that people had getting to and from, but I had to be very careful as I was Her Majesty's representative in Berlin, I was still a soldier."

Corbett's excellent language skills (he spoke German and French fluently) had perhaps pushed him to the front of the queue to handle this high-profile yet pressured position. To his great good fortune, he realized that his French counterpart would be General François Cann. Both men had served in the same elite French parachute regiment (though not at the same time), the 3rd Parachutistes d'Infanterie de Marine ("French Marine Parachute Regiment"). "We needed to understand and trust one another," he recalled. In fact their paths had crossed unwittingly many years before.

When on his attachment to the 3rd Marine in 1975, Corbett had taken part in a Special Forces exercise in the Montagnes Noires, Tarn, where they would parachute into a drop zone at dusk. It went badly wrong. A number of his unit soldiers landed well short of the drop zone and were injured with varying degrees of severity. Corbett himself landed in a quarry, among huge blocks of stone, breaking a leg. Needing to raise the alarm, he had dragged himself for miles until he had succeeded in getting help for his injured men. No inquiry was held in the UK, but the French authorities had conducted one, and as a senior and highly experienced airborne officer, Cann had been involved.

Lieutenant General François Cann was a born soldier and built like the boxer Rocky Marciano. Hailing from Brittany, his father was

a highly decorated hero from the Second World War who after distinguished service with the French Resistance for his role in rescuing Allied
aircrews, had landed at Normandy and served on US General Patton's
staff as French liaison officer. His eleven-year-old son was inspired to
follow in his footsteps. Cann Senior had then served postwar in the
French Sector of Berlin as a police commissioner. His son, then twenty,
would visit him and take in the sights of the city. "I had known Berlin
without the Wall and already what was called then the Soviet Sector
of the city contrasted with the western sectors where the reconstruc-
tion of the city was in full swing, while in the east the ruins remained
unchanged." By 1954 he was a second lieutenant in the colonial infantry,
qualifying a year later to the colonial paratroopers. Like Corbett, he
would rise quickly through the ranks, from one elite unit to another—
seeing service in Algeria, Cambodia, and Lebanon—commanding the
11th Parachute Division. By 1987 Cann was ready to take command of
the French Sector and garrison in Berlin. For Robert Corbett, there
was an unspoken bond between the two leaders. "It was a good start
to what became a strong personal friendship—important in the light
of what lay ahead."

The American commander would be Major General Raymond Earl
Haddock, a tough, plain-speaking, and resolute leader from Oklahoma.
After graduating from West Texas State University, he had enlisted in
the US Army, qualified as an officer in the artillery. He was a lieutenant
serving in West Germany when the Wall was erected in 1961. He had
gone on to serve as an adviser in Vietnam in the 1960s and by the
1970s had transferred to the Federal Republic of Germany to serve as
first a company commander, then battalion commander, and finally
commander of the 56th Field Artillery Command. Haddock also commanded the artillery of the 9th Infantry Division at Fort Lewis, Washington. As part of the defense doctrine of the US having an "umbrella
protection," President Ronald Reagan's administration had begun the
process of installing their medium-range nuclear missile system—
Pershing II—throughout Western Europe. More than 108 would be
eventually deployed, despite much public outcry in the region, such
as the Campaign for Nuclear Disarmament (CND). Speaking fluent

German allowed Haddock to be chosen as one of the key American officers to speak with local West German leaders throughout southern and southwestern Germany, to gently push the policy through successfully. The deployment of Pershing II was the final straw for the Soviets as Gorbachev had realized they could not match the Americans in an arms race and still restructure and modernize their country. After a brief stint in the Pentagon, Haddock had in 1989 been in charge of the American Sector since June 1988. As with all previous members of the Allied *Kommandatura*, the three commandants in 1989 would work well together, would socialize with their wives, and would handle the biggest crisis in the city's history since 1961.

Within hours of arriving to begin his new command, Robert Corbett was horrified by how the GDR treated its own people, specifically those choosing to escape through the Wall or swim the canals. Six weeks after he arrived to take up his post, Christopher Gueffroy (a young East German waiter) was shot by the border guards—the last person to be killed attempting to cross the Wall—at the Britz Canal area. Later in March of that same year, the last fatalities crossing the actual border were Winfried and Sabine Freudenberg, who tried to escape in their makeshift balloon, which they had filled with helium. Sabine was captured by the Stasi before they took off, and Winfried almost certainly died falling to earth.

In his first week in the garrison, the Corbetts were guests of the Catholic Archbishop of Berlin at St. Hegwig's Cathedral on Babelplatz, and it was here they saw up close just how unsettled the population was with their government. As they took their seats at the front of the congregation with the commandant of the French garrison—François Cann—and his wife, they were immediately made to feel very welcome by the local worshipers. By contrast however, six grim-looking members of the politburo who were ushered in late and out again at the end of the service, received no recognition at all from the congregation. Once the service was finished, however, as the couple departed back to their vehicle and escort, they were mobbed by East Berliners shaking their hands and thanking them for attending. Others were in tears pleading for them to stay and help. Pushing through the throng, the East Germans began to hammer on the car roof once the Corbetts were safely inside. It was a shocking initiation into the state of the GDR in 1987, and both wondered what was going to happen next.

By the summer, Corbett had spent a lot of time in East Berlin, trying to get a feel for himself of what was going on in the country as it suffered the upheaval of large demonstrations of popular unrest and the sudden emigration of hundreds of its citizens across the Hungarian border. He had concluded that the pressure cooker of discontent in the country was going to blow. He was a firm believer in seeing a problem up close, so when a young East German border guard crossed into the American Sector via swimming a canal, Corbett was keen to speak with him. With the permission of US Major General Raymond Haddock, the British officer sat down to speak in German with the young soldier. "It was absolutely fascinating, and toward the end of our conversation, I said to him, 'What was it that made you risk your life and throw yourself into the canal when you could so easily have been shot or drowned or both? Why did you do it?' He replied, 'We had no hope for the future. We were not able to travel. We couldn't see that there was anything opening up for us. We wanted out!' Those were his very words." Despite his sending reports back to Bonn and to London of how he felt things were changing, Corbett's comments went unheeded. "I always believed that we were dealing with a formidable opponent," he said, "who was now defending a really formidable obstacle—much more so than when I first encountered it in 1961. It was as brutal as ever but now much more sophisticated and, if anything, more formidable than ever."

The life of an army wife could be boring and eventful in equal measure, depending on where your spouse might be posted. Susan "Susie" Corbett had traveled the world with her husband for many years, as she brought up their three children. Like thousands of Allied personnel before them, they had undertaken the journey to West Berlin by car—traveling via the checkpoint at Helmstedt and, once in the GDR itself, the autobahn. "As we drove along," Susie recalled, "we had a British security car in front of us and one behind us and all three vehicles were traveling at one hundred kilometers [about sixty miles] per hour—double the national speed limit. Robert calmly reassured me that he'd been told by the Royal Military Police we had to make a statement and driving at this speed was all about politics."

Their residence would be the Villa Lemm. It had been the British Commandant's residence since being selected by Field Marshal Montgomery at the end of the war in 1945, as it was intact and lay in the district of Spandau, which had been assigned to the British Sector. Originally built in 1908 by the Berlin shoe polish manufacturer Otto Lemm, it was designed by Max Werner in what was then the popular English country house style—a two-story building with an attractive high tiled roof and bay windows throughout the ground floor to give excellent views to the gardens and the banks of the River Havel beyond. A large gatehouse led out to the main road and was guarded by the German Security Unit (GSU) formed from local enlisted civilians trained and administered by the Royal Military Police. There was a large estate designed in the classic Edwardian style, and from one open section of lawn at the back of the house General Corbett would regularly take a helicopter to work. You would think you were in Kent, rather than Eastern Europe.

The house had an elegant and tragic history. It had been the holiday home of the famous Berlin pathologist and physiologist János Plesch, who was a lover of the arts and held lavish parties there, hosting the likes of Marlene Dietrich and Albert Einstein. With the rise of the Nazis in 1938, Plesch was warned he needed to flee the country and so quickly sold the property to a Jewish banker, Hans Seligmann, and relocated to London, where he established himself as an innovative heart specialist. Seligmann's fate under Hitler's regime is unknown, but it is thought he died in the Holocaust, and the house subsequently came into occupation of the Nazi *Gauleiter* of Spandau from 1939 until 1945. The villa was close to the East German border and to the massive Soviet artillery firing range at Döberitz. There seemed to be a permanent state of armed forces on exercise, and the Corbetts could hear the shattering noise of tank guns firing virtually every day. "It was ominous but one got used to it," the general recalled.

The residence employed twenty-eight staff altogether (financed by the federal German government), including four gardeners to maintain the estate and two chefs who oversaw the kitchen and planned banquets. Head of the household was a house sergeant, and Corbett's was a special man indeed. Brian Andrews had first met the Berlin commandant at the army's training center in Pirbright, Surrey, England, when Andrews was beginning his training to become an Irish Guardsman. Robert Corbett was then a major and Andrews's first company commander. "I will never forget his first words to me," the house sergeant recalled. " 'The Irish Guards are not only a great regiment but are a family who will care for you. You will make friends for life here.' *What a load of rubbish,* I thought to myself, but I couldn't have been more wrong. As soon as I qualified, I was posted to Hong Kong, and Major Corbett left to join the Guard's paratroops. The next time our paths crossed was when I was posted to the 1st Battalion, Irish Guards, in Münster. On returning to the battalion from Gibraltar, I was then a lance sergeant and was enrolled into the staff of the officer's mess, which I helped to run, but never thinking that from here, under Lieutenant Colonel Corbett's command, I would one day find myself as house sergeant for his official residence in Berlin."

A large part of the job would include working closely with Susie Corbett, who was herself slightly intimidated at first with the amount of entertaining the commandant was expected to do. "Within the first week of arriving, we had all the city mayors throughout the Federal Republic travel to West Berlin to greet us. After that we then entertained all the senior clergy. I remember confiding to Robert's chief of staff, 'I feel just like the new girl at school and I don't know where my locker is!' The house felt like a prestigious hotel and I was the manager."

One of the events to be hosted would be a monthly lunch for the French and American commandants, for which hosting duties rotated among the commandants. Each general always wanted to "best" the others, to see who could put on the finest lunch. There would be no one in the room except for the generals themselves, sitting at a round table, with a spare place set for their Soviet counterpart—who never turned up. As Sergeant Andrews recalled, "The lunches lasted usually two hours.

General Corbett and General Cann were on very good relations with one another, and to a degree with General Haddock, too. He, however, had a more serious idea of what his primary role in West Berlin was—to fight! He took security very seriously indeed and would arrive in an armored car and [with] a large protection team. It was rather amusing to see all this as necessary just to enjoy lunch."

The social life for an Allied commandant was hectic—more so than in any other military posting. A typical day for the Corbetts would begin with the general leaving in the morning for work, but he would have to vary his departure and method of travel due to terrorist threats—a helicopter from the garden, or a boat from the banks of the Havel, or a car journey under guard. Susie Corbett would then start her day, which could begin with a mid-morning meeting with delegations, or parties, of businesswomen, or large numbers of diplomats' wives. Lunch would usually be for about twenty people, with some of them actually resident in the Villa Lemm itself. By the evening, it was a quick change into their best attire to attend possibly two different cocktail parties, which were a mixture of military and business events. Finally was a dinner, where the Corbetts would find themselves flanked by guests speaking fluent French or German, and needing to focus extra hard on the speeches being delivered in these languages. This diplomatic life did have its high points, too, such as hosting very charismatic VIPs, like Princess Anne, Labour Party leader Neil Kinnock, various VIPs, and of course, Her Majesty Queen Elizabeth, the Queen Mother.

Outside of official duties as the commandant's wife, unlike her husband, Susie did enjoy a great deal of freedom to travel around the city and into East Berlin. "I was assigned my own driver—a Greek-Cypriot called Herr Georgio who insured I was safely driven wherever I wanted to go. If we went to a restaurant, there were always two bodyguards from the Royal Military Police Personal Protection Unit on the next-door table." Most guests wanted to go over to the east to shop, for the exchange rate and because some of the things one could buy were unique to East Germany—such as handmade toys and Dresden porcelain, which was very sought after. They would enter the eastern side always via Checkpoint Charlie. "There was a particular favorite shop," Susie said, "run by this kindly old man I would regularly visit in the northeastern sector of the city, and it took an hour's drive to get there. It had lots of little wooden farm animals and toys in the front window, which everyone loved to have as a memento for their children. We would arrive and patiently wait for his local clientele to depart, and he would then shut and lock the door, greet me, and usher us all behind a gold curtain toward the rear of the shop. Here one would fine a treasure trove of china. Sometimes he'd have lovely things, and just as we valued the opportunity to purchase such rarities, so he very much valued and appreciated Western currency."

Official visits alongside Robert would involve outings to the opera at the Admiralspalast on Friedrichstrasse, where they would be front row watching performers such as Luciano Pavarotti. "When we ate out in East Berlin, we always had to be on our guard as we knew we were under constant surveillance from the Stasi and KGB. There was a restaurant we used to go to and we'd always be seated at the same table away from the public gaze just to enforce the feeling we were secure, but perhaps more to allow their security services to listen in on our conversation. We were obviously careful as to what we discussed. If we traveled to the British ambassador's house in East Berlin [Sir Nigel Bromfield]—he and his wife Valerie were great friends of ours—we were very careful when we spoke to them as well. Robert and I would even resort to going out to stand in the middle of the lawn with our hands over our faces just to talk." After the fall of the Wall, it was discovered that the residence contained over 15 kilometers of hidden wiring.

All three commandants had at their command an effective deterrent to any enemy encroaching on the city's borders. Despite this, they were under no illusion as to their fate should the Warsaw Pact powers mean business. François Cann said, "In the unlikely event of attack, the first step was to evacuate French civilians [about six thousand]. Our mission was then to sacrifice ourselves in the face of the 'tsunami' of the Red Army." Robert Corbett concurred, "From a purely military perspective, we were a very powerful garrison. There were ten thousand Allied troops there. The British also had our squadron of Chieftain tanks, and various other specialized units, so we had a powerful brigade, and anybody who understands anything about urban fighting will know what a difficult form of warfare this is. We would have had a hell of a problem if the Warsaw Pact had decided to take the city, I mean we would have all been goners. So we took our training extremely seriously, and we would have given them a lot to think about."

Susie Corbett, as a civilian, realized what an invasion would mean for the population. "The plan for the Allied garrison's families was to slowly evacuate to the west, but in such a way as to not cause a panic with the general population. Those that remained would have retreated to the British military hospital, where there were solid, protective basements and cellars, where we would attempt to find shelter as best we could—who knows what that would mean if it really had been World War Three coming. I would stay with Robert in any event, and if our children happened to be with us home from boarding school—then they would have been evacuated—I would always stay with Robert. The general consensus of planning for any eventualities was that the garrison had ninety minutes to react to any Warsaw Pact incursion."

Dealing with the Soviets was never dull, and all three commandants generally tried to always have constructive relations with them. But when the British troops started putting ropes and ladders into the River Spree to lend those trying to swim across to freedom a helping hand, the Soviet officials remonstrated with General Corbett. "I wouldn't want to have to fight them, I can tell you," he said and smiled, "I *would not*, because quantity has a quality all of its own—three hundred and fifty thousand troops and two thousand tanks do focus one's mind as to an enemy's capabilities. However, I think the Soviets saw the winds of change in what was happening in terms of the collapse of the East German regime, and they saw in that potentially the loss of everything that they regarded as the fruits of victory in their 'Great Patriotic War.'"

The buildup in 1989 saw the Allies monitoring the protest movements that were going on in the East—such as in Leipzig and in Dresden, and the growing clamor of East Germans to travel abroad, or even within the Eastern Bloc. The opening of the Hungarian border in June was the flash in the powder keg, with thousands pouring across the now unprotected border, many of whom came right the way back around into West Berlin itself. Such was the flood that the garrison was very busy helping the West Berlin authorities run refugee centers.

"We were watching events very carefully, as you may imagine. But I don't think we thought that, even until quite late on, that the GDR would collapse. Primarily there was a great fear of potential for violence in the great industrial cities in the southern part of the GDR—Dresden, Leipzig particularly—that if that had turned to violence and the violence had perhaps moved up north all the way, as it threatened to do, right the way up to Rostock, washing past East Berlin. There was a strong possibility if we had had people attempting perhaps to flee to what they might have regarded as freedom and the West, in particular in West Berlin, say for example trying to get across the Wall into the Western sectors, and perhaps being shot at, what were we going to do about it? Well, we were going to try and help them and if needed by the use of armored vehicles, but that obviously would have meant dramatically increased tensions."

When First Secretary Mikhail Gorbachev arrived on October 7 to participate in the East German regime's fortieth anniversary celebrations, Susie Corbett was in East Berlin on a regular shopping trip. "As far as I could see from touring the center of town in my car," she recalled, "it seemed the whole place was enjoying a fête, with red Soviet flags dressing up the main thoroughfares and government buildings and the population seemingly keen to celebrate, too. Nothing seemed any different to my previous visits." After a massive military parade, the Soviet leader's pronouncements to the media in a public walkabout (unheard of by any Eastern Bloc leader until then) shocked Honecker and those closest to him in the SED hierarchy—Gorbachev announcing to the cameras, "A party that lags behind the times will harvest bitter fruit." This was a clear and honest appraisal of the pressure the country was under from internal protests and his knowledge of the perilous financial state of the GDR. The planned torch-lit parade that evening, which would praise the creation of the GDR, the rule of the SED, and of course the leadership of Erich Honecker, turned into a farcical spectacle. Gorbachev looked on incredulously, standing alongside the grimacing East German leader, as they watched supposed loyal party activists shout to the Soviet general secretary, "Gorbi, Gorbi—help us!"

For the ailing Honecker, this was a disaster, which had quickly followed a fiery meeting, with the German and Russian men clashing verbally in private and in a meeting of the East German politburo, Honecker deriding Gorbachev's reformist policies compared to what he believed were the GDR's economic success. The Soviet leader had audibly hissed his derision at the old East German, with Honecker's excuses met by deafening silence around the politburo table.

Robert Corbett received a request from Britain's ambassador to West Germany, Sir Christopher Mallaby, to discuss the situation. Televised coverage of an October 16 march in Leipzig had been aired on West German TV following secret video recordings that were smuggled out of the GDR. Now the world could see hundreds of thousands of East Germans demonstrating, instead of just the hundreds who were trickling into the West German embassy compound in Prague seeking asylum. It was a far bigger story.

A general atmosphere of unease gripped Berlin, reinforced when the sudden news came through that Erich Honecker had been forced to step down. The younger generation within the East German politburo, led by his deputy Egon Krenz, had taken Gorbachev's visit and his official rebuke on the need for the regime to change as a signal to make a grab for power. Krenz had long been seen as the heir apparent and had risen through the SED ranks to become secretary of the central committee. Crucially, he oversaw security for the country and was able to persuade the head of the Ministry of State Security, Erich Mielke, to support his bid to oust the ailing leader. The week after this bloodless coup, more than 350,000 people took to the streets of Leipzig for a second mass rally. Secret dossiers had been prepared for the new leader that outlined what kind of state he was now inheriting from the man he had unceremoniously ousted. The GDR was in effect bankrupt and surviving on enormous loans from the Federal Republic just to keep going in the short term. Debt was piling on top of debt to the international markets. Was the game up? Ambassador Mallaby and his fellow ambassadors of the USA and France were deeply concerned and this was reflected in the by now constant updating of plans by the three Western Allied Commandants and their staffs.

But events would take a quite unexpected and significant turn at what was supposed to be an insignificant press conference.

CHAPTER NINETEEN

The Memo That Ended the Cold War

On the mundanity of a daily press briefing can world events spin out of control. It had been a tiring day for sixty-year-old Günther Schabowski, the Berlin Party secretary and now press spokesman for the East German Communist Party politburo. Just returned from a much-needed break, his journey into the history books on November 9 began at 6:53 p.m. A seasoned journalist who had been the editor in chief of the Party's official news organ, *Neues Deutschland*, Schabowski had endured a chaotic day of meetings to bring him up to speed on events, and now the loyal Party secretary just wanted to get back home to his wife, Irina, for dinner.

A few weeks prior, Deputy Secretary Egon Krenz had led a bloodless coup d'état. This "new Socialist Unity Party" now aimed to show the watching world—and the East German people themselves—that it could change for the better and survive. The shocking state of the country's finances was only known to a select few, and was a consequence of the economic path Erich Honecker had laid out once he took control in 1971. Under Walter Ulbricht, the GDR's borrowing on international markets had totaled two billion marks. Honecker had heavily invested more Western loans, to the tune of twenty billion marks, but instead of investing to overhaul the country's industrial infrastructure, he instead increased consumer consumption for the population. He had been robbing Peter to pay Paul. By 1989 the country was bankrupt. Insolvency was literally days away.

By November 4, an even bigger rally had taken place in Berlin—where half a million protestors gathered in Alexanderplatz to not only hear speakers from the country's leading democratic movement that had been set up that September—New Forum—but Krenz himself, who spoke to the crowd promising change. Whatever way the country would reform, he hoped the SED would coordinate that evolution—i.e., they would retain power. To achieve this, they needed to promote change, and the Party leadership would soon be purged to be replaced with younger reformers loyal to him. The great survivor, Erich Mielke, retained his power base as head of the Stasi after pledging loyalty to the new order, despite thousands now gathering outside his headquarters calling for the destruction of the security service. Could the regime manage a bloodless transition? Acknowledging to the people and the world's media that it would embrace change meant answering their questions as to the way forward. This meant a daily press conference, beamed live around the country, and to the world.

This briefing was now a cornerstone of Krenz's planned pushback against the growing internal unrest. It was now nearly an hour since the press conference had started at 6 p.m. in the Party's International Press Centre in Mohrenstraße—a tall room of polished wooden walls, with rows of red foldaway seats. Plodding to the platform to take his place, flanked by three SED colleagues, Schabowski thus found himself monotonously reciting his section of the daily news, linked to the urgent matter dominating East German society—freedom of travel.

The reverberation and smell of thousands of East German Trabant cars trundling their way across Eastern Europe had been a dark precursor of the storm that would envelop the GDR that autumn in 1989. The entire country seemed on the move as its citizens collectively decided enough was enough. Theirs was not a panic-induced desire to flee persecution, but rather a growing realization that their bonds of captivity had finally been severed, that a longed-for better life was out there waiting for them. The general consensus that summer had been to get to their neighboring socialist "cousins" of Hungary and Czechoslovakia, find the West German embassy, and demand asylum. The irony of this crisis for the diplomats of the Federal Republic was not lost on their chancellor Helmut Kohl—as the West German embassy in Budapest was closed to newcomers on August 13, twenty-eight years to the day that the Berlin Wall had been erected under Erich Honecker's direction. The man himself had six weeks earlier declared that the Wall (and with it, the GDR) was here to stay. Events were proving otherwise that summer.

Sweating under the many camera lights, an impatient Schabowski looked out onto the throng of journalists, the television crews at the rear of the room, and the thicket of microphones arrayed before him—a new experience for a man used to "managing" the news, not relaying it. With a heavy-set face, sunken eyes behind half-rimmed glasses, and a double-breasted gray suit, he looked every inch the worn-out bureaucrat. He eyed the clock on the nearby wall, determined to get this conference over with soon. He had clearly forgotten, or failed to appreciate, Krenz's final words when pressing the news conference paperwork into his hands at the ministry offices: "Announce this, it will be a bombshell."

The quick-fire irregularity of these daily briefings didn't sit comfortably with Schabowski's instincts, but he knew he had to move with the times if the situation was to be saved. The day before, more than twenty thousand of his countrymen had moved from their initial camps inside Czechoslovakia into Austria and freedom; more than five hundred a day were fleeing across the Hungarian border. The GDR was bleeding to death.

He rummaged around on the desk in front of him, mumbling that he had one final piece of news to convey to the packed newsroom. Finally locating the two-page memo, Schabowski scanned the text again to ensure he knew what it said. He was keenly aware that he had not fully digested its meaning while his limousine had taken him the short journey to the news conference. Without looking up—as if he were a schoolmaster facing an assembly—he began to recite, "So, we want . . . through a number of changes, including the travel law, to [create] the chance, the sovereign decision of the citizens to travel wherever they want." He paused to reread what he had just said to himself. Satisfied, he continued, "We are naturally concerned [about] the possibilities of this travel regulation—it is still not in effect, it's only a draft.

"A decision was made today, as far as I know . . ." Schabowski continued, without seeming to show any urgency about what he was saying, as he looked at his colleagues flanking him for their confirmation. No one moved. Unperturbed, he continued, ". . . a recommendation from the politburo was taken up that we take a passage from the [draft of] travel regulation and put it into effect, that . . . as it is called, for better or worse . . . that regulates permanent exit, leaving the Republic."

At once, there seemed a sudden spark in the room as the audience cottoned on as to what these words actually meant. Taking no notice, Schabowski mechanically read on, "Since we find it . . . unacceptable that this movement is taking place . . . across the territory of an allied state . . . which is not an easy burden for that country [Czechoslovakia] to bear." He now quickened the pace of his delivery as the end of the memo was in sight. "Therefore . . . we have decided today . . . to implement a regulation that allows every citizen of the German Democratic Republic . . . to . . . leave the GDR through any of the border crossings." He then took off his reading glasses to emphasize his task was done.

Immediately, hands shot up. Schabowski looked to his left and acknowledged an Italian journalist—Ricardo Ehrman of the ANSA Press Agency—who asked the obvious question in the room: "At once? When does that come into effect?" Ehrman then spoke louder, to make himself heard amid the many voices now coming from the audience: "At what point does this come into effect!?"

"What?" Still unused to the process of a "question and answer" session after a government announcement, Schabowski peered into the audience, scratched his chin, and wearily replaced his glasses in exasperation. "You see, comrades, I was informed today that such an announcement had been distributed earlier today. You should actually have it already." He held up the memo once more to repeat the key line to answer the question. " 'Item One: Applications for travel abroad by private individuals can now be made without the previously existing requirements [of demonstrating a need to travel or proving familial relationships]. The travel authorizations will be issued within a short time. Grounds for denial will only be applied in particular exceptional cases. The responsible departments of passport and registration control in the People's Police district offices in the GDR are instructed to issue visas for permanent exit without delays and without presentation of the existing requirements for permanent exit.' " Again, Schabowski sat back; surely there were no more questions.

The press pack could smell a story, and more hands went up; this time it was the American NBC network man, Tom Brokaw. "When does it come into effect?" he asked. Schabowski casually sifted through his pile of paperwork on the desk to find the memo again. "That comes into effect, according to my information, immediately, without delay . . ." He studied the memo again a final time, as if to confirm that statement to himself. His colleague to his left concurred quietly in his ear, ". . . without delay," while to his right another hissed, "This has to be decided by the Council of Ministers."

The questions from the floor continued quickly. "Does this also apply for West Berlin? You only mentioned the FRG." With a dispirited shrug of his shoulders, Schabowski studied his papers again.

"So . . ." He paused before he stated, "Permanent exit can take place via all border crossings from the GDR to the FRG and West Berlin, respectively." Clearly out of patience, he wanted to conclude the day's business, and repeated, "I haven't heard anything to the contrary" to all other queries. One final question chased him out of the room, and into history:

"Mr. Schabowski, what is going to happen to the Berlin Wall now?"

Unwittingly, he had made the fatal error of not stating that the press release was embargoed and would come into effect the following day at 4 a.m. More significantly, Schabowski had also failed to state that there would be strict criteria each applicant would need to fulfill in order to get access through the border checkpoints. He had inadvertently fired the starter's gun. The unrest that had been brewing since the start of the year, the protest marches in Leipzig and Dresden, the mass migration into border states, and the shifting political alliances in the Warsaw Pact—this had bubbled for months. Now, after this press conference, the time frame for the GDR's very survival could be measured in days and hours.

Brokaw rushed out to follow Schabowski upstairs, his NBC crew toiling behind him with their camera still rolling. Asking the Party spokesman to confirm what he'd just announced, Brokaw anxiously questioned him further about the lifting of the restrictions, and logically would East Germans need, therefore, to have free access through the Berlin Wall? "It is possible for them to go through the border," Schabowski replied, and with a sardonic grin he added, "It is not a question of tourism. It is permission to leave the GDR." The American correspondent stood stunned, realizing what it meant for the country. He raced back to the NBC offices in West Berlin, impatiently traversing through Checkpoint Charlie to file his explosive story back to New York. As the border guards waved the TV crew through, back toward the American Sector, Brokaw asked one guard what he thought of the new policy. "I am not paid to think," came the deadpan reply.

As Brokaw spoke with New York, his colleagues at Reuters, DPA, and the Associated Press were already reporting on the new travel arrangements, but it was the Associated Press that decided to run the story (incorrectly) that East German citizens could cross into West Germany by any border crossing point. West German television news programs followed suit and focused on the fact that the Berlin Wall was opening, replaying the words from Schabowski's own mouth. Within a few hours, a trickle, then a flood of Berliners, from both sides, began making their way to the Wall. The world's media now scrambled after them to all the crossing points in the city, and in particular Checkpoint Charlie.

_____

CHAPTER TWENTY

The Flood

November 9 was just another normal day of duty for Sergeant Michael Rafferty of the 287th US Military Police. He was in a great mood, having just picked up his wife and daughter from Tegel Airport that lunchtime, after their trip to the United States. "I was keeping up on the news and the East Germans traveling to Hungary and Czechoslovakia. They were making the big swing in order to get into West Germany and freedom. I don't think they wanted to move to West Germany as much as they wanted change in their hometowns. Even when I watched the news and they stated that East Germans would have the right to travel I wasn't sure what that meant for me." Rafferty called his buddy Staff Sergeant Nate Brown at the checkpoint and asked him for a picture of what was going on. "Nothing to report" came the succinct reply. "Nate was a man of few words." Thinking it might be a fuss over nothing, a worn-out Rafferty headed off for some much-needed sleep. The landscape of the city would be radically different when he awoke.

Corporal Kevin May of the Royal Military Police had enjoyed a great day in East Berlin, taking his wife shopping followed by a beautiful and cheap meal in a Chinese restaurant that had just opened. In his platoon he was known as "Mr. East" as he quickly got to know where to buy the best things in East Berlin, such as Meißen china. He also organized the platoon's regular nights out into the city, where he'd book the biggest table in the smartest restaurants, well aware they were still saving a fortune due to the exchange rate—and he'd generously tip the grateful maître d'. "When I got to 'Charlie' in the evening of the ninth, I booked in with the Duty Corporal. He asked if there was anything happening, as he had heard that they were lifting the travel restrictions. I told him there wasn't and everything seemed normal. On my drive home, however, I was urgently contacted by my unit and recalled to work. After a briefing I was sent as NCOIC [Non Commissioned Officer in Charge] at the Brandenburg Gate. I made several trips to Checkpoint Charlie to change over staff and to check on activities. I remember the moment people entered the no-man's-land and began climbing onto the Wall. Initially being sent off by the guards."

Welshman Sergeant Chris Toft of the Royal Military Police, based at the Olympic Stadium, was hoping for a quiet night as he assembled the men who would carry out the patrols that evening. It was half an hour before Schabowski began his press conference. After briefing his men, Toft oversaw the issuing of their weapons, and he watched each team climb into their Volkswagen combi vehicle and head off on their respective tours of the "wire." Toft had a three-man team supporting him—a desk NCO, an interpreter, and a liaison officer from the West Berlin police's riot squad—just in case any drunkenness in town turned nasty. "The first time we had any inkling that something was going to happen," he recalled, "was about 19:42 hours. I got a telephone message from my Officer Commanding [OC], telling me that the BBC World Service had reported East Germany had lifted all travel restrictions to West Germany." Toft composed himself, went to his desk, took out a blank piece of paper, and began to record events for the logbook; he would be the only Allied policeman to do this. "My first job was to get my day interpreter to phone to everyone else and say, 'What the hell is going on?' He phoned the West Berlin police, the East German police, the East German border guards. We phoned the Americans, too. We managed to speak to someone in the French side who could speak English, and none of them knew what was happening. We eventually phoned the West Berlin Customs, and they were the only ones who knew that the border was possibly coming down at midnight. And that was at 19:42 hours."

For Major General Corbett, out on official duties in his role as British Commandant and Head of the British Military Government, the news of the border opening came without warning. "I was opening a German-speaking radio station in West Berlin. At the official reception, my driver, Corporal Martin Burnell, came running across the room. He was usually a very staid and careful man, so not one to be flustered. 'Sir, sir,' he blurted, 'you're needed urgently on the radio telephone. Something very important is happening!' I bade farewell to my hosts, went quickly to my official car, and there was Michael Burton [Minister of the British Military Government], and my deputy—a brilliant man—saying, 'Robert, they're coming across!'

"I said, 'Steady on, Michael, *who's* coming across?'

"He said, 'I think the Wall's opening!'"

This was at the time when the barriers were being raised at 9 p.m., as the crowds started to multiply at the various crossing points and the border commander at Bornholmer Straße—Harald Jäger—was faced with thousands of East Berliners demanding entry into West Berlin. Unlike Checkpoint Charlie, Bornholmer Straße was situated in a residential area, and so a buildup of people hearing the news from Schabowski's announcement were eager to seize their chance. Without any official advice, orders, or sanctions to do anything, and faced with by now twenty thousand impatient Berliners, Jäger was left with little option but to begin letting them through. To have used force to keep the crowds back was not an option—it would have led to a stampede, or at worst a massacre. History would say Jäger was not prepared to take that risk. In single file, hundreds walked through calmly, having their passports stamped as they went. It was a pivotal moment for the Wall, the city, and for the GDR. By allowing the first batch through, however, the border commander had only slightly relieved the situation—the pressure from the thousands waiting behind the barriers was immense. Jäger knew he had little option, and time was rapidly running out with still no word from his superiors.

Over at Checkpoint Charlie, the staff at the nearby Café Adler were serving the final customers of the evening, even though there were always a few stragglers coming in late at night for a drink or a coffee.

The waitress that night, Astrid Benner, had expected a quiet shift, but news of the border checkpoints opening had startled everyone, and soon the few regular barflies of the Adler were being joined by dozens of West Berliners eager to see what was happening for themselves. Brenner called her boss, Albrecht Raw, who soon arrived with his wife to get the place ready for what they expected to be a flood of people over the next few hours. Armed with the information from the news conference they had heard on the radio, they were convinced a giant party would begin anytime soon as they hurriedly unearthed extra glasses, plates from the café's cellar, and stocked up the shelves with drinks and snacks. Such was the carnival atmosphere that Brenner, her boss, his wife, and a local journalist managed to summon up the courage to walk directly toward the white line of the border crossing—where twenty-eight years ago tanks had famously faced one another—to present the East German guards with bottles of champagne. The guards refused the offer, but they didn't point their weapons, or bark out warnings. It was a surreal moment as the joyous posse from the Adler walked back to the café and prepared the bar for guests—lots of them. The American MPs on duty, commanded by Major Bernie Godek, kept a steady eye on their opposite number, from the Mitchell Suite rooms above the café. Although they could see nothing unusual, they could detect pockets of people cautiously approaching the checkpoint from the eastern side. Previously, it would have been unheard of for Berliners to do this, especially as the checkpoint was so detached from the city environs. There was no reason to be there unless you had a permit to travel. But not tonight. Godek had been enjoying a BBQ at his house with his family when he'd heard the call after 6 p.m. and had rushed to the checkpoint with his superior officer Lieutenant Colonel Greathouse, who, among other duties, was the commander of the 287th Military Police. Both men now peered into the distance, toward the illuminated border complex in the east. West Berliners were milling at the checkpoint, more than two hundred of them, waiting to see what would happen. Meanwhile the commander on the eastern side—Günter Möll—eyed the numbers arriving at Checkpoint Charlie with growing unease. What would the night bring for him and his men?

*   *   *

That evening, USAAF airman Mitt Law was with his family in the Kreuzberg part of Berlin, approximately a kilometer from Checkpoint Charlie. He had just returned from Tegel Airport, picking up his wife and daughter, who were flying back from a vacation in the United States. Law had met and married a local Berlin girl from the Turkish quarter near Friedrichstraße. Back at their family home in Dahlem, he turned on the television to catch the 7 p.m. news. "We were shocked to learn that the Wall was to be opened," he said. "Up to this point, we knew nothing about it. After about five minutes of watching the coverage of the press conference in disbelief, I looked around the room and asked who wanted to go to the Brandenburg Gate and Checkpoint Charlie? One person, my brother-in-law—Kurt Sopora—said 'let's go.' In the thirty minutes it took to drive to the Brandenburg Gate, there were no signs of anything unusual until we got real close. As a local who had grown up in postwar Berlin, Kurt was in shock and insisted the news was nothing more than GDR propaganda, was a hoax."

They arrived at the Brandenburg Gate area by 8 p.m. A large crowd had formed, but not as large as the crowds would be in the coming days. A big group was milling around by the base of the Wall, with another five hundred people standing or sitting on the top and helping others climb up. "The easiest route up the high wall was the 'buddy system,'" recalled Law, "someone on the ground lifting a person up and a complete stranger grabbing you from the top and pulling you to the top of the Wall. The Brandenburg Gate portion of the Wall's design did not have the cylindrical sewer piping covering the top section, thus allowing room for people to stand and walk around on top of it. "The overall feeling at the gate that night was joy and love. Strangers hugging one another and a general feeling of goodwill, though we couldn't see any East Berliners at that point. On our side, the gate was surrounded by West German police, but they didn't stop people from climbing the Wall or hitting it with hammers. They were simply there and enjoying the spectacle.

"While walking around the Brandenburg Gate in an amazement of seeing people standing on the Wall, in front of it, and a general feeling of inspiration and happiness, I spotted NBC News legend Tom Brokaw on a makeshift platform conducting a live news broadcast. Honestly, I was a little shocked to see him there. I couldn't believe I was looking at the people standing on the Wall with Tom running a live feed. Since I looked like a photographer with cameras around my neck, I simply walked up the steps and onto the platform where there were a few camera operators, Tom, and me! I took pictures of him and, after about thirty minutes, got bored and continued on my journey. I felt pretty good having the chance to witness history.

"Driving was not an option due to the size of the crowds gathering in the streets. And walking was the only way to get from the Reichstag to Checkpoint Charlie. At one point we were near Potsdamer Platz on the west side and watched a crane remove sections of the top of the Wall off. Eventually, two sections were knocked down with East German guards standing on them as the crowd cheered. This was late in the evening, after midnight if I recall. There were no cell phones or internet and the best information was word on the street. We'd hear of work on a new opening and head there to see what was going on."

West Berlin police president Georg Schertz had been attending the fiftieth birthday party of a good friend, the film director Peter Schamoni, in the Kindl Hall. "At the party whilst I was chatting to guests, my driver came in to find me and said: 'Mr. Schertz, come out for a moment, please, you have an urgent phone message.' I went to the phone and was informed of the situation at Bornholmer Straße. A meeting was ordered at Schöneberg town hall. It must have been about 10 p.m. Even though we were discussing how these events would play out in terms of people crossing into the west of the city in large numbers through the crossing points, there was a certain helplessness in the room. We didn't know how the GDR regime would react—would they tolerate this? I decided to travel down to the crossing point Invalidenstraße by Sandkrug Bridge to see the situation for myself. The border was already open with dozens of Trabants slowly coming across. On the Wall itself stood an officer of the *Grenztruppen* and directly in front of the Wall one of our own police officers—though he was actually standing in East German territory. I called to him to come back as he might be in danger of being shot by the border guards, when all of a sudden, the East German guard shouted back, 'That's all right, we do that together here!' I was shocked. I could never have imagined having that kind of conversation with a border guard right by the Wall." But as personnel covering all the checkpoints that night would encounter—this kind of communication began to happen all along the Wall, for several days.

American student Gillian Cox, from Boston University, had traveled to Berlin on an exchange program to study history and German. In her hometown of Miami she had always been intrigued by the Cold War, as her Cuban friends talked about Castro, the missile crisis of 1963, and watching the summits held between Reagan and Gorbachev. Traveling to the epicenter of the Cold War that autumn, through Checkpoint Charlie to visit East Berlin, was exciting and would be an eye-opener for her. She moved in with a Berlin host family, the Koslowskys, who lived in Steglitz, and attended classes in the mornings (a language school outside of the center of the city) and the occasional lecture at the Berlin Free University in the afternoons. Six weeks before the Wall opened, Cox had encountered the customs control guards at Friedrichstraße, who kept her sweating for nearly an hour alone in a cubicle while they validated her papers. Although she enjoyed the day trip and met various locals who were happy to converse with her, by the time she came back across the checkpoint she felt like kneeling to kiss the ground on the western side. But the experience radically altered her perceptions of the East Germans—she now felt they were just like her, but without the access to the freedoms she enjoyed. On November 9 she was visiting a German friend in Schöneberg, who had tuned his TV onto the BBC in order to practice his English skills. "My friend's roommate said, 'Oh my God! Did you just hear?!'

"I said, 'What?!'

" 'Travel restrictions on East Germans were just lifted. Let's take a walk.'

"It was bitterly cold that night, so I zipped up my leather jacket, grabbed my camera and my school bag, and walked outside. We started heading in the direction of the Wall, which wasn't far from my friend's apartment. We could hear the crowds and knew this was it. I recall walking all over the city that night, gaining and losing people as we moved further into town. So many folks were coming through the border that when we got to Checkpoint Charlie, we were overwhelmed with the numbers of East Germans coming through it. I remember how everyone from East Germany wanted a banana, so I went in search of some with a few friends. We ended up in Ullrich's underneath S-Bahnhof Zoo, and we were told there weren't any bananas. We left the store singing 'The Banana Boat Song.'"

By 10:30 p.m. a sizeable crowd had built up around the Allied positions at Checkpoint Charlie—thousands had now arrived and were flooding the side streets nearby, too—making it impossible for vehicles to drive through. The crowd stood on the borderline facing the Wall, anxious to get across. They edged closer and even began sitting down just in front of the Wall, with the East German guards allowing them to do so. Commander Günter Möll of the *Grenztruppen* was in a position similar to Harald Jäger's at Bornholmer Straße—no orders from above and faced with an impossible situation to his front. His men looked anxious, confused, and scared, but still held their positions. Möll had no way of knowing what was happening at the other checkpoints, for they were not connected via any telephone system, but he could guess they were in the same predicament. The restless crowd by now had actually started climbing up onto the Wall itself, without any interference from the guards, who obligingly even helped some up. A carnival atmosphere was brewing as the Berliners relaxed, realizing they were not in any danger. They started asking for the caps of the guards as keepsakes, and offering presents, drinks, and handshakes—with the young soldiers from the *Grenztruppen* refusing.

The crowds at Checkpoint Charlie now numbered more than three thousand, but still the atmosphere was more one of excited anticipation than violence. Even when four uniformed Soviet soldiers at the Allied checkpoint, queuing in their car to return to the east, were spotted by the West Berliners, the crowd simply rocked the car in mock celebration rather than to attack them. The situation couldn't go on for Günter Möll, as he ordered his men to retreat behind the Wall rather than confront the swelling numbers who were edging closer to the crossing point.

Sergeant Chris Toft's logbook states:

23:23 Hours: Large crowd of East Germans on Checkpoint Charlie border crossing. East German side crowd building up onto West Berlin side.

23:35 Hours: German TV reports East Germans crossing border at Osloer Strasse / Bornholmer Strasse.

Commander Jäger had seen what he had to do, a dozen men under his command facing well over twenty thousand impatient civilians wishing to cross into the west. He was impotent to prevent what he knew would now have to happen, otherwise bloodshed would soon follow and he was not prepared to see that. At 23:35 hours, German TV reported that East Germans were crossing the border at Heinrich-Heine-Straße. The flood had begun. At 11:40 p.m. Oberbaumbrücke and Chausseestraße checkpoints opened to the Berliners. Bornholmer Straße, Checkpoint Charlie, and all other checkpoints would follow suit at two minutes past midnight—the biggest party in Berlin's history could now begin. Café Adler was besieged by people hugging, kissing, singing, crying, and all wanting to toast freedom.

Airman Mitt Law had by now reached the checkpoint from the Brandenburg Gate. "Checkpoint Charlie was a madhouse and I don't recall even speaking with the US Army that night. You couldn't even get close to the guard hut it was so crowded. Keep in mind by the time we walked from the Brandenburg Gate to Checkpoint Charlie, the crowds intensified one-hundred-fold. I was in civilian clothes and blended in well amongst the throng, but standing and watching the mass of people waiting for the East Berliners to come through was unreal. Feeling a little sneaky, I walked across the painted border on the ground and entered East Germany illegally—again. I felt stealthy, and it was the first time on foot without being challenged for my ID or Soviet pass."

Meantime Sergeant Chris Toft was listening to all of this on his radio back at the Olympic Stadium, trying to make sense of what was happening as his men reported in one by one. "The East German border guards and passport control were overwhelmed. They couldn't have controlled it if they tried, without shooting people. If someone had given them the order, then there would have been a bloodbath, because there were thousands. Berlin was surrounded by East Germany, and Checkpoint Charlie was what everyone knows. But nobody knows about Checkpoint Bravo. That's at the bottom end of Berlin, and that's where we would come along the Autobahn from the British zone in West Germany, which was controlled by the British Military Police and passing through Checkpoint Bravo. There were just as many people coming in through Checkpoint Bravo and the Glienicker Bridge as at the Sandkrug Bridge and Checkpoint Charlie."

At the beginning of November 1989, Vera Knackstedt had to fly to Berlin to be with her mother, who had fallen ill. That evening, she had stayed up very late while her parents slept—reminiscing about the life she had enjoyed in the city in the 1950s and early '60s with Adolf, who was now back at their home in Fort Bragg, North Carolina. She had watched the news on the television declaring the border checkpoints were opening but had paid little attention to it before heading off to bed. "Sometime between 1 and 2 a.m. I heard loud and excited voices out in front of our house on the street, which caught my attention. I walked onto our balcony and saw a fairly sizeable group of people standing in front of our house entrance door, laughing, singing, and shouting. One of the ladies in the group was calling her aunt to open up the door, since they just came through the Berlin Wall to visit her!"

Vera tried to call Adolf back in the United States, wanting to tell him what was going on in the city, but he didn't answer. Her parents lived only ten minutes' walking distance from the border checkpoint at Heinrich-Heine-Straße, so she dressed and got out into the city to see for herself. As soon as she walked out onto the street, she was engulfed by long lines of East Berliners being greeted by West Berliners, whether they knew them or not. "The confusion out on the street was tremendous; a carnival atmosphere. West Berlin had changed a lot over the last twenty-eight years since the construction of the Wall, and these East Berliners needed a lot of help finding their relatives and friends. Emotions were high and freely flowing amongst all of us. We were all in shock."

While the US Garrison Commander Major-General Haddock was touring his sector to get a front-line view of what was going on, and personally greeting East Berliners coming across, back in Washington, DC, the White House was stunned by what it witnessed on television as East Berliners began pouring through the checkpoints. Secretary of State James Baker recalled that many of President George H. W. Bush's cabinet were caught unaware. "I was hosting a luncheon for President Corazon Aquino of the Philippines. An assistant passed me a note toward the dessert course that detailed the circumstances of this historic occasion. I read the note aloud to my table, raised my glass, and proposed a toast to an event the West had anticipated for more than twenty-eight years. I then rushed to the White House and spent the rest of the afternoon and much of the night with the president crafting our response to this important event and watching television as young Berliners danced atop the barrier and chipped it away as souvenirs."

At a more local level for the US forces, Sergeant Michael Rafferty awoke at 5 a.m. as his day began for his relief shift starting at Checkpoint Charlie an hour later. He knew nothing of what had happened until he called the desk sergeant to ask for a ride into the city. "I was briefed on the night's events," he said, "but it still didn't register what it meant until I arrived at the checkpoint. Then it dawned on me—history in the making!"

As he drove down into the city, all Rafferty could think of was that the next day was Veterans Day, and like his colleagues, he'd been briefed to expect hundreds of military personnel who would come to the checkpoint sightseeing, adding to the many garrison personnel who would be out to enjoy the long weekend, too. Upon arriving he was stunned by the mass of people, both on the Allied and the eastern end of the crossing. "I got to Nate [Staff Sergeant Nathan Brown], and I said, 'You told me nothing was going on!' He just shrugged his shoulders and didn't say anything, but just looked at me like I was crazy. 'It's all yours.'

"How it normally worked was Nate would brief Berlin-based soldiers going over to the east, and I would be inside the checkpoint dealing with anybody that was brand-new. On that day of the 10th of November I was sitting in there in my misery, processing soldiers and families that had never been to the east. And these people didn't know what they were doing. At the start of the shift, the first fifty or so people received a professional briefing from me. 'The East German checkpoint . . . As you see the checkpoint . . . This is how you process it. When you're done, you come right back here. Here's your book. It's got a number on it.' By the time I got to two hundred people, I was simply handing them a book, pointing eastwards, and saying, 'Good luck to you, guy. Read the book.' Nobody expected the Wall to fall. We had traffic jams on the corridor. We had people screwing up—coming back or going to Checkpoint Alpha from Charlie. It was just a mess. The tracking of people was just horrendous."

Hours into Rafferty's "shift from hell," by midmorning, student Gillian Cox realized she was caught in a pivotal moment in history, that the Wall was falling and Europe was changing before her eyes. "I wanted to document all of it," she remembered, "the picture of the graffiti on the Wall declaring, 'Charlie's Retired,' I shot fairly early in the morning on the tenth. I recall walking from there to get breakfast at Anderes Ufer because they had good coffee, and I was bound to run into a few people I knew. I walked in there, grabbed a cup of coffee, and found myself among my friends Mike and his roommate Chris. We had started out together but got separated due to the crowds. They had been running around Berlin in the same state of euphoric disbelief as I and probably gaining and losing people along the way, until they knew they needed to eat something, and landed at Anderes Ufer, too. It also helped that David Bowie's 'Heroes' was playing in the background.

That was a moment I will never forget. It was, 'Wow, I just saw history. I am in the middle of all this. David Bowie is playing in the background. What a day! What a time!'"

By lunchtime Sergeant Rafferty was taking frantic calls at Checkpoint Charlie from headquarters at the Clay Compound, asking how many people were passing through the border. "I looked across and I said, 'How do you expect me to count?'

"'Count for ten seconds, and then multiply it by six, or whatever you have per minute, and then times that by sixty. It's a math equation,' came the instruction.'"

The East Germans coming through all the checkpoints were in the main ecstatic, and some in a state of drunken happiness. The first thing the majority of them did was collect their "welcome money" of one hundred west marks at any bank open, a welcome gift promised to them by Chancellor Helmut Kohl, resulting in long lines at banks throughout West Berlin. "The majority of them came into West Berlin for a day trip, see the sights, spend some money, and then return home. They simply wanted the freedom to travel—that is what it was all about," stated Rafferty.

Taking a much-needed break, and to escape the car fumes for a few precious minutes, Rafferty left the checkpoint and walked toward Café Adler. "I climbed the steps above the café to enter the VIP Mitchell suite that we owned and decided I wanted to capture the moment on the balcony and take photos of the crowd below. I yelled at all the people, 'Look up and smile!' And thousands of people looked up and smiled and waved. They were having a good ol' time—and so was I. But those first days were just a total nightmare for all four of the NCOs in charge. There was really no celebrating, we were stuck in this tiny checkpoint, which was basically just a mobile home, a single white trailer, and constantly processing people. I'd get hot, open the window, and the Trabants would sit next to me and blow the exhaust fumes in, which made me sick, forcing me to close it again and suffer the heat."

By 6 p.m. on that day, Rafferty had been forced to remain at his post an extra two hours as no patrol would come to pick him up; driving through the massed throngs of celebrating Berliners was still impossible. "I was feeling sick from all the fumes I had consumed and decided to go to Kochstraße Lübar. I sat there at the U-Bahn stop, and one train went by full of people. The next train went by full, too. Finally, I had to decide and push my way on. The train stopped, the doors opened, and I took one step on—it was like a miracle. The press of bodies just parted before me as if I was somebody important. I was nodding thankfully, telling everybody, '*Danke*' all the way back to the American Sector— which took about forty minutes.

"Finally, I got to the U2 route, which runs from Wittenbergplatz to Krumme Lanke. Sitting across from me was a little girl from Potsdam, and her father. The train started moving, but I was trying so hard not to be sick that it took all my concentration not to throw up on the poor girl. To take my mind off the nausea I just started up some small talk with the father, who told me that they were from Potsdam and this was their first time in the city. Before I alighted, I took the Berlin pin off my sweater and put it on her scarf, saying, 'Welcome.' The father became so emotional, but I was still not feeling well and got off the train quickly; she smiled and I was gone. It was a lovely moment for both of us."

There would be one episode that could potentially have blown up in the Allies' faces if General Corbett hadn't been able to react quickly to the events that were occurring all along the Wall that night. The morning of November 10 there were now tens of thousands of civilians milling around that great Soviet war memorial beside the Brandenburg Gate, the majority just celebrating the suddenness of events, and a tiny minority perhaps looking to cause trouble. Corbett was more concerned that a large percentage of those in the crowds were East Germans who in the main *hated* the Russians—the British who controlled the Sector were concerned there might be an excuse for violence. "I had jurisdiction over the civilian police in the British Sector of West Berlin," said Corbett, "and so I asked the police president, Georg Schertz, to put some of his people in that sensitive area in order to protect the monument. Schertz put two platoons of the *Bereitschaftspolizei* in place."

Over the course of these crucial forty-eight hours, Corbett was moving around the city quickly to get a handle on events, the size of the actual situation they were facing, and to gauge the morale of his garrison and of his allies. By four o'clock in the morning he went to see that all was well there at the Brandenburg Gate. There were Russian sentries on duty, and they had a photograph of him in their guard box for identification purposes, "but I looked absolutely white," he recalled, "and hardly recognizable to your average Russian private soldier! He got on his telephone calling for assistance, and his officer came running, luckily with a German interpreter. I said, 'Can I come in to calm the situation down? Because I want, if I can, to tell you what is going on.'

"Immediately, the relief in his face was clear, even in the gloom of the sentry box light. A young officer in the center of a world event, and under extreme pressure to protect his country's national monument. Backed up with thirty, or so, soldiers, with fingers on the trigger, and live ammunition in the chambers. Equally, I was very aware the Soviets were notoriously trigger-happy. They had shot quite a lot of people one way or the other, including the killing of Major Nicholson of the US Military Liaison Mission in March 1985—which had caused huge upset between East and West. With this, as well as what had happened at Tiananmen Square in China some months before, I said, 'Now, look, what I want you to understand is there's a hell of a lot happening tonight along the border. I cannot guarantee what will occur in the other sectors, but what I can say is above all else, I will guarantee to you, that your memorial, and your responsibility, will not be breached, and you will be protected.'

"Instantly, he relaxed. My confidence boosted by this reaction, I then asked him, 'Do you think I could talk to your soldiers?' There was an interminable pause as this was translated, but he soon smiled and said, 'Yes, sir, absolutely, give me a moment.' We then slowly walked into the guardroom, which was just in behind the memorial itself, not particularly big, but it accommodated this assembly with a little room to spare. The Russian officer had his men form up in sort of a half square, there was a chair for me at the front facing them all, and he stood to my right and our interpreter on my left. One could feel the nerves of them all as the volume of the crowd outside increased, and the traffic of military vehicles and helicopters overhead could be heard distinctly, too. For the next twenty minutes we talked about the things that soldiers always talk about. What's life like in a foreign country? What's it like being so far away from home? What's the training like, and of course, the food? The tension in this small room simply ebbed away as we chatted, and slowly began to understand one another.

"And then I said, 'I must go now, I have to go back to my headquarters.' And my young Russian officer said, 'Will you give me a moment?'

"'Yes, absolutely,' I replied with a grin.

"And coming to attention, the whole Russian garrison filed out in precise step to one another, all saluting, it was impressive. He and I then marched back to the gate and the British Sector. 'Look, don't worry,' I said, 'at least things will remain quiet here. And good luck.' And we shook each other by the hand."

As Corbett quickly sped back down Heerstraße toward the Olympic Stadium, where he had to get back to his headquarters, the car phone buzzed. It was Brigadier Ian Freer, the Chief of the British Mission (BRIXMIS) to the Soviet Commander in Chief in East Germany, needing to speak with the General urgently. "Something very remarkable has happened!" he said.

"I laughed at this," remembered Corbett. "'Well, you can say that again, there's an awful lot of remarkable things going on around here.' He was waiting for me on the steps of HQ and walked me into the main Operations Room. Speaking quietly, he said, 'You will not believe this, but using a channel of communication that has been closed for decades because of the bad blood between the Soviets and the Western Allies, has come this message uniquely by name from Army General Boris Snetkov [the Commander in Chief of what was then Soviet Forces in Germany (GFS(G))]. This message is addressed to you specifically by name; using this defunct channel of communications. It says, *Thank you for what you have done. It will not be forgotten.*' We both stared at the communication for a time. I couldn't believe it.

"Back in Bonn, at NATO headquarters in Brussels, Belgium, and in London, events in Berlin were taking everyone by surprise. I always believed we were supported to the hilt, though we were an isolated garrison, an outpost in a Communist sea. I was telling them as much as I knew at the time but reports from right across the city were sketchy and fluid, so it was difficult to paint a complete picture for them. Perhaps they believed I was sitting on my hands! General Walters was the United States ambassador, who'd been a soldier, and he really understood, and he was immensely supportive, as was our own ambassador, Sir Christopher Mallaby—who I had known since childhood, which was crucial. General Sir Peter Inge was the Commander in Chief of the British Army of the Rhine [BAOR], and a senior NATO Commander. I had two bosses, one was Her Majesty's Ambassador in Bonn, and the other was the Commander in Chief. Essentially, we on the ground had to get on with it and make the thing work."

On November 9 one of Corbett's key men, Lieutenant-Colonel Ron Tilston, Royal Military Police, Corbett's Assistant-Provost Marshal (APM) and commander of all RMP assets in Berlin, had been back in Britain, scouting schools for his son. "I received a phone call from my elder daughter in Berlin," he recalled, "that General Corbett had phoned and wanted to speak to me. I phoned the Provost Company Officer Commanding, Major Mark Watson, who told me that the Wall was to be opened up that night, and that the GOC Berlin wanted me back." Tilston then spent the next two hours desperately trying to get a seat, and finally got one, on a flight the next morning to Berlin. And on the tenth, he traveled from Heathrow, first class, which was probably the only time Her Majesty would pay for an officer to go first class. He arrived mid-morning. "I got a quick brief from the Company Commander as to what had happened, and then I went straight up to see Major General Corbett himself in the operations room. He just reconfirmed that the Royal Military Police were his eyes and ears on the border, the Wall, and the wire. 'Get on with it. Carry on what you're doing but keep us all informed of what's happening.' I . . . went out and did a complete tour of the Wall and wire, to all the permanent posts, like Checkpoint Charlie and the Soviet War Memorial in the Tiergarten. I was then briefed by the Helmstedt (246 Provost Company) Officer Commanding, Major Terry Hollingsbee, who described the hundreds of East Germans driving from East Germany, long queues of Trabants, and many breaking down. Our own vehicles were going up and down this line, providing sandwiches and water to those who sat in the queue. In some cases, towing broken-down vehicles into West Germany itself!"

Tilston would be present at many of the major Wall openings. Probably the main one was at Potsdamer Platz. "The East Berlin authorities would inform, certainly, the West Berlin authorities and the police that they would be opening such-and-such road or the closure tomorrow morning at 8 a.m. or 8:30 a.m. or whatever. So, work would be done during the night to sort of break away the concrete base of the Wall. They would attach spikes to the sections and have a crane ready to lift it at the due time. Once it was open, then they allowed people through. We would have a presence, and that was respectful and simply monitoring. The locals were so happy—groups coming through with young children on the shoulders of parents. In many cases, meeting relatives who they hadn't seen for a long time. Even if they weren't relatives, they were being welcomed with open arms by West Berliners, some of whom had placed flowers on our vehicle's windscreens [windshields]. I was in full Service Dress Uniform, with my Sam Browne belt, famous red Military Police cap on. The emotion got to me, tears were running down my cheeks."

Meanwhile, one of his men, Corporal Mark Horton, was now situated atop the RMP's Observation Post (OP) in the Reichstag, with orders to monitor the situation at the Brandenburg Gate and report in what he witnessed. Still hungover from a farewell party his Company had held for a colleague, he had been roused from his sleep abruptly with the news the Wall was opening. "We'd all woke up to be scrambled out to the border. I knew nothing about the press conference. It was freezing cold, and I spent the whole night taking turns on the roof of the Reichstag looking directly down over the Brandenburg Gate sitting in my small tent with a Calor gas burner inside to keep me warm. From my observation point I watched the iconic scenes of more and more people climbing and dancing on the Wall, with Pink Floyd's 'Another Brick in the Wall' being played repeatedly the whole evening. I was pleased for the East Germans to get their freedom, as we had been aware of several failed escape attempts in the months prior to the Wall coming down, so it was good to see."

In Fort Bragg, North Carolina, meanwhile, Adolf Knackstedt was catching up on events in the city he called home. "I couldn't go to Berlin with Vera on this trip, I was a civil servant and worked for the Defense and State Departments and couldn't get away from my duties that week. The night the checkpoints opened, I was invited for dinner at a friend's house. During our evening conversation, they mentioned something was going on along the Berlin Wall, but I put it off by mentioning something always was happening along that border, and thought no more about it. After getting home, I read my newspaper without turning on the television. A short while later the telephone rang. My daughter, who lives in Texas, was on the line and wanted to know what I was doing. I told her.

"She further questioned me: 'You don't have the TV on?'

"'Why should I?' I replied.

"'Well,' she continued, 'they are dancing on top of the Berlin Wall!'"

The man who had spent so much of his life, as a citizen, refugee, and spy, in the city he loved gazed at his television in disbelief with tears in his eyes as his fellow Berliners danced on the Wall by the Brandenburg Gate.

Lights, Cameras, Action!

Amid the dazzle of overhead lights, the bustle of camera crews setting up, and the buzz of thousands of Berliners milling around the Brandenburg Gate, three British journalists stood waiting for their cue to broadcast live to the public back home. Alastair Stewart, Jon Snow, and John Suchet were all well known, highly experienced, and savvy newsmen, and the A team for ITN sent rapidly across to cover the breaking story the night before. In their earpieces they could hear the director sitting in the trailer parked some way off, counting down the seconds until they went live.

As the three men began their broadcast, if the ITN camera crew had panned a few feet to the right or left they would have seen correspondents from ABC, NBC, the BBC, and other major broadcasting companies—all vying for the best spot in front of the gate, and all wanting to have the best story to tell. The next few days would be a pulsating, nerve-shredding, and iconic period, when the world's best news networks delivered the story of the Berlin Wall opening to the rest of the world. It was their D-Day, JFK assassination, moon landing, and death of Elvis all rolled into one. It was what they lived for. And they had the perfect backdrop—the Berlin Wall was coming down, and it had defined an era for them, with all the possibilities that gave them to offer debate live on air of what it all meant for the country, Europe, and the Cold War itself.

Stewart was at the height of his career as a news correspondent for ITN, both in the studio and as a roving reporter for the key events since the mid-1980s. He had already reported from Poland where Solidarity had established a permanent presence as a democratically elected body under its charismatic leader Lech Walesa, who would create an international platform that was powerful enough to take on the Communist regime. Stewart was among the international press that would cover this story—which to a degree had turned violent, with the regime implementing marshal law at one stage. Mass arrests and hundreds of deaths had resulted before the situation had stabilized. Would East Germany follow suit? That is one of the things the networks' correspondents all discussed live on air, with the Brandenburg Gate as the iconic backdrop.

Stewart's journey to cover the story had been one that all foreign correspondents would find familiar. With his wife, Sally, he'd been at a black-tie dinner in Knightsbridge on November 6, three days before the Wall opened. Called away to the phone by his news desk, they informed him their contacts in the city were telling them something big was about to happen and so he was instructed to get to Berlin as soon as possible, he would be anchoring ITN coverage in the city for the lunchtime news the next day. "I was absolutely fizzing when I got to the center of Berlin, because at that point—I've had it clear in my mind that one of the lines I wanted to deliver was 'Unlike 1968, unlike 1956, this is different. Something very different is happening in Moscow, that means Berlin is going to be totally different. These people have not been stopped from doing what they are determined to do.' And I remember even now with great clarity, thinking this is the biggest story I will cover."

By the time Stewart arrived at the west side of the Brandenburg Gate, the place was buzzing with civilians mulling around everywhere, and a big presence of the military and West Berlin police. In the distance stood the imposing Brandenburg Gate, with dozens of figures standing on the Wall itself in front of it. A surreal sight, enhanced with the continuous noise of joyous Berliners chipping away pieces of the Wall while impotent East German border guards looked on not knowing what to do other than scowl forlornly ahead. "For a live broadcast, covering such a momentous time as the Berlin Wall falling," Stewart recalled, "then if you do what I do for a living, there are two questions that matter: Where am I standing? Is this backdrop as good as John Simpson's or

Tom Brokaw's? Secondly, one is sniffing the air and looking around for the great shot that will capture the viewer's imagination. It needs to be iconic. The legend of people recalling seeing the smiling faces of East Berliners peering over the Wall is simply not true. Where we were all filming it was too far away."

Stewart was surrounded by the broadcasting giants from the United States and the UK: the legendary Dan Rather of CBS, who'd covered President Kennedy's assassination in 1963; Peter Jennings, another veteran broadcaster from ABC; and the BBC's number one foreign correspondent, John Simpson. Vying for the best backdrop was an ongoing affair, depending on when each network's news cycle was imminent. "John actually told me off at one point for standing too close to his spot when he was doing his piece to camera, because the BBC were then on at 9 p.m. and we were *News at Ten*," recalled Stewart. The day would be made famous by the sudden appearance of Dan Rather above everyone else's head, thus gazumping the world's media. "Suddenly, we're on our little stage, when this huge metal arm swings down and it's Dan standing in the bucket of a huge overhead crane, thus giving him an incredible, jaw-dropping backdrop of the Brandenburg Gate, the Wall, the celebrating Berliners, and the military and police presence. It was perfect and he'd scooped everyone. It's the one image we all now remember. Very clever!"

By November 10, with events quickly unfolding, Stewart fronted the ITN lunchtime news at 1 p.m., followed by a live broadcast at 5:45 p.m. and then the ubiquitous *News at Ten*—with the Brandenburg Gate brilliantly illuminated in the winter light by the beams of the press and the authorities. "We then cobbled together an hour-long special, I think it went out early on the 11th of November, and by then all networks were sending out reporters into East Berlin to get stories from the population. Our jobs as the anchors was obviously to segue all these pieces together to present to the viewer as a complete a story as was possible. Typically, we wanted to cover both the political as well as human interest stories of the day."

Ben Bradshaw, who would later enter politics as a Labour MP in 1997, serving as minister for culture and then as minister for health in the governments of Tony Blair—was a young, local radio reporter in Devon, who was then plucked at the start of 1989 to be the BBC's main radio correspondent in West Berlin. "I think it probably was the most important event in my lifetime," he said. "When I headed out to Berlin, I never thought that something like this might happen, that the Wall would come down in my lifetime. Historically, it was something which had a permanency to it. For me personally as someone who had studied and spoke German, I was fortunate to now be there to cover this event. It was so exciting."

Standing there by the Brandenburg Gate and seeing this unique pivot in world history happen before his eyes, the ITN anchor, too, couldn't help but think of his father who'd led a squadron of RAF fighter jets in the 1950s and '60s and for a time had been stationed in Germany. "As a teenager growing up, I led a pretty normal life, went to university, and though I was suspicious of the nuclear bomb and its threat to humanity, I still wasn't quite CND [Campaign for Nuclear Disarmament]. I would argue quite profoundly with my father, even though I worshiped him. I always remember him saying with the greatest clarity the 'Big Stick' theory. 'So long as we've got a nuclear deterrent, it reduces to absolute minimal the likelihood of Britain ever using it; and if we give it up, the odds change fundamentally, and therefore my humble belief is that we should keep it. Democracy will win.' *You were right, you old bugger!* I muttered to myself on several occasions as I looked out onto the Wall."

Lieutenant-Colonel Ron Tilston, now back in action commanding the Royal Military Police, watched the media crews with mild bemusement. The British Sector had never been so busy, or so crowded with people. "The whole of the world's media seemed to have set up camp, and of course, the big networks all came with massive trucks, equipment, and large teams. It would be Dan Rather with the famous mobile crane with a cage on it where they could go up to fifty or sixty feet and look over the Wall at the Brandenburg Gate area and film what was going on. It proved a real coup over the other networks and I always thought it was a bit of a cheek. When things would go quiet, they might allow some lesser agency from some country to use it, probably at a cost. As things went on and sort of quietened down a little bit after that initial surge, everyone from the media realized that they were there on a permanent basis in this little hut and we mapped out a schedule for them.

We established a sort of key rack; they handed the keys to their vehicles to us to hold, while they went off to eat or sleep or whatever it was. Then they could come back as and when necessary, draw their keys to open up their trunks. We 'controlled' a lot of valuable equipment! One of the Brandenburg Gate shift commanders, Welshman Staff Sergeant Burgess, was very popular and helpful to the media and even caused an upset between two agencies who wanted to get 'the first interview' with him, accusing each other of poaching him!"

As the hours progressed, every network correspondent, radio journalist, and newspaperman was on the hunt for "the" story, whether it was with a local from east or west, a policeman, politician, or soldier. Etiquette went out the window—it was dog eat dog, as General Corbett and his bodyguard Corporal Ornsby were to find out. The general was in uniform to be interviewed live on ITN *News at Ten* by [Sir] Trevor McDonald, with the backdrop of the Brandenburg Gate. Unfortunately for Ornsby, the party were accidentally dropped off a mile away from the actual interview site, but unperturbed, Corbett decided to walk the remainder of the way and, as a novelty, along the Wall's exclusion zone, which was twenty-five yards wide. Corbett, his aide-de-camp Captain Carter, and Ornsby would have space to move around as the barriers now set up would keep the press pack at arm's length. The plan went awry straightaway.

"If you're a close-protection officer," Ornsby recounted, "one of the fundamental rules is you've got to stay within one easy reach of the shoulder of your principal; so in an emergency you can quickly direct him, or her, out of harm's way. You never leave their side." Unfortunately for Ornsby, as Corbett approached the media area, he was identified by dozens of journalists, and the barriers gave way, as the world's press descended, sweeping Ornsby unexpectedly aside, and out of reach of the general. "Picking myself up, I could see the general disappearing from view as the crowd of eager journalists and civilians pressed around him, most wanting to ask questions, others simply wanting to shake his hand. It was chaotic. I adjusted my beret, checked my sidearm, and grimly marched back into the fray—if needs be, I would fight my way back to his side."

One of the discretionary tactics he had been taught at close protection school, in order not to be photographed punching anyone in the face, was to instead aim lower and punch them in the groin. "I sized up the route to get straight back to the general's side, targeted the first few reporters holding microphones, and in I went." Once the first few reporters had been felled with swift punches, others farther forward in the scrum began to turn around to see what the commotion was, caught Ornsby's fierce expression, and vacated as quickly as they could. He quickly reached General Corbett, who was occupied answering several questions at once, but remaining completely calm and polite. "He must have felt my presence once again on his shoulder and turned to look at me. 'Ah, Corporal Ornsby, how nice of you to join us.' And that was it. Panic over. He never blamed me or called into question my actions. I could have easily drawn out my firearm and shot it into the air to reclaim the situation, but I hadn't, and I think he knew and appreciated that." Now *that* would have been a story!

For journalist Hans-Ulrich Jörges, now a veteran of the twenty-four-hour news cycle, what the media achieved in 1989 was very special. For him, the coverage was a unique, once-in-a-lifetime experience, the fulfillment of what he and his family had endured since the 1950s encapsulated through the power of the media. "Those incredible pictures of the East Germans walking and driving through the checkpoints, singing, smiling, and crying; hugging long-lost relatives and friends. I remembered my hometown as a boy, how as a family we had always been in tears at the border. When we arrived at the railway station on holidays to see my East German relatives, there were always tears when we left. Now here we were, all of us watching these incredible scenes unfold and all our dreams had come true. Everybody was crying at that time the whole day. That weekend, I traveled along the Baltic coast from Hamburg to Lübeck and encountered many people from across East Germany, not just from East Berlin, who had traveled there, too. A lot of whom had very little, if any money to spend. We gave them what we had and hugged and celebrated, sharing memories of the Cold War, families being split up, struggling to survive, and escaping."

CHAPTER TWENTY-TWO

Aftermath

The opening of the border checkpoints and the gradual lowering of any threat of a potential aggressive act by the security forces of the GDR over the next few days lent a surreal atmosphere to the city as both sides figured out what their next moves would be. Tens of thousands of East Berliners had now traveled into West Germany and were returning home, having seen what they wanted to see, bought some luxuries, or embraced long-lost loved ones. For the civil and military authorities, on both sides, it was a very delicate dance as neither wished to overstep their perceived authority or encourage any escalation toward confrontation.

For Corporal Richard Ornsby, serving with the Royal Military Police's close protection team, having only been in the city for the first time in a matter of days, the following weeks would prove to be a baptism of fire. The next morning after the Wall was opened, "after establishing the plan of action for the day [considering the situation of the borders opening up, it was highly unusual], I then escorted the general down to his car," Ornsby recalled, "a Mercedes 300 SEL, and I was sat in the back with him, and my role was just to give audible instructions to the driver, if they hadn't picked it up, such as warning of a figure lurking too close to the car as we drove past, or a vehicle we didn't recognize tailing us, or trying to come alongside, or overtake. The general was absolutely lovely to work for. I've bodyguarded some guys that have been hugely disrespectful and arrogant, always expecting you to carry their briefcase, and running around after them on errands. Yes, one expects an element of this on behalf of whom you're protecting, but bear in mind, if they're in a suit, I'm carrying a briefcase as well that's got a machine gun in it. So you press the button in the handle, and pull it into you, and the sides fall apart, and you're firing bullets. Therefore, to carry another briefcase just isn't feasible, or sensible. General Corbett was not like that at all and he understood what my primary role was—to protect his life—and so he didn't burden me with other jobs."

For General Corbett, the work of stabilizing the situation in Berlin, while at the same time ensuring that his own assessment of what would happen to Berlin and to Germany was being heeded by his superiors, kept him frenetically busy. A battle was going on at the highest international levels as the Allies seemed to be in two camps of thought as to the future of a reunified Germany. Secretary of State James A. Baker III recalled, "It soon became evident that there was a separation between Kohl and his West European counterparts about what to do next. Kohl was ready to reunite his country with East Germany, and he remained steadfast. Thatcher and Mitterrand, on the other hand, were very skeptical. Remember, Germany had twice invaded its neighbors during the first half of the twentieth century. . . . It was an extremely emotional moment. President Bush's response to the historic incident [was] a model in effective diplomacy. He knew that we had a lot of work still to do with the Soviet Union. As a result, he refused to gloat about winning the Cold War. . . . His measured approach attracted domestic criticism from those who espoused triumphalism. But it was the right thing to do."

Foreign Secretary Douglas Hurd arrived to see the situation for himself. As Corbett recounted, "I took him on a helicopter tour of the city so he could actually understand the lay of the land and the issues we all faced in dealing with this sudden collapse of the GDR. He was hugely helpful and then gave a really excellent press conference in the Reichstag. Straight afterwards, I spoke with him. 'Sir, there's just one thing I want to say about what's going on here [German reunification], this thing has an unstoppable momentum behind it. Chancellor Kohl clearly sees it as being a narrow window which he will take, and anybody and anything who stands in his way is going to come off worse. I'm terribly sorry, but this is the situation, this is the way it will be.' "

Corporal Ornsby could see the heavy toll the amount of work was taking on the general. "He worked incredibly hard across those days and weeks after the Wall came down—twenty hours straight, late into the night. He would have a ten-minute power nap in the back of the car, and then he'd wake up and say, 'I need to phone the minister for Berlin Michael Burton, or the American commandant General Haddock, or the head of the West German *Polizei*. I need a phone now!' he'd order. His brain never stopped. Luckily for mobile communication in the car, driving around Berlin, we had one of the first mobile phones installed for him. It was like a brick even though it was state-of-the-art stuff back then, but he was on it constantly."

As the days progressed, so activity at the Wall increased from one of celebration and shock at being able to cross through, and even climb onto it, to one of wanting to destroy it. House Sergeant Brian Andrews was leaving the Villa Lemm to pick up his wife, who worked for the British civil administration, and drive her back home to their quarters in Spandau. Her office had been extremely busy since November 9 as they were inundated with questions from the media back home in London as well as dignitaries and politicians wishing to come over to see it for themselves. Andrews recalled, "I immediately put the television on to watch *Sky News* to see what might be happening at the Wall that evening. Low and behold there was a shot of a bulldozer ripping part of the Wall down! Our first reaction was 'Does General Corbett know about this?' I decided to phone the ADC [Captain Carter]. 'I don't want to worry you, sir,' I said, 'but I'm watching *Sky TV News* here at home and part of the Wall's just come down!' The line went dead for an instant. It rang again and it was the captain asking,

'This is a joke, isn't it?'

" 'No, I'm quite serious,' I replied.

" 'Where are you getting all this information from?' he demanded.

" 'I'm watching it on TV,' I stammered. 'Do you not know about it?'

" 'Of course not!' "

*   *   *

It was then things started happening quickly, marking the beginning of the end of the Wall itself, igniting the wholesale destruction of it by the Berliners themselves.

As they danced on the Wall, none of them knew how close they were to a highly volatile situation. The Allies and the West German civil authorities were keenly aware, however, of the risk of a heavy-handed reaction by the GDR regime, as Georg Schertz, head of the West Berlin police in 1989, recounted. "By the 10th of November, the border crossing points were open, but not at the Brandenburg Gate itself, which the GDR had always regarded as a symbol of its sovereignty. There were no crossing points at the Brandenburg Gate, and the Wall was shorter than elsewhere due to its high-profile location, and several people, probably West Berliners, were now standing on top of it. Some were drinking alcohol and were throwing fireworks in the direction of East Berlin. The GDR border guards became understandably nervous and more men were brought in to support them—though, thank god, they were unarmed.

"I went down to review the situation myself," Scherz recalled, "worried that a tense situation could easily escalate, especially if for whatever reason the East German guards or *Vopos* started using water cannon to get the West Berliners off their wall. My fear was if there were any casualties from people falling from the Wall due to being knocked off it, then that might give the East German security forces an excuse to intervene.

"Though we hadn't known what their leadership was thinking on the 9th of November when the borders were opened, by the night of the tenth we were having some communication with our counterparts in East Berlin. We spoke to their local commanders, telling them if they were going to use water cannon, then do not have it as a strong jet of water, which would knock people off the Wall, but rather spray them instead and they'll eventually get fed up being wet and cold. They took our advice and did this, and by the time I reviewed the area again later that night, the West Berliners were now slowly going home. Some would come back, but the overall atmosphere was far less confrontational. Both sides started the process of withdrawing personnel to thin out the numbers at the Brandenburg Gate, again making it seem less confrontational, and by 3 a.m. the next morning (November 11) there were hardly any civilians there. With approval from the British commandant, we then placed many police vehicles next to the Wall on our own side in order to prevent more people gaining access to scale it. The crisis had been averted."

What the Allies didn't know at the time was that the previous day at noon, the GDR's minister of defense Heinz Keßler had declared a state of emergency for the NVA and that as a result thirty thousand troops were now on standby, which included the Felix Dzerzhinsky Guards Regiment. This was an elite Stasi-run, motorized formation—comprised of veteran troops loyal to the party and trained to protect all government buildings in Berlin. They would be supported by other NVA troops. All units had their vehicles made ready and troops fully armed to respond at a moment's notice. General Keßler had called the secretary of the National Defense Council [and deputy chief of the armed forces] Fritz Streletz, asking him, "Are you ready to march with two regiments to Berlin?" Streletz replied:

"Is that an order or a question?" He didn't wait for an answer from Keßler and continued: "If it is a question, it needs to be considered. We are too late to move as the streets are congested with traffic and we'll have logistical problems getting the units to Berlin."

Keßler sighed. "Wait, we will inform you."

The measures the West Berlin police had put in place for de-escalating crowd trouble at the Brandenburg Gate were only reported to the GDR leadership by noon of November 11, and by that time Keßler's state of emergency had already been suspended. Why? Because their reason to actively intervene at the Brandenburg Gate had evaporated—the crowd had now dispersed and the atmosphere was far less volatile. Even the East German guards standing on top of the Wall were behaving in a less threatening manner—many of them even accepting gifts of hot coffee and bars of chocolate from the throng below them. At Potsdamer Platz, which for decades had been a wasteland where once it had been the busiest square in Europe, the British had started to open a new checkpoint—removing sections of the Wall with a crane—again, much to the approval of the Berliners watching. As a memo from the British military command back to Bonn summarized: "Today is a day to sigh with relief in West Berlin, because there was no major incident and because the numbers who decided to stay permanently were far fewer than had been feared." This had been a major worry for all of the Allies—how could West Berlin cope with the flood of humanity they feared would want to claim asylum? As the weekend progressed, each of the sectors reported the same scene; East Berliners were coming across in the thousands, and staying awhile before returning home, to start work again that Monday. Reinforcing the picture of major changes lying ahead, the reports also noted the lack of activity by the *Grenztruppen* at the Wall. Many watchtowers were now unmanned, and the patrol boats so ubiquitous on the River Spree had now vanished.

Though it was clear that the reactionary wing of the GDR's leadership had failed in their desire to defend the border through force, to the Allies, the carnival-like atmosphere in Berlin was hanging by a thread and could change at any minute. They would realize through various contacts that the Russians had not been aware of what Schabowski was going to announce on November 9 but had clearly decided to stay out of it. For Timothy Garton Ash, this decision was influenced months before, and thousands of miles away from Berlin. "On the 4th of June, 1989, you have the free elections in Poland, and I'm coming back very excited in the evening because it's all gone very well for Solidarity," he said. "I come back into the newspaper office in Warsaw, and there on the tiny black-and-white television screen are the first shots from Tiananmen Square [in China] of this worker or student being carried on a board. From that moment forward, Tiananmen was on everybody's lips, and people talked about it constantly. You remember the one moment in Leipzig when it nearly came to violence, and Dresden also, and then it was prevented? The fact that it had happened in China is one of the reasons it didn't happen in Eastern Europe. Tiananmen was very bad for China, but in a paradoxical way it was good for the change in Eastern Europe."

The Allies had no idea what was happening in the rest of the country, or indeed that other elements within the NVA, and indeed the Soviet armed forces based around the city, were either in the dark as to what was happening, or back in their barracks awaiting orders. But the Red Army would stay in its barracks, and a young Vladimir Putin would stay behind the doors of Stasi headquarters in Dresden, too.

Lieutenant Torsten Belger, from Scharnebeck, near Magdeburg by the Elbe River, was in his third year at the NVA's training academy in Sietow near to the Polish-Czechoslovak border, awaiting to graduate as an artillery officer. Twenty-one years old, he was a classic product of the SED system, loyal, not fanatical, but never questioning the system he lived in and wise enough to know he had to conform—signing up for twenty-five years of service once he was qualified.

Now Belger was safely ensconced in his academy as the news of events happening in Berlin slowly dripped into their consciousness. The GDR was crumbling before their eyes over a period of weeks, but not before the authorities attempted to train the students in riot control. But it was too late; even the cadets began to question the system. "The demonstrations and discussions of what was going on," Belger recalled, "and how we had been deceived by the regime, were now going on in our own barracks. We demanded to know what was going on and what did the government plan to do to remedy the situation. We didn't think we were listened to by the commandant of the school, but the news kept changing every day with more updates, it was a very fluid situation. Change was coming, and quickly."

Life in East Germany had been very good thus far to reconnaissance platoon leader Vitaliy Denysov and his comrades serving with the elite Soviet Berlin Brigade. "The soldiers stationed in Germany were very lucky for several reasons," he said. "First and foremost, the war in Afghanistan was in full swing and a lot of eighteen-year-old conscripts following a short boot camp were sent directly to a slaughterhouse. Second, it was a dream of an average Soviet individual to have a foreign trip at least once in a lifetime. The restrictions on leaving the country even for a short trip made it almost impossible. By the time a Soviet soldier would be discharged from service in the DDR, one would have a stash of money enough to buy a pair of jeans and maybe even a stereo cassette recorder!"

The events of November did not come as a surprise to Denysov or his fellow officers. "There was no violence and it was the first time in my life that I witnessed events of such scale. Moreover, it looked like all the events were sanctioned by and under complete control of the Soviet Union. Having said that, the 10th of November was one of the most memorable days in my military career. There was a lot of hesitation with our supreme command as to whether to direct uniformed patrols to West Berlin that day. Finally, two crews consisting of just officers were sent across. Our mission was to make it through Checkpoint Charlie and proceed to the Soviet War Memorial next to the Brandenburg Gate, where we were to remain until further notice and keep reporting live on the developments. At a briefing prior to the mission we were told that the crowd may be extremely aggressive toward us and we may be subjected to violence." The unit drove through the crowd toward the white line dividing the two halves of the city and were stunned at what they saw.

As they arrived at the checkpoint, a mass of people greeted their arrival, creating a dangerous bottleneck. If someone was going to attack them, it would be here, and Denysov and his companions braced themselves. To their amazement the Germans welcomed them as heroes, throwing flowers onto their vehicles and shoving bottles of wine and champagne and bars of chocolate through their windows. "Not a bad day!" as Denysov recalled. Under strict instructions from their commanders, the Soviet armed forces would remain in barracks, or keep a low profile. Like tens of thousands of his fellow troops, Denysov welcomed this policy. "Our leadership was very skillful in handling the situation, as it prevented any bloodshed and standoff between the superpowers." The Warsaw Pact was standing down.

As the situation settled down to a degree at the checkpoints, more and more military personnel decided to take their chance and get across the border to see for themselves what was happening. One of them was the British commandant's wife, Susie Corbett. "I probably was the only British person going into East Berlin," she recalled, "as everyone else was coming back into West Berlin. The mixture of euphoria, wariness as to what might happen next, and of course confusion was a heady mixture during those first forty-eight hours. Seeing the many Trabants on the Glienicker Bridge, making their way slowly back into East Berlin, having explored the west, was incredible; all the passengers with smiles on their faces, waving bottles of wine and champagne and greeting friends—it was widely emotional.

"I also drove to Steinstücken, which is a very remote little island stranded between the GDR and Western Powers–controlled territory. There I was, trying to get a bit of the Wall—the size of a coffee table—into the back of my car, when a young man in a pair of jeans suddenly appeared and offered to help me and my driver. We were ladling this enormous piece of masonry into the car boot, and I just said to him, 'What do you do?' He sheepishly replied, 'Well, I was an officer of the *Grenztruppen* until four days ago!' I think this summed up how dramatic and surreal this whole period was for everyone in the city."

Possibly the most surreal story from those early weeks was the mission to get Prime Minister Margaret Thatcher a piece of the Berlin Wall. The armed forces minister Archie Hamilton arrived in the city soon after Douglas Hurd on November 12, to see for himself how the British garrison was coping. He was met by General Corbett and enjoyed an aerial tour of the city by helicopter, "It was a magical thing to do," Hamilton recalled. "We flew over the Wall and one could see people still pouring through the border crossings, as well as through holes made in the Wall itself. It was one of the most moving things I've ever experienced." Corbett then toured the minister around the British Sector, taking in the massive tents the army had erected near the Brandenburg Gate to offer tea and buns to the thousands of East Germans pouring through. The party then returned to the commandant's residence at the Villa Lemm for dinner. During after-dinner drinks, the plan to venture out to the Wall to gather mementos was hatched. For close protection officer Corporal Ornsby, the fun was just about to begin.

"At about midnight," he said, "I sat having a cup of coffee in the kitchen with the staff of the Villa Lemm, when suddenly, General Corbett came in, with Archie Hamilton and his aide-de-camp [Captain Carter]. 'The Minister would like to go down into the center of Berlin and chip his own bit off the Wall,' announced the general, looking straight at me." Despite Ornsby's protests about security and the fact it was the dead of night, the general smiled and gently told the corporal he was ordering him. "It was the only time I've ever had a general order me to do anything," Ornsby said. The main issues now were adequate clothing to keep out the freezing Berlin winter chill, and transport to get to the Wall—using the general's car was out of the question should they be stopped.

As the group stood in the hallway, Ornsby began instructing his charge. "It was the sort of speech I gave when on duty and everyone knows what's at stake and how to behave. The minister had enjoyed a few drinks at dinner, but out of nowhere, he jumped up in mock salute, stood to attention with his arms down by his side, and cried out, 'Yes, Corporal!' General Corbett couldn't keep a straight face and burst out laughing, 'I've just witnessed the minister for all of the armed forces taking an order from a corporal of the Royal Military Police,' he said. It was a bizarre night and we were just getting started."

The group would drive down to the border in Captain Carter's Peugeot 205 coupe, complete with a soft top. It was a British right-hand-drive vehicle, and Captain Carter got in the driver's seat, with Ornsby in the front passenger seat, pulled as far forward as possible to accommodate the long legs of the minister, who was squeezed up directly behind him. It was about minus eight Celsius (about seventeen degrees Fahrenheit), wintertime, in the middle of the night. Off they went, into the Berlin dark, four tall men in a small Peugeot 205 soft top, with the top down.

Not wishing to draw attention to themselves as they arrived at the center of town, they looked for a quiet side street near the border to park without being spotted and attempt to chip a bit off the Wall. The authorities were now beginning to crack down on what they termed

"*Mauerspechte*" ("wall woodpeckers"). Archie Hamilton remembered, "There was nothing but this sort of chipping noise going on, lots of it—mainly West Germans, I suspect—chipping away at the Wall, having bits to take away in the freezing night."

Ornsby continued, "We did get discovered a few times—a West Berlin police foot patrol with torch [flashlight] beams shining, spotted us and ordered us to 'Move on!' without any further checks—they must have been doing this for days and were getting tired of it. We dived back into the car and sped off looking for another site. At the next stop further along we were almost apprehended, this time by an East German guard who actually stood on the Wall pointing at us all and shouting at us to stop. Again, we had to jump back into the car and speed off.

"Finally, we came to a point in the Wall where there was an actual hole as people had already punched through it with hammers. The minister got out and chipped off a small chunk—he finally had his piece of the Wall at last." "The interesting thing is," Hamilton said, "was that the Wall wasn't very thick. It was made of very hard slabs of concrete, about three to four feet across, and about ten to twelve feet high. And they tapered toward the top. And when you chipped away at them, you were very lucky to get even tiny bits off, because it was so hard. But they'd been concreted together, so there was a sliver of concrete going down between the slabs, and you could get much more of that out with your chisel. So we chipped away at that, and got some quite large lumps." The night would continue with Hamilton visiting a British army checkpoint, much to the shock and amazement of the troops as the minister was dressed as if on a walk through the countryside, and chatted with them over a cup of cocoa.

Finally, Hamilton had his piece of the Wall to take back to Downing Street. "Because I was parliamentary private secretary to Margaret Thatcher, I had wrapped her a piece of the Wall in tissue paper. It must have been very near Christmas, because the prime minister always gave parties for all the parliamentary party in Downing Street, spread across two evenings as there was so many to get into the place. As I went in, I said, 'Prime Minister, I've got a little present for you here. These are parts of the Berlin Wall.' Her reaction was rather interesting. She said,

'Oh that would be wonderful. Would you get them framed for me? And inscribed to Margaret Thatcher, not to the Prime Minister?' She was obviously wary about people saying, 'Oh, well, this was a gift to the office.' . . . We had it framed for her and it was sent across to Downing Street. Once she had left office in 1990, I used to go to her house occasionally, and I'd look for this thing in the loo as I was intrigued what had become of it. I never saw it again."

The destruction of the Berlin Wall effectively started on November 9, 1989, once the Berliners were tolerated to climb onto the Brandenburg Gate section by the *Grenztruppen* stationed there. Within hours, civilians were taking hammers and chisels and whatever else could wreak havoc on it. Television crews recorded the new border crossings the East German authorities had announced were being created, with heavy bulldozers and cranes removing huge chunks of the Wall. At historically significant points such as Potsdamer Platz, the Brandenburg Gate, and Bernauer Straße vast crowds cheered the destruction. The military and West Berlin police soon became more flexible in allowing people through unauthorized points (holes) in the Wall, and by December 23, applying for and obtaining a visa to visit East Berlin and East Germany had been annulled. By the summer of 1990, the military would be systematically destroying the whole barrier, creating 1.7 million tons of rubble in the process, and repairing every road that had been blocked off between East and West Berlin. All that would remain were the sections we see in the city today.

Goodbye Checkpoint Charlie

The Wall was now in pieces and becoming a novelty, rather than the deadly obstacle that had taken hundreds of lives since 1961. By February 1990 Allied military sapper units had been ordered in, using cranes to systematically dismantle the Wall, piece by piece. Events had spun out at a frenzied pace since the Wall had been opened, as Helmut Kohl strove to push forward his goal of a reunified Germany quickly, to keep his allies on his side, and to have the Soviets on board and ultimately removed from the country. The SED's hold on East Germany was over. The Wall's destruction had seen to that, as the politburo, led by Egon Krenz, were forced to resign, to be replaced by the existing prime minister Hans Modrow—who knew how close the GDR was to total financial collapse.

The vehicle for Germany's reunification would be through Article 23—where as long as the majority of the GDR population voted to accept the FRG's laws and institutions—reunification could be processed within a six-month time frame. The GDR's first free elections on March 18 pointed the country to a brighter future: The Christian Democratic Union, campaigning for speedy reunification with the Federal Republic of Germany, with 40.8 percent of the vote, joined forces with the Social Democratic Party (21.9 percent) to establish a majority in the *Volkskammer*. The old SED, now rebranded the Party of Democratic Socialism, came in third with 16.4 percent. The Wall was dead, and so were the dreams of Ulbricht, Honecker, Mielke, and Krenz. Under a new prime minister, Lothar de Maizière, the Treaty of Monetary, Economic and

Social Union was signed on May 18. Though Margaret Thatcher and François Mitterrand were reticent to support a reunified Germany, their concerns were neutralized by the United States supporting Chancellor Kohl to the hilt. The Soviets needed to pull out their occupational forces due to their own dire economic situation—and Kohl's offer to underwrite the bill for their relocation, as well as substantial loans, smoothed the issue for the Kremlin.

The main players would come to Berlin for the necessary meeting that would cement the country's reunification, and the departure of the old powers. Thus, at Friedrichstraße, it was time to say goodbye to Checkpoint Charlie, as another crane towered over the simple hut. This icon of Cold War history was now obsolete and being put out to pasture.

Assistant provost marshal Lieutenant-Colonel Ron Tilston of the Royal Military Police picked up the story. "The 'Two Plus Four' talks were taking place between the foreign ministers of the FRG, the GDR, and the Soviet Union, France, USA, and Britain, planning the reunification of East Germany to West Germany. It was an opportune time to close Checkpoint Charlie, which after all was only meant to be a temporary requirement, a porta-cabin mounted on blocks. On June 22, 1990, Checkpoint Charlie would be closed.

During the previous night, the Americans brought down a mobile crane and a flatbed truck to the location. They put strops under the building and tested to confirm the crane could take the weight. The structure was lifted a couple of inches and eased back down again. Then they swung the crane over the top of some adjacent trees to the little car park and the flatbed to make sure the event would run smoothly in front of the world's press. For the next day, they built a temporary stand for the many officials who would be present.

For the military personnel selected for the ceremony it had already been a long morning. The day before Sergeant Michael Rafferty had been the NCOIC (noncommissioned officer in charge) at the checkpoint, dealing with the scrum of media looking for a story prior to the closing ceremony on Friday. He had decided to take it easy and remained within the privacy of the checkpoint hut as he watched the younger MPs on duty being interviewed. "It was kind of neat to see the young eighteen- and nineteen-year-old 'kid' privates being interviewed by the press such as *Stars and Stripes* and their photos taken by tourists," he recalled.

Rafferty's commanding officer, Major General Haddock, had also arrived to meet the media and answer their questions and attempt to quash any local rumors that the checkpoint would be transported back to the USA. To the Berliners, this small piece of real estate was now part of the city's heritage. American government officials had refused to comment, instead simply stating they were removing the hut to prevent vandalism or damage. Haddock's impromptu appearance seemed to allay any concerns for tomorrow's much-publicized removal. *Stars and Stripes* quoted him as stating, "Charlie's removal was highly symbolic for all concerned. . . . It is an indication that freedom and democracy are certainly on the ascent and is something that we can share together with the people of all nations. But it's something we view with joy and with a bit of caution, because the future is still uncertain—but we're optimistic."

Staff Sergeant Rafferty knew Friday would be a long one. "I got off at six o'clock that evening, the following day I had to be there at 5 a.m., which meant I woke up at 3:30 a.m.! I got into my Dress B uniform, with white gloves and helmet and made it to Tempelhof, where we practiced how the whole thing was going to go down. We worked on it and worked on it."

The honor guard to close the checkpoint was a cross section of twenty-one Allied military policemen who had served their time and deserved the opportunity—seven from each sector. For the Americans, Staff Sergeants Nathan Brown, Michael Yount, Michael Newton, and Michael Rafferty were the current NCOICs of the checkpoint, and they also added Staff Sergeant David Hadley and Sergeant Robert Baldwin, who had previous experience at the checkpoint. The final member was Specialist Robert Rashke, a Russian linguist who, like Rafferty, had been trained for Berlin Access, processing civilians and military personnel in and out of East Berlin. The guard would be commanded by one officer, Major Bernard J. Godek—also of Berlin Access—who had witnessed the scenes at Checkpoint Charlie the previous November when the GDR checkpoints had opened up and the Wall had fallen.

For the British and French forces within the honor guard the ritual was equally significant. Corporal Mark Horton of the Royal Military Police had been serving on "the Wire" since 1988 and had witnessed the chaotic scenes on November 9 from his observation post above the Reichstag. "I was fortunate to be one of those British NCOs chosen for the ceremony guard," he recalled. "It was very humbling to be part of such a significant moment and it gave a great feeling of pride to have been such an important part of protecting the freedom of the Berliners. The crowds were cheering and waving madly, it was pretty emotional, though it did feel strange to have such powerful people as the Soviet foreign minister there, who had been our enemy for so long."

Friedrichstraße was never as busy—it teemed with people as the noise and bustle steadily built in anticipation of the foreign diplomats and commandants to arrive. The street had been split into thirds as one looked down past Checkpoint Charlie's hut and into the Eastern Sector. The middle third had been cordoned off with folded seats in several rows for dignitaries, their wives, military personnel from each of the garrisons, and VIPs. On the right would be space for the military band—the US Army's 298th, the longest serving unit in Berlin since 1945—and the honor guard, who would officially close and "deactivate" the checkpoint. And on the left third room was made for the dozens of international press and media.

The buildings flanking the ceremony, including the Café Adler, housed hundreds of Berliners eager to witness this historic event. Many could be seen hanging out of their windows to take photographs, film it, or simply enjoy the view in the bright summer air. One overlooking flat displayed a small white banner with a message painted in red, *Schade lieber Checkpoint Charlie!* ["It's a shame, dear Checkpoint Charlie!"]. The flags of the three Allied powers—symbols for over four decades of West Berlin's security—flew everywhere, as well as those of the Federal Republic of Germany. The iconic symbol of the city, the black bear, was in evidence, a fitting tribute to the warm applause afforded to the hero of 1961 and VIP guest Willy Brandt. Sergeant Rafferty was called upon to usher VIP guests up to the second floor of the Café Adler—where the Mitchell Suite would offer a splendid view of the ceremony. "I didn't realize it was such a big thing," he said, "until I saw the international media. I escorted Tom Brokaw and John Chancellor of NBC *Nightly News.* I then walked up Peter Jennings of ABC *World News* so he could look down on the 'mess' that was Friedrichstraße. He made a couple of comments which led me to believe he was thinking of 1961 and how things were changing in front of his eyes."

A fleet of limousines slowly came into view. The diplomats and politicians were now arriving. The commandants were already on hand to greet them, with Major General Haddock taking the lead. The size of their individual retinues of civil servants, and bodyguards, gave the crowd watching an indication of who was coming. Military police and members of the West Berlin *Polizei* stood to attention, the French gendarmes looking especially elegant in their service uniforms, and sternly taking in the event behind their aviator sunglasses. Over the next fifteen minutes the main players took to the stage, as first Haddock, then François Cann and Corbett shook their hands, said a few pleasantries to their assistants, and bade them to the relevant seating situated on the wooden platform right in front of Checkpoint Charlie.

For the British commandant the significance of the day was almost overwhelming. His thoughts drifted back to that autumn morning of 1961 when, as a young Irish Guards officer, he had taken in the view of the Berlin Wall for the very first time from atop the RMP observation post within the ruins of the Reichstag. He may have harbored deep animosity toward the Wall and its architects, but his role now was to bring closure. Meeting someone of the Soviet foreign minister's stature finally revealed to him the pressures of the past months. "Before the official ceremony began, we found ourselves arriving too early and so I sat with Eduard Shevardnadze in a side room with an interpreter talking about the whole process and what was going on. I could see he was exhausted—both physically and mentally. A telling aspect of his demeanor from my soldier's eye were his shoes, worn right down to the uppers. This was quite telling as to the amount of traveling he had been doing on Gorbachev's behest, across the USSR and throughout the West, too." Corbett sat next to his French brother-in-arms General François Cann as both watched the American commandant prepare to give the opening address.

Major General Raymond E. Haddock stood tall and erect, bringing all the authority of his years of service to bear on this one final duty. The man who had come to Berlin "to fight" was now the peacemaker. "Charlie" loomed behind him and the dignitaries seated in front as he stepped up to the wooden lectern. He studied his surroundings as the sunshine of this crisp early summer sky bathed Friedrichstraße. He could feel the buzz of expectation among the crowds standing, as well as among the Allied military personnel, politicians, reporters, and policemen waiting for this iconic moment. The world's press was arrayed to his left, anxious to get the right image of "Charlie" finally being winched away with the East German border still ominous in the background. He watched admiringly as the military band of the 298th marched in formation to their position. The honor guard followed and came to a halt to the right of the stage, adressed their ranks, and stood easy.

The press focused on the foreign dignitaries sitting behind Haddock. West Berlin's deputy mayor Ingrid Stahmer and East Germany's foreign minister Markus Meckel looked nervous as they prepared themselves for their turn in the spotlight. This was their city, and country, so their sense of responsibility to provide a historic sound bite was huge. In the center of the seating British foreign minister Douglas Hurd and American secretary of state James A. Baker III gave off an aura of calm self-assurance, as did their French counterpart, foreign minister Roland Dumas. All were seasoned politicians, whose place on this sort of stage was a regular duty. In this new era of cooperation and openness with the Soviet Union, West German foreign minister Hans-Dietrich Genscher and the Soviet foreign minister Eduard Shevardnadze sat motionless, though Shevardnadze's young translator sitting by his shoulder looked anxious as he readied himself to keep his master informed over the coming hour.

For Secretary Baker, a child of the Cold War, a military man himself, and one of President Ronald Reagan's key lieutenants when the Cold War was blowing hot, the events since November 9 had developed a momentum of their own, but the White House staff had remained focused on their goals. "Once the Wall came down, President Bush had one plan—to reunite Germany," Baker said. "There was no plan B for the United States. American leaders had been talking about unification for forty years, and when the chance came, the opportunity came to do it, we took it. It would not have been feasible to walk away. This was the moment. Though the Soviet Union, United Kingdom, and France initially opposed reunification, President Bush and Chancellor Kohl remained steadfast." Now here was Secretary Baker, in Berlin, finalizing the historic agreement that would eventually reunify Germany. But today was closure on a different level.

Haddock, keen to begin, reviewed the pages of his speech as the audience settled down. He turned to officially welcome his fellow commandants and the invited guests. "We have come together for a different kind of ceremony. Not to dedicate a building, but to close one. When the Berlin Wall was built twenty-nine years ago, optimism was in rather short supply, and the new reality of concrete and barbed wire appeared to many as insurmountable," he said. "What was a new reality twenty-nine years ago has not withstood the test of time." Looking at the elongated hut, Haddock then remarked that the unimpressive appearance of the latest MP station, which was installed in 1986, disappointed many visitors. "There was something unfinished, something temporary about it," he said. ". . . These impressions, however, were altogether accurate. For the temporariness of the structure reflects the permanence of the determination of free men to uphold the freedom of movement in Berlin." James Baker and Hurd nodded at these words, while Generals Corbett and Cann looked ahead steadfastly; though they had heard these words practiced days before, the message the words conveyed was both touching and honest.

Haddock then turned to the honor guard and other military personnel in the audience. "As representatives of all those who have served here before you—for nearly three decades, day and night, you have served at this crossroad between East and West. You have done so loyally, and with dedication." Coming to the end of his speech, the American commandant paid tribute to the place they had served, and what the

Allies' role had now brought about: "A city long divided is repairing its severed arteries, and its pulse is growing stronger. For the contribution you have made to the freedom and the well-being of Berlin, you have earned the thanks of all free men." The audience burst into applause.

The foreign ministers rose one after another to give thanks, pay tribute, and look to the future—with passing references to the bigger picture for a reunited Germany. Secretary Baker was magnanimous in his words. "At this checkpoint, the United States stood with its allies and with the German people, resolved to resist aggression and determined to overcome the division of the Cold War. And now, with the help of a new generation of Soviet leaders, that time has come. . . . Germany will be united in peace and freedom. Europe will be whole, and it will be free." Eduard A. Shevardnadze's words caught the audience's imagination with part of his short speech that proposed the withdrawal of all Allied troops from a reunified Germany within six months of a treaty being signed. For a Soviet minister announcing this in Berlin, after twenty-eight years of the Wall being in place, and an implacable foe ensconced behind it, must have been startling to so many Cold War warriors arrayed before him.

It would be British foreign minister Douglas Hurd who captured the mood and perhaps stole the show, when he addressed the audience and evoked a level of emotion about the little hut on a street. "We should not forget—and our children should not forget—the reasons for which Checkpoint Charlie stood here for so many years. . . . At long last," Hurd said, "we are bringing 'Charlie' in from the cold." It perfectly captured the mood for the many military and civil personnel. Both Cold War warriors, Cann and Corbett, didn't blink. But Staff Sergeant Rafferty, standing at ease in the honor guard, smiled at these words. "If he only knew how cold the checkpoint could get on cold days," he later said. "Then it felt like a refrigerator in the middle of the road!"

Major General Corbett now addressed the audience. "Ladies and gentlemen, in acknowledgment for twenty-nine years of service by the military police at Checkpoint Charlie, we ask you to please rise for the final dismissal of the detachment." Commandant Cann walked to the podium as Major Godek took his cue and stood to attention before him, with the honor guard waiting for the signal. General Cann solemnly gave the order, "Please close the Checkpoint Charlie control point." One MP from each nation then marched to the side of the building to ceremoniously lock its doors and remove the Allied checkpoint sign.

They then marched the sign back to the podium as though carrying a family coffin. Some members of the press corps, wanting the photograph that would light up the next day's newspapers, shouted at the men to raise the signpost. The MPs ignored them. Following the carefully practiced choreography, Major Godek returned to the front of the stage and saluted—the silence was deafening. Standing in front of the microphone, Cann's order of "Dismiss your detachments" reverberated around the street. The guard marched off.

General Corbett replaced Cann at the lectern. Thinking back to the previous year's dramatic events, his final words were from the heart. The Cold War was officially confined to history. "Checkpoint Charlie has served the cause of Berlin well, and has now been retired with honor. . . . I, for one, will never forget—could never forget—the scene which we saw here on the 9th of November last year. And now, we look forward to a future where Berlin will be one city again."

The United States Berlin Brigade 298th Band's rendition of "*Das Ist die Berliner Luft*" ("That Is Berlin's Air") serenaded the crowd as they watched as the fifty-foot-long hut was lifted by crane. It momentarily hung ten feet in the air for one final photograph with the ministers out front—and a clearly emotional Willy Brandt ushered into the shot—then swung onto a flatbed truck in an adjacent parking lot. The audience was surprised at how basic the foundations of the checkpoint actually were. A simple bed of sand and timber remained as workers had the previous day dug up the foundation stones—which now lay near to the site. The crowd quickly made a beeline to grab a souvenir.

Sergeant Rafferty and his buddies had been busy handing out their white service gloves to the Berliner spectators. They now did something extraordinary. "Those foundation stones became quite the collector's item," Rafferty recalled. "So Staff Sergeants Brown, Baldwin, and I quickly moved to the site to grab some of those stones. We then went over to the East German border guards and gave them one each. They were surprised, but very polite and friendly. They just said thank you and posed for some pictures with us." It was a touching moment the media failed to capture.

For others witnessing the event, despite their years spent serving in the city, the closure was fairly straightforward. Lieutenant Colonel Ron Tilston had been busy overseeing the security of the event from the British side. "I actually didn't feel much emotion that day," he said. "I saw its removal as just part of the process. Right from November through to that point, so much had been happening. If someone had said to me back in October 1989, 'In eight months' time, Checkpoint Charlie is going to close and be taken away,' I'd have said, 'You're mad!'" For the French ADC Philippe Sandmeyer, another Cold Warrior who worked alongside General Cann, the significance of the hut's removal allowed him to look back on how wrong the entire GDR experiment had been. "Winston Churchill," he said, "was correct in *Blood, Sweat, and Tears*, to write: 'The dictatorship-fetish devotion for a man is an ephemeral thing. A state of society where it is not possible to express his thoughts, where children denounce their parents to the police, such a state of society cannot last long.'"

The following day the world's press had their front pages declaring "Checkpoint Charlie Closes," with photographs of the hut dangling above the ministers' heads. Haddock had by this time developed a strong rapport with the people of Berlin, having enjoyed mingling with them during the fall of the Wall the year previously. He decided to leave the Checkpoint Charlie hut for the German people despite a call to have it shipped back to the United States. The structure would come to rest at the Allied Museum, situated in the old American Sector, on Clayallee (named after the hero of the Berlin Airlift, Lucius D. Clay). It still stands there today. Sergeant Michael Rafferty is full of praise for Haddock's actions. "It showed a greater understanding that this change wasn't about us but the German people themselves," he said. "His role and his calm command during that November displayed what President Bush himself stated, 'We shall not dance on the Wall.'"

From a wider, geopolitical perspective, Secretary of State James A. Baker III shared that sentiment. "The events that started November 9, 1989, at the Berlin Wall—and ended October 3, 1990, when Germany was officially unified—went very well. A lot of people deserve the credit for it. It could not have happened without the dedication of Helmut Kohl. It could not have happened without the decision of Mikhail Gorbachev and Eduard Shevardnadze that they would not keep the Soviet empire together using force. It could not have happened without the leadership of every American president from Harry Truman on, all of whom generated bipartisan support for America's successful effort to resist Soviet expansionism. It could not have happened without the wise and deliberate response of President George H. W. Bush, who refused to metaphorically dance on the ruins of the Berlin Wall. And perhaps, most importantly, it could not have happened without the indomitable spirit of the people of East Germany and the other captive nations of Eastern and Central Europe. They never gave up."

The building of the Berlin Wall had been a last throw of the dice by a desperate regime, taking advantage of the global confrontation between two superpowers in order to keep afloat its totalitarian, repressive authority. The people of the GDR, as well as West Berlin, would pay the price for this act of inhumanity. The twenty-eight years of its existence not only scarred this beautiful city but cowed the East Germans into accepting their way of life as permanent, while offering itself up as the pressure vent for the Cold War in general. Nowhere else would the superpowers come as close to one another with loaded weapons. This dystopian place was celebrated in Hollywood films and best-selling books, but they only scratched the surface as to the human tragedy the Wall epitomized. White crosses around the city each mark where a human being was killed by the East German border guards. But for every official cross, there were thousands more who failed to get across, who were shot or injured and taken back to a life of imprisonment and surveillance. Checkpoint Charlie was central to this period—not just from the spectacle of world leaders visiting the crossing point—but because the Western powers could send their people in unmolested to visit East Berlin. As many witnesses in this book have attested to, this presence showed the East Germans they were not forgotten, and that the world was watching. Checkpoint Charlie physically may have been a small wooden hut, but it stood as a beacon of hope to the east—for freedom. It served its purpose. The men and women who served there, the people who went across—whether officially or illegally—and the people who died nearby should never be overlooked for the significant role they played in the fall of the Wall and the GDR, and the end of the Cold War.

I hope these pages have done them some justice.

Four Memories

The Café Einstein, Unter den Linden, August 2018

It is a beautiful Berlin autumn morning. The Wall is long gone; the city is whole again and rejuvenated. Everywhere one looks there are signs of major building works, as yet another piece of wasteland is rebuilt in the Mitte district where I am meeting my guest. Checkpoint Charlie is now a popular tourist destination, still standing sentinel on a street lined with souvenir shops, burger bars, and the museum dedicated to its memory.

I sit enjoying my exceptionally strong coffee in one of the city's historical venues of the Cold War on *Unter den Linden*, watching the tourists file past to take a snap of the restored Brandenburg Gate. Opposite me sits Hans-Ulrich Jörges chuckling as he recounts his adventures reporting in East Berlin decades earlier. Since the Wall fell, he has become one of Germany's most renowned journalists and media commentators. In the UK he would be Andrew Marr, or in the USA Tom Brokaw. The Cold War, the Wall, and reunification are at the forefront of his mind.

"The majority of West Germans did not want the reunification of the country. They knew it would cost them financially. Lots of money! Erich Böhme, editor of *Der Spiegel*, wrote at that time: 'I don't want to be reunified.' Chancellor Helmut Kohl and a minority of West Germans, including Willy Brandt, thought and acted in the opposite direction. They demonstrated historical responsibility. They were true German patriots. I, on the other hand, am extremely happy with the unification because of my personal history."

It is as we touch upon his own experiences that Uli, as I have seen many Germans I interviewed for this book do, erupts with deeply held emotion. "When the Wall collapsed, I sent a telegram to my family in Bad Salzungen with just one sentence: 'Congratulations for a peaceful revolution!'" Suddenly, he stops talking and his infectious smile freezes, and tears fill his eyes. It was one of the most moving interviews I did. We stop for a minute as he composes himself, drinks some coffee, and I ask him about the problems the country faces. "There was a reckoning of sorts—from an economic perspective. The industrial and commercial power of West Germany was overwhelming and the East German economy was systematically destroyed. Too many East Germans lost their jobs and their confidence in this new order. That is one of the reasons, in my opinion, for the rise of Neo-Nazi movements in East Germany today. But only a very small minority still feel nostalgic for the Wall and for the GDR—and most of these people belong to the Stasi!

"Today, Berlin is a great city where I am so proud to live and work. I do not want to live anywhere else in Germany. The city is more multicultural than any other in the country, and thus more liberal and more international (much like London). But it is still not one whole city. East and West will always differ, I believe, as North and South always differ in the USA. You just have to take a walk across Friedrichstraße, where Checkpoint Charlie used to be—the symbolic US Army sentry hut now stands alone, like a sentinel—and you feel it quite quickly. The memories come flooding back. I can picture the windows of the war-torn apartment blocks staring out across the Death Strip. It never leaves you."

A conversation with Professor Timothy Garton Ash, Oxford

Following our interview, in conclusion, Timothy offered up this final piece of his issue with East German nostalgia: "I had the very curious experience of visiting Erich Honecker when he was an old sick man in prison in West Berlin, in his prison uniform. He said to me— still slightly defiant, 'I get lots of letters from East Germans'—and he continued—'they say they lived more calmly in the old days.' And of course, there is that. It's true, and the famous joke was: 'We pretend to work, and they pretend to pay us.' There weren't the stresses of a market society. They moved much more slowly. There was more time. There was more leisure. So, I understand that people would genuinely miss that, but not the system. Not the famous achievements of socialism."

An email from Secretary of State James A. Baker III, January 2019

The Secretary had been very gracious to answer my many questions, despite having recently laid to his rest his great friend President George H. W. Bush, and naturally he singled out Bush 41 as pivotal in shaping Europe after the Wall crumbled. "I was the first and the last US Secretary of State who visited East Germany, and my first impression was that it was in very bad shape. Shortly after the Wall opened, at Christmas time 1989, I drove across the Glienicker Bridge to the Potsdam Inter-Hotel to meet Hans Modrow, the hope of the Socialist Unity Party of Germany. That was a surreal experience for me. It was as if someone had switched the world from color to black and white. Everything was gray, the clothes, the houses, the people, the atmosphere. Everyone around the world was surprised by the speed of events that led up to the fall of the wall. Even more amazing was how quickly the world responded to the events that had unfolded. Within a year, the two Germanys joined the United States, Soviet Union, France and England to work out a plan to put Germany back together again. We accomplished it despite all sorts of resistance and it brought the desired goal: Unification of the two German states, NATO membership for Germany and the withdrawal of the Red Army from the former GDR."

Secretary Baker had always been keen to single out his president for leading the way in ensuring that neither the USA nor its allies descend into triumphalism once the Wall had come down, but he was now keen to tell me how events could easily have spiraled out of control had it not been for the foresight of Bush's opposite number in the Kremlin. "Fortunately, Soviet leaders did not respond to the peaceful protests in East Germany and the Warsaw bloc like Chinese leaders did to the protesters at Tiananmen Square and elsewhere in China. Mikhail Gorbachev and Eduard Shevardnadze made the fundamental decision not to keep the Soviet empire together using force. It had been built by force. Until that point, it had been maintained by force. So, theirs was a remarkable commitment. That decision, as much as anything, helped lead to a peaceful end of the Cold War."

Presents from Russia, Dorset, September 2018

This story began with Sir Robert Corbett, anxiously traveling on a supply train to the surrounded British garrison in Berlin in 1961. Many years after the Wall's demise and his retirement from the armed forces, after which he spent a decade in the charity sector, he now resides with his wife, Susie, in a quiet village in the southwest of England. Which is where, he, Lady Susan, and I talked at length over lunch in their beautiful back garden.

As our talk was ending, Robert gestured toward the house. "I want to show you something," he said. We went inside to his study where, one by one, he showed me a series of objects: a Russian general's full-dress cap decorated in gold braid, gray fur, and surmounted by the Red Star embossed with the hammer and sickle of the Soviet Union; a memoir of Marshal Zhukov (Stalin's greatest general of World War Two); training manuals of the Soviet army; greeting cards; and an impressive medal. What was not present, however, was the supply of high-quality vodka that had somehow not survived the passage of the years! And the reason for these mysterious gifts? He smiled. "What happened at the Brandenburg Gate all those years ago on that November night in 1989. If those young Russian conscripts had felt threatened by the West Berlin protestors storming the two-meter-high perimeter, then there would almost certainly have been shooting around that Soviet memorial, and all our fears would have . . . where would that ever have ended?"

Robert was remembering how that shooting did not break out, that soldiers on all sides displayed restraint and kept their weapons down. "In all the dramatic moments about what was happening that night which we all remember so well, and are still portrayed on countless television programs, it is worthwhile remembering that the small things are those on which so much can turn."

How right this grand old soldier was.

Fatalities at the Berlin Wall 1961–1989

This book has been about the ordinary people whose lives were affected by the Berlin Wall. It is only right, therefore, to commemorate those ordinary Berliners who died because of it. Figures vary, but records released by the Berlin Wall Memorial, based on Bernauer Straße, show that at least 140 people were killed or died at the Wall in connection with the East German border regime. This total comprises 101 East Germans who were killed, died by accident, or committed suicide while trying to flee through the border fortifications; 30 people from the east and west without any escape plans and 1 Soviet soldier who were shot or died in an accident; 8 East German border soldiers who were killed by deserters, comrades, a fugitive, an escape helper, or a West Berlin policeman, by accident or intentionally while on duty. Added to this total here are at least 251 others who died during or after they had gone through checkpoints at the Berlin border crossings. Unknown numbers of people attempted to escape and were injured and taken back into the GDR—there are few, if any, records detailing their fate.

1961

Ida Siekmann—Günter Litfin—Roland Hoff—Rudolf Urban—Olga Segler—Bernd Lünser—Udo Düllick—Werner Probst—Lothar Lehmann—Dieter Wohlfahrt—Ingo Krüger—Georg Feldhahn

1962

Dorit Schmiel—Heinz Jercha—Philipp Held—Klaus Brueske—Peter Böhme—Horst Frank—Lutz Haberlandt—Axel Hannemann—Erna

Kelm—Wolfgang Glöde—Siegfried Noffke—Peter Fechter—Hans-Dieter Wesa—Ernst Mundt—Anton Walzer—Horst Plischke—Otfried Reck—Günter Wiedenhöft

1963
Hans Räwel—Horst Kutscher—Peter Kreitlow—Wolf-Olaf Muszynski—Peter Mädler—Klaus Schröter—Dietmar Schulz—Dieter Berger—Paul Schultz

1964
Walter Hayn—Adolf Philipp—Walter Heike—Norbert Wolscht—Rainer Gneiser—Hildegard Trabant—Wernhard Mispelhorn—Hans-Joachim Wolf—Joachim Mehr

1965
Unidentified Fugitive—Christian Buttkus—Ulrich Krzemien—Peter Hauptmann—Hermann Döbler—Klaus Kratzel—Klaus Garten—Walter Kittel—Heinz Cyrus—Heinz Sokolowski—Erich Kühn—Heinz Schöneberger

1966
Dieter Brandes—Willi Block—Jörg Hartmann—Lothar Schleusener—Willi Marzahn—Eberhard Schulz—Michael Kollender—Paul Stretz—Eduard Wroblewski—Heinz Schmidt—Andreas Senk—Karl-Heinz Kube

1967
Max Sahmland—Franciszek Piesik

1968
Elke Weckeiser—Dieter Weckeiser—Herbert Mende—Bernd Lehmann—Siegfried Krug—Horst Körner

1969
Johannes Lange—Klaus-Jürgen Kluge—Leo Lis

1970

Christel Wehage—Eckhard Wehage—Heinz Müller—Willi Born—Friedhelm Ehrlich—Gerald Thiem—Helmut Kliem—Hans Joachim Zock—Christian Peter Friese

1971

Rolf-Dieter Kabelitz—Wolfgang Hoffmann—Werner Kühl—Dieter Beilig

1972

Horst Kullack—Manfred Weylandt—Klaus Schulze—Cengaver Katranci

1973

Holger H.—Volker Frommann—Horst Einsiedel—Manfred Gertzki—Siegfried Kroboth

1974

Burkhard Niering—Czeslaw Jan Kukuczka—Johannes Sprenger—Giuseppe Savoca

1975

Herbert Halli—Cetin Mert—Herbert Kiebler—Lothar Hennig

1977

Dietmar Schwietzer—Henri Weise

1979

Vladimir Ivanovich Odintsov

1980

Marienetta Jirkowski

1981

Hans-Peter Grohganz—Dr. Johannes Muschol—Hans-Jürgen Starrost—Thomas Taubmann

1982
Lothar Fritz Freie

1983
Silvio Proksch

1984
Michael Schmidt

1986
Rainer Liebeke—René Groß—Manfred Mäder—Michael Bittner

1987
Lutz Schmidt

1989
Ingolf Diederichs—Chris Gueffroy—Winfried Freudenberg

East German border soldiers killed while on duty
Jörgen Schmidtchen (1962)—Peter Göring (1962)—Reinhold Huhn
(1962)—Günter Seling (1962)—Siegfried Widera (1963)—Egon Schultz
(1964)—Rolf Henniger (1968)—Ulrich Steinhauer (1980)

Acknowledgments

There are many people I would like to thank for their advice, support, and kind contributions to my research, and of course also those who agreed to be interviewed for this book. First and foremost I wish to acknowledge the invaluable assistance I have received from my longtime German researcher Sabine Schereck. She has been with me on this journey to locate many of the German interviewees across the country, and in some cases has sat in with me on interviews. Her skills in translation and fact-checking are second to none, and any praise this book might receive is shared with her.

The narrative of *Checkpoint Charlie* is populated by many voices of people who lived, worked, and served in both East and West Berlin, as well as the city's hinterland. In keeping with the zones of Berlin itself, I wish to thank, by nationality, first from the British contingent: Major General Sir Robert Corbett for his generosity of time, the hospitality he and his wife Lady Susan showed me on my visits to their home, his thorough retelling of events, and the bravery of spirit he displayed through all of this while undergoing treatment for a serious illness. I cannot praise him enough and I consider it a highlight to have met with him. His son, Professor Jonathan Corbett, was also kind enough to be interviewed to recall his memories of student days in Cold War Berlin. General Corbett's house sergeant during that pivotal period, Brian Andrews, was invaluable in detailing what life was like in the commandant's residence during 1989. Grateful thanks to former leader of the Conservative Party Lord Michael Howard for recollecting his own experience of witnessing President John F. Kennedy's visit to Berlin in 1963, and to former minister of the armed forces Lord Archie Hamilton for sharing his story of a very cold winter's night attempting to find a piece of the Berlin Wall for Margaret Thatcher in November 1989. Thanks also to the following: The officers and men of the Royal Military Police who all gave up their time to talk to me or conduct further research on my behalf; Lieutenant Colonel Ron Tilston OBE for supplying me with so many documents; Colonel Jeremy Green of the Royal Military Police Museum for his enthusiastic backing of this project from the start; Provost Marshal Barry Davies for his generosity in passing paperwork to me for my initial research; Sergeant Christopher Toft for supplying the actual logbook he updated at Checkpoint Charlie on the night of November 9, 1989; Sergeant John Walker for the valuable insight into the care of prisoner Rudolph Hess at Spandau Prison in the 1970s; Sergeant Robert Wilmhurst for memories of what life was like on "the Wire" just when the Wall was being constructed in August 1961; and Corporals Kevin May, Mark Horton, and Richard Ornsby for willingly giving up their time to answer all of my questions about key events in Berlin from 1989 to 1990 (special mention to their honorary unit "the Wallbusters," who will be attending the upcoming thirtieth anniversary celebrations this year in their old stomping ground). From BRIXMIS I am extremely grateful to General Peter Williams, Major Nigel Dunkley, and Sergeant Michael Opsako for revealing just a portion of their incredible service monitoring the Warsaw Pact forces in East Germany during the 1980s. Three very brave and resourceful men who wear their incredible achievements with undue modesty. I hope my book has at least shone some praise on their unit's work for a new generation. In the British media, broadcaster Alastair Stewart of ITV was an invaluable source of information on life growing up with the RAF in Germany, as well as his experiences reporting in Berlin in 1989. Mark Wood, then of Reuters, was superb at detailing what life was like reporting inside the East German state in the 1970s. His love for the country and its people shone through each of our meetings, and he was immeasurably helpful in fact-checking and introducing me to some of his contemporaries who worked alongside him. Timothy Garton Ash was kind enough to invite me to his office in Oxford for an afternoon to hear his thoughts on how morally corrupt a state the GDR really was. Former BBC radio and television correspondent, and current member of Parliament for his Exeter constituency, Ben Bradshaw gave unique insight into events post–November 9, 1989, when he was on assignment.

From the American sector, I would first wish to praise every man and woman who belong to the Berlin United States Military Veterans Association. Their reunions coordinator, Colonel Berry A. Williams, could not have been more generous in assisting me to contact the relevant people within that organization so as to get a taste of the American military experience in West Berlin during the Cold War. His kind invitation for me to join as a guest at the BUSMVA's reunion in Berlin in August of 2018 was a highlight as the city officially commemorated the seventieth anniversary of the Berlin Airlift. I was honored to attend. At the event I befriended Adolf and Vera Knackstedt, a very special couple who have lived remarkable lives that I have tried to describe herein. I want to thank Colonel Verner Pike for recounting his unique role at the tank standoff at Checkpoint Charlie in the winter of 1961. It was a pleasure to meet with Vern and his wife for lunch in New York. Privates Tom Ables and Wayne Daniels of the US Military Police were a historian's dream in the information they gave me of their service in West Berlin when the Wall was built. Sergeants Lynda Harvey of the US Military Police and Allen Lawless of the 298th USARMEUR Military Band deserve special mention for being valuable sources of information, too. It was a unique and thrilling experience to interview some key figures from one of the Cold War's forgotten units—the 39th Special Forces Operational Detachment, or, Detachment A. James Stejskal, Robert "Bob" Charest, who was recently inducted into the Green Beret Hall of Fame, and Colonel Darrell Katz willingly gave of their time to detail the unique role their unit played in West Berlin. Colonel Lawrence Kelley was a font of knowledge in aiding my understanding of the vital and hazardous role the USMLM (US Military Liaison Mission) played in surveillance behind the East German border. I am grateful to Jon Landau for discussing with me the significance of Bruce Springsteen's legendary concert in East Berlin in 1988, as well as Tracy Nurse for connecting us for that interview. For the pivotal year 1989, Sergeant Michael Rafferty gave much of his time to answer all of my questions, however trivial, as to events at Checkpoint Charlie after the Wall was opened. USAAF airman Mathew "Mitt" Law was also a key eyewitness to events of that fateful night. Gillian Cox allowed me to view the fall of the Wall from the perspective of a young foreign student caught up in historic events. Secretary of State James A. Baker III was extremely insightful in supplying the wider implications of the Wall coming down for Europe and the world as a whole in 1989. I very much appreciated him taking the time to answer all my questions fully. He is a remarkable man.

The book's narrative has many stories told by the East and West Germans I interviewed. Günter Heinzel kindly flew to London to answer my questions on his daring escape from the GDR. Margit Hosseini welcomed me to her West London home for an afternoon to describe her childhood and teenaged memories of life before and just after the Wall was built. I thoroughly enjoyed interviewing Hans-Ulrich Jörges of Stern magazine and for his helpful comments in follow-up emails. On my various trips to Berlin I was fortunate to be made welcome by Bernd von Kostka at the Allied Museum, who supported all my efforts to contact various potential interviewees, as well as fact-check my research. Hans-Peter Spitzner was tireless in answering my many questions over the past twelve months via email. Thanks also to Major Peter Bochman for his hospitality when interviewed, and to Stefan Wolle of the DDR Museum for taking time out of his busy schedule to talk. I want to express gratitude to the following who spent time either via telephone or email to recount their unique stories related to the Wall: Andreas Austilat, Dirk Bachmann, Astrid Benner, Torsten Belger, Brigitte Geschwind, Wolfgang Göbel, Manfred Höer, Professor Andreas Nachama, Rosemarie Platz, and Georg Schertz.

Finding and interviewing French and Soviet witnesses was tricky, but I am honored to record the memories of General François Cann, his ADC Commander Gilbert Sandmeyer, and Jean Pierre Vido. Sergeants Jean-Louis de Moulins Beaufort, Raymond Teske, and Emmanuel and Ghislaine de Geoffrey gave insightful information on what life was like for the French garrison in West Berlin in the 1970s and 1980s. For the Soviet sector I enjoyed talking with Vitaliy Denysov to see the disparity between what one might read of life for the ordinary Soviet soldier in the GDR and the reality for this young officer in 1989.

Constructing a narrative such as this, involving multiple story lines and historic events to interweave, means one spends a great deal of time in the archives. I wish to express thanks to the staffs (London unless otherwise stated) of the Allied Museum (Berlin), the Berlin Wall Memorial (Berlin), the British Library, Hohenschönhausen Prison (Berlin), the Imperial War Museum, the Marienfelde Refugee Centre Museum (Berlin), the National Archives, the National Army Museum, the Royal Military Police Museum (Hampshire), the Spy Museum (Berlin), the Stasi archives (Berlin), and the Wende Museum (Los Angeles). My local libraries of Dulwich and Forest Hill in London, where I wrote the majority of this book, are fantastic places that are highly valued by their respective communities. Long may they flourish.

It is rare to find a literary agent with Mark Lucas's breadth of historical knowledge and excitement at being involved in a project such as this. His constant advice from proposal stage all the way through the process has been exceptional. *Checkpoint Charlie* wouldn't be the book it is without him. Thanks also to his "brother in arms" George Lucas at Inkwell in New York. Both my editors at Constable (Andreas Campomar) and Scribner (Colin Harrison) have been enthusiastic and supportive. In Colin's case, from our very first discussion his notes and editorial pointers have been hugely beneficial to the book's final structure, as has the tireless work on the material by his associate editor Sarah Goldberg. At Simon & Schuster I would like to thank Carolyn Reidy and Nan Graham for their support, and Ian Chapman and Suzanne Baboneau in the London office for giving me time to finish writing the first draft. Fellow editors and authors who have been supportive and offered assistance with the research are: James Barr, Karen Farrington, Jonathan Fenby, Joshua Levine, Sean Rayment, Barney White-Spunner, and Chris Whipple. With the logistics involved in finding, talking to, and researching all the interviewees listed, I could not have managed to set their memories to paper without the help of my efficient transcriber Nick Chen.

Friends and family have taken the brunt of my absences due to the nature of traveling many times in the researching of this book. They know who they are and I value all of them, but I will thank those dearest to me. My wife, Jo, and my children, Cameron and Isla, have watched over the past three years as this initial idea I discussed at the breakfast table morphed into what it is now. I can never repay them enough for their support in giving me the time and space to write this book. Our trip as a family to Berlin was memorable as Bernd von Kostka generously gave them a personal tour of the Allied Museum on his weekend off. My children must now be the most knowledgeable twelve-year-old students of the Cold War in London.

Finally, to the people of Berlin. You live in an incredibly vibrant, exciting, and open city—a spirit that has seen you come through many hard times since the end of the Second World War, and the Wall was a traumatic fissure for generations of Berliners. I truly hope this book captures some aspects of that for future generations to comprehend what a seismic episode it was.

Naturally, all errors and inaccuracies within this book are my own.

Notes

The city of Berlin is a complicated and diverse place and this is reflected in how I have gone about constructing this narrative. For simplicity's sake, I refer to West and East Germany with a capital W and E, except when generalizing. The East German state is referred to as the German Democratic Republic (GDR), and the West German state as the Federal Republic of Germany (FRG). I have adhered to calling Russian troops "Soviets" for ease of use through the period of the Berlin Wall's existence. Where possible, I have tried to use the German spelling of streets, places, bridges, and buildings, such as the Glienicker Bridge.

Prologue: October 1961

1 *He knew there would be ample time wasted at the Inner German border at Helmstedt*: Per map on p. 8, the Helmstedt-Marienborn border crossing from West Germany into the GDR was the shortest transport route to West Berlin. Therefore, most transit traffic crossed through here between 1945 to 1990.

1 *where Checkpoint Alpha was situated*: This was one of three checkpoints the Allies set up alongside Checkpoint Bravo for entry into West Berlin, and Checkpoint Charlie for entry into East Berlin.

2 *Out of the gloom came at least a dozen East German Transport Police— Trapos*: The *Transportpolizei* of the GDR were an element of the country's *Volkspolizei* and numbered approximately 8,500 men organized at district and national level to oversee all forms of transit.

2 *East German border guards—Grenztruppen*: They were the primary force guarding the Inner German border, as well as the Berlin Wall, numbering approximately 47,000 troops.

3 *"Oh, sir," one of them said*: Interview with Major General Sir Robert Corbett.

5 *He walked through the Tiergarten, past the Soviet War Memorial*: The Soviet War Memorial was one of three constructed after the end of the Second

World War by the Soviet Union to commemorate the 80,000 soldiers it lost capturing Berlin between April and May 1945.

PART I: EXODUS

Chapter One: Island in the Communist Stream

9 *The city was now divided, as the Potsdam Conference had agreed:* Held from July 17 to August 2, the conference was officially titled the Berlin Conference of the Three Heads of Government of the USSR, USA, and UK and was attended by Joseph Stalin, Harry S. Truman, Winston Churchill, and Clement Attlee.

9 *Under the leadership of Secretary of State George C. Marshall:* Marshall became secretary of defense in 1950 under President Harry S. Truman after being his secretary of state and advocated for a huge economic package to aid postwar Europe that would ultimately bear his name.

10 *at the Allied Control Council:* Also known as *Allierten Kontrollrat*, it was the governing body of the Allied Occupation Zones in Germany and Austria at the end of the Second World War.

10 *"This act merely formalized what had been an obvious fact for some time, namely, that the four-power control machinery had become unworkable":* Robert E. Griffin and D. M. Giangreco, *Airbridge to Berlin*, (Novato, California: Presidio Press, 1988), 186.

10 *Under the leadership of General Lucius D. Clay:* Clay had previously served under General Dwight D. Eisenhower and rose to become commander in chief of the US Forces in Europe and military governor of the American zone in Germany from 1947 to 1949.

11 *"more and more planes could be seen flying":* Interview with Adolf Knackstedt.

11 *Crystal City, in Texas:* The Crystal City Internment Camp housed people of Japanese, German, and Italian descent during the Second World War. It accommodated just under 3,500 people and was run by the Department of Justice. It was the United States's largest civilian internment camp.

13 *"I found it frightening":* Interview with Margit Hosseini.

13 *Marienfelde refugee center:* One of three camps (the others being in Giessen and in Uelzen) set up by the authorities of the FRG and West Berlin to cope with the wave of refugees fleeing East Germany from 1950 to 1961. Marienfelde was in that same-name district of West Berlin and set up in 1953 with a capacity to house 2,000 people at any given time.

13 *Stalin's successor, Nikita Khrushchev:* Khrushchev served as first secretary of the Communist Party of the Soviet Union from 1953 to 1964.

14 *In 1953, in the days after the uprising:* An initial strike by East Berlin workers mushroomed into the East German uprising across the whole country between June 16 and 17, which was brutally suppressed by the Soviet tanks and resulted in more than 500 deaths and 1,800 people injured.

14 *"Where I lived"*: Interview with Günther Heinzel.

14 *"My father and mother were members"*: Interview with Stefan Wolle.

14 *"I actually remember a happy childhood"*: Interview with Hans-Ulrich Jörges.

15 "Stasi [*Staatssicherheit*]": The official East German Ministry for State Security set up in February 1950 by the ruling SED Party under Walter Ulbricht.

15 *Stalin's foreign minister, Vyacheslav Molotov*: Molotov was a key member of Stalin's Politburo and minister of foreign affairs twice from 1939 to 1949 and from 1953 to 56.

15 *By June 1952,* Republikflucht: "Flight from the republic" was the official term given by the East German authorities for emigration legally and illegally to West Germany, West Berlin, and non–Warsaw Pact countries.

17 *As Walter Ulbricht*: Born in 1893 and a committed communist from 1920, Ulbricht would play a leading role in the creation of the GDR post–Second World War and ruled as first secretary of the Socialist Unity Party (SED) from 1950 to 1971.

17 *"The people in the East looked towards the West with longing"*: Cambridge University Library.

19 Nationale Volksarmee: Abbreviated NVA, the National People's Army was set up in 1956 and disbanded in 1990. At its height it numbered more than 175,000 men and women.

19 *"When I was a child, it was exciting even when we crossed the street"*: Interview with Wolfgang Göbel.

19 *He would reside in the notorious Stasi-run prison at Hohenschönhausen*: For more information go to: https:/www.berlin.de/mauer/en/sites/commemorative-sites/berlin-hohenschoenhausen-memorial/.

21 *Bay of Pigs fiasco*: The CIA-backed failed military invasion of Cuba by the rebel group Brigade 2506 from April 17 to 20 in 1961.

21 *His first meeting with Khrushchev, in Vienna at the start of June, was a disaster*: The summit was held from June 4 to 6 in 1961. For details of the whole summit I recommend reading Frederick Kempe, *Berlin 1961* (New York: Putnam, 2011).

23 *Erich Honecker was the man to implement Operation Rose in two weeks' time*: Erich Honecker, born in 1912, was a committed communist since he was ten years old.

24 *Erich Mielke was a political mercenary*: Born in Prussia in 1907, Mielke had grown up in a communist neighborhood of Berlin and joined the Communist Party of Germany (KPD) in 1925.

Chapter Two: The Spook in Berlin

25 Primarily based on extensive interviews with Adolf Knackstedt.

25 *then became a returning* Volksdeutscher *in the Second World War*: The Nazi Party defined Germans in terms of their race, not their actual citizenship;

therefore, as long as they were not of Jewish origin, they qualified to return to the Third Reich to reside.

Chapter Three: In a Mousetrap Now

31 *"If I were you, I wouldn't leave Berlin this weekend"*: Adam Kellett-Long's account of what the situation was like in a BBC podcast *The Day the Wall Went Up*: http://downloads.bbc.co.uk/podcasts/worldservice/docarchive/docarchive_20110816-1000a.mp3.

32 *"At my [prep] school, for days afterwards, we discussed with both fear and incredulity"*: Interview with General Peter Williams, British Army.

32 *"Do nothing!"* Feldwebel *Eduard Schram watched too"*, Interviewee requested name not used, so Eduard Schram is a pseudonym.

36 *border patrol—"Bravo 3"*: This subsequent story from an article appearing on pages 10–12 of the 1979 Second Quarter edition of *The Royal Military Police Journal*, courtesy of the Royal Military Police Museum.

38 *"With a very stern voice"*: Interview with Adolf Knackstedt.

40 *Meanwhile, Assistant Provost Richards watched the ever-increasing buildup of forces"*: *The Berlin Bulletin*, Richards, L.F. Brigadier.

41 *the* Betriebskampfgruppen *[factory fighting units]*: These are basically armed workers of good enough socialist fervor that they were recruited by the authorities to act as armed militia.

41 Freie Deutsche Jugend *[Free German Youth, FDJ]*: The youth wing of the Socialist Unity Party.

42 *The mayor of West Berlin, Willy Brandt*: Brandt was a totemic figure in West Berlin and West German politics for more than four decades. By force of personality he held the city together during the crisis of 1961. He would go onto lead the Socialist Democratic Party and ultimately become chancellor of West Germany (1969 to 1974).

42 *veteran opponent, Konrad Adenauer*: Adenauer was a bulwark against Communism and the Federal Republic's first chancellor in 1949, leading the country's Christian Democratic Union.

42 *Robert Lochner, head of RIAS*: Association for Diplomatic Studies and Training, "The 54th Anniversary of the Berlin Wall," *Huffington Post*, updated December 6, 2017, https://www.huffpost.com/entry/the-54th-anniversary-of-t_b_7978398.

43 *"We had obviously had practice alerts"*: Interview with Private Wayne Daniels, US 287th Military Police.

44 *"When I climbed out of my cab"*: John Wilkes, "The Berlin Wall—Aug. 13, 1961: An eyewitness account of the first day's action at the Brandenburg Gate," *Santa Cruz Sentinel*, August 13, 2011.

47 *"As they replaced the barbed wire"*: Interview with Lieutenant Vern Pike, US 287th Military Police.

PART II: A TALE OF TWO CITIES

49 *"At all costs we must avoid any kind of dispute"*: Keith Hamilton, Patrick Salmon, and Stephen Twigge (eds.), *Berlin in the Cold War 1948–1990: Documents on British Policy Overseas, Series III, Volume VI* (London: Routlegde, 2015), 228.

Chapter Four: Split Asunder

51 *"It was still a terrible experience"*: Interview with Günther Heinzel.
53 *"Never have I seen so many tears"*: Interview with Adolf Knackstedt.
55 *"I was a ten-year-old Pioneer"*: Interview with Stefan Wolle.
57 *Charité Hospital:* The Charité - Universitätsmedizin Berlin was the city's primary hospital and had originally been built in 1710 in response to a plague epidemic in East Prussia.
57 *"Looking across to the western side"*: Interview with Rosemarie Platz.
58 *"There was very little reaction coming"*: Interview with Margit Hosseini.
59 *The most famous of these escapes:* Peter Liebling worked for the Hamburg Picture Agency. His photograph of Schuman would win the award of Best Photographs, Daily Newspaper or Wire Service, from the Overseas Press Club of America in 1961.

Chapter Five: A New Border to Patrol

66 *The thousands of men and women:* Interview with Colonel Jeremy Green and Assistant Provost Marshal Ron Tilston.
67 *For the Americans, after the creation of the Berlin Brigade:* Interview with Lieutenant Vern Pike, 287th US Military Police.
68 *"On traveling by train to get to Berlin"*: Interview with Private Tom Ables, 287th US Military Police.

Chapter Six: Who Blinks First?

75 *He was battling with Chinese disaffection:* Nikita Khrushchev and Mao Zedong loathed each other. The former because he resented the lack of respect the Chinese displayed at the XXII Congress of the Communist Party of the Soviet Union, and the latter due to Mao firmly believing Khrushchev was leading the Soviet Union away from the true path Stalin had bequeathed him.
75 *President Kennedy had bowed to the "Berlin Mafia" in the White House:* Chief among them was US ambassador to the Soviet Union Llewellyn E. "Teddy" Thompson Jr. (1967 to 1969) who enjoyed a close relationship with Nikita Khrushchev during the Berlin crisis.

76 *of the US Army's 1st Battle Group:* This 1,500-strong unit from the 18th Infantry travelled to West Berlin in 491 vehicles and was commanded by Colonel Glover S. Johns Jr.

76 *By this point, the physical wall was taking shape:* See full description in Gordon L. Rottman, *The Berlin Wall and the Intra-German Border, 1961-89* (Oxford: Osprey Books, 2008), 63.

78 *Lightner himself was a fan of General Clay:* Lightner was in close contact at all times with General Clay and shared the American commander's concerns of a lack of allied resolve to stand up to the Soviets in the city. He was keen to test how much the East Germans would push the issue of requesting allied diplomatic personnel to show their identification.

81 *"One evening after the 13th of August":* Interview with Lieutenant Vern Pike, US 287th Military Police.

85 *"The tank standoff at Friedrichstraße":* Interview with Private Tom Ables, US 287th Military Police.

85 *"This crisis nearly got us to the brink":* Interview with Adolf Knackstedt.

Chapter Seven: Elvis Is Dead

87 *Peter Fechter:* Born in 1944, Fechter was an East German bricklayer whose older sister lived in West Berlin and, recently before his attempted escape, had been refused permission by his company to travel to West Germany on a sanctioned trip. He attempted to scale the wall with his friend Helmut Kulbeick.

87 *"I was staying with friends":* Interview with Margit Hosseini.

90 *"After the Peter Fechter incident":* Interview with Adolf Knackstedt.

Chapter Eight: Let Them Come to Berlin!

93 *Kennedy's actions in the first half of 1962:* Kempe, *Berlin 1961,* 175. Khrushchev fervently believed that Kennedy didn't have the stomach for a fight with the Soviet Union, especially if it involved nuclear confrontation. The Vienna Summit had given the first secretary an imaginary insight into what the America president would do, and it was to prove ultimately costly for his own job prospects.

95 *DEFCON 3:* The DEFense readiness CONdition is an alert state implemented by the armed forces of the United States of America that unifies all land, air, and sea under one command structure with the president at the top of the chain of command. It has five levels of readiness, DEFCON 5 being the least severe and DEFCON 1 being the most severe.

97 *It was agreed that a "hotline":* Set up in 1963, the Moscow-Washington, DC, hotline provides direct communication between the Kremlin and

the White House. Popular myth has it as a red telephone, when in fact it was originally a teleprinter, which was replaced by a fax machine in 1988 and in 2008 by email via a secure computer link.

98 *"The more the East Germans"*: Interview with Adolf Knackstedt.

100 *"I was in the audience,"*: Interview with Lord Michael Howard.

101 *Law student Dietrich Weitz:* "A Passion for Justice," Free University Berlin, June 6, 2013, https://www.fu-berlin.de/en/sites/kennedy/zeitzeugen/weitz/index.html.

101 *Schoolgirl Eva Quistrop:* "Greatly Influenced by Kennedy's Speech," Free University Berlin, June 8, 2013, https://www.fu-berlin.de/en/sites/kennedy/zeitzeugen/quistorp/index.html.

102 *"I experienced both of Kennedy's speeches"*: Interview with Wolfgang Göbel.

103 *Khrushchev himself had been ousted:* Led by Leonid Brezhnev, then chairman of the Presidium Supreme Soviet, and supported by Central Committee members such as Alexander Shelepin and the head of the KGB Vladimir Semichastny. The plotters struck in a bloodless coup on October 14, 1964, with Brezhnev being elected first secretary the following day.

104 *The city itself was now undisputedly linked:* For his work in driving this process through successfully, Willy Brandt would be named Man of the Year by *Time* magazine in 1970, as well as awarded the Nobel Peace Prize the following year.

PART III: THE INTELLIGENCE WAR

Chapter Nine: The Secret Army

107 *Special forces were created, or re-created, in the footsteps of the Office of Strategic Services (OSS):* Formed in June 1942, reporting to the Joint Chiefs of Staff, to coordinate espionage activities behind enemy lines.

108 *"The military was really focused"*: Interview with Chief Warrant Officer James Stejskal.

109 *was based at Fort Bragg, North Carolina:* Fort Bragg is the largest military installation in the world, accommodating more than 50,000 military personnel.

111 *Leibstandarte SS Adolf Hitler:* An elite unit overseen by Heinrich Himmler that would evolve into a fully fledged Panzer division of the Waffen-SS.

111 *"In Berlin I think we had a higher"*: Interview with Lieutenant Colonel Darrell W. Katz.

114 *such as in the Grunewald Forest:* The largest green area in Berlin, it is situated on the western side of the city and comprises more than 7,400 acres of woodland.

Chapter Ten: Searching for a Grain of Truth

119 *Erich Honecker now took over the mantle of leadership:* He had bided his time throughout the remainder of the 1960s, obediently following Ulbricht's plans for a "New Economic System" that was hoped would improve the country's flagging economy and poor consumer market. Deteriorating relations between the two men by the summer of 1970 led to Ulbricht demoting his protégé until Brezhnev himself stepped in to move the GDR leader aside on "health grounds" in favor of the younger man the following year.

120 *"I loved my 'tour of duty' in East Berlin":* Interview with Mark Wood, Reuters.

121 *"There was the excitement of getting across the Wall":* Interview with Timothy Garton Ash.

121 *"By the time I managed to get to Berlin":* Interview with Hans-Ulrich Jörges.

Chapter Eleven: Catch Me If You Can!

134 *British Lieutenant General Sir Brian Robertson:* One of the UK's most senior army officers during the Second World War who had seen service in East African, North African, and Italian campaigns. He was the deputy military governor of Germany from 1945 to 1948, and then promoted to military governor in 1948 to serve for a year.

134 *Colonel General Mikhail Sergeevich Malinin:* A long-term member of the Red Army since the Russian Civil War in the 1920s, he had steadily risen through the ranks, survived Stalin's purges in the 1930s and the onslaught by the Nazis in the Second World War, becoming army chief of staff in 1941. He would lead the Western Group of Forces (WGF) until 1948.

136 *or in flights within the agreed airspace constraints of the BCZ:* The Berlin Control Zone was coordinated by the Berlin Air Safety Centre (BASC) for Allied air traffic to fly safely through the three air corridors linking West Germany over West Berlin airspace to the designated airports of Tempelhof, Tegel, and Gatow.

138 *"People used to mark on their maps":* Tony Geraghty, *BRIXMIS: The Untold Exploits of Britain's Most Daring Cold War Spy Mission* (London: HarperCollins, 1997).

141 *"This charade could go on for hours":* Geraghty, *BRIXMIS*, 166–72.

142 *"A normal tour by car":* Interview with General Peter Williams.

144 *"I learned a lot about diplomacy":* Geraghty, *BRIXMIS*, 133–35.

145 *"My initial impression of Berlin":* Interview with Major Nigel Dunkley.

151 *"During the Cold War":* Taken from article written by Colonel Lawrence Kelley, US Marine Corps (retired), and the U.S. Military Liaison Mission for Association newsletter, 1985.

153 *"The liaison missions were always originally designed as a reassurance mechanism"*: Interview with Major General Sir Robert Corbett, British Army.

Chapter Twelve: Death of a Soldier

This chapter was conceived and written after lengthy discussions via email with Colonel Lawrence Kelley, US Marine Corps (retired) and the author of a report of the incident.

PART IV: THE STRUGGLE TO BE FREE

Chapter Thirteen: The Singing Jew of Checkpoint Charlie

This chapter is based on a lengthy interview conducted by Sabine Schereck with Professor Andreas Nachama in Berlin.

Chapter Fourteen: Going Underground

176 *Operation Gold:* The total bill to finance this operation would come to $6.5 million.

177 *MI6 had gestated the "Cambridge Spy Ring":* Comprised of Donald Maclean, Guy Burgess, Kim Philby, Anthony Blunt .and John Cairncross. To the KGB they were known as the "Magnificent Five."

177 *George Blake was different:* Born George Behar in 1922, he was of Dutch and Egyptian parents who had ties to the British Commonwealth, allowing him to claim British citizenship. After working for the secret service in the Second World War, he would be captured in the Korean War by the Communists who turned him while in captivity. From there he would migrate to the KGB and become one of its most successful spies until his arrest in 1961.

179 *"We went into the house":* Kirsten Grieshaber, "Secret tunnels that brought freedom from Berlin's Wall," *Independent,* October 18, 2009, https://www.independent.co.uk/news/world/europe/secret-tunnels-that-brought-freedom-from-berlins-wall-1804765.html.

181 *"They tried to create a picture of the West":* Interview with Manfred Höer.

183 *Manfred's job as a boiler man for the Bewag:* Set up in 1923, "Berliner Städtische Elektrizitätswerke Aktiengesellschaft," *Bewag* for short, it was the city's main electricity supplier during the Cold War.

Chapter Fifteen: Chimes of Freedom

188 *David Bowie's concert near the Wall:* Bowie's Glass Spider Tour played outside the Reichstag building on the Platz der Republik in West Berlin on

June 6, 1987, followed by the Eurythmics and Genesis during a three-day concert series. On the last night of the festival, the East German authorities would clamp down on protestors congregating by the Wall, arresting as many as two hundred people.

188 *"By the time of being at university"*: Interview with Andreas Austilat.

189 *The Tunnel of Love Express tour: Tunnel of Love* is Bruce Springsteen's eighth studio album, released in October 1987.

190 *"It was a different society"*: Bruce Springsteen, *Born to Run* (New York: Simon & Schuster, 2016), 288.

191 *"When we arrived"*: Interview with Jon Landau.

195 *"We'll keep pushin' till it's understood"*: "Badlands," Bruce Springsteen, track 1 on *Darkness of the Edge of Town*, Columbia, 1978.

196 *"As majestic bells of bolts struck"*: "Chimes of Freedom," Bob Dylan, track 4 on *Another Side of Bob Dylan*, Columbia, 1964.

Chapter Sixteen: At the Edge of Control

This chapter is based on an interview with Major Peter Bochman, East German Border Control.

Chapter Seventeen: The Last Escape

This chapter is based on an interview with Peter Spitzner.

PART IV: THE WALL FORMS

Chapter Eighteen: A Family in Berlin

226 *"I said to him"*: Interview with Major General Sir Robert Corbett, British Army.

227 *"I had known Berlin without the Wall"*: Interview with Lieutenant General François Cann, French Army.

229 *"As we drove along"*: Interview with Lady Susan Corbett.

231 *"I will never forget his first words to me"*: Interview with House Sergeant Brian Andrews, Irish Guards.

235 *"A party that lags behind"*: William Taubman, *Gorbachev: His Life and Times* (New York: W. W. Norton & Co., 2017), 485.

Chapter Nineteen: The Memo That Ended the Cold War

239 Neues Deutschland: At its height during the Cold War, this publication enjoyed a circulation of 1.1 million East German readers; whereas today,

though still in business, this figure has shrunk to just 21,000 (its political affiliations are now more social democratic).

239 *Egon Krenz:* A product of the Socialist Unity Party of Germany (SED), having joined the Free German Youth (FDJ) in 1953, and after national service in the National People's Party (NVA), Krenz would rise through the ranks and join the central committee of the SED in 1973. Within a decade he was on the Politburo as Honecker's deputy in 1984. By the time of the press conference, he was in control of his party, but not of events.

Chapter Twenty: The Flood

245 *"I was keeping up":* Interview with Sergeant Michael Rafferty, 287th US Military Police.

245 *"When I got to 'Charlie'":* Interview with Corporal Kevin May, Royal Military Police.

246 *"The first time we had any inkling":* Interview with Sergeant Chris Toft, Royal Military Police.

247 *"I was opening a German-speaking radio station":* Interview with Major General Sir Robert Corbett, British Army.

248 *The waitress that night:* Interview with Astrid Benner.

249 *"We were shocked to learn":* Interview with airman Mitt Law, USAAF.

250 *"At the party whilst I was chatting":* Interview with Georg Schertz, president of West Berlin Police.

251 *"My friend's roommate said":* Interview with Gillian Cox.

254 *"Sometime between 1 and 2 a.m.":* Interview with Vera Knackstedt.

255 *"I was hosting a luncheon":* Interview with Secretary of State James A. Baker III.

261 *"I received a phone call":* Interview with Lieutenant-Colonel Ron Tilston, Royal Military Police.

262 *"We'd all woke up to be scrambled":* Interview with Corporal Mark Horton, Royal Military Police.

263 *"I couldn't go to Berlin":* Interview with Adolf Knackstedt.

Chapter Twenty-One: Lights, Cameras, Action!

265 Interview with Alastair Stewart of ITN News.

268 *"The whole of the world's media":* Interview with Lieutenant-Colonel Ron Tilston, Royal Military Police.

269 *"If you're a close-protection officer":* Interview with Corporal Richard Ornsby, Royal Military Police.

270 *"Those incredible pictures":* Interview with Hans-Ulrich Jörges.

Chapter Twenty-Two: Aftermath

271   *"after establishing the plan of action for the day"*: Interview with Corporal Richard Ornsby, Royal Military Police.

272   *"It soon became evident"*: Interview with Secretary of State James A. Baker III.

272   *"I took him on a helicopter tour of the city"*: Interview with Major General Sir Robert Corbett, British Army.

273   *"I immediately put the television on"*: Interview with House Sergeant Brian Andrews, Irish Guards.

274   *"By the 10th of November"*: Interview with Georg Schertz, president of West Berlin Police.

276   *"On the 4th of June, 1989"*: Interview with Timothy Garton Ash.

277   *"The demonstrations and discussions"*: Interview with Lieutenant Torsten Belger, NVA.

277   *"The soldiers stationed in Germany"*: Interview with platoon leader Vitaliy Denysov, Red Army.

279   *"I probably was the only British person going into East Berlin"*: Interview with Lady Susan Corbett.

279   *"We flew over the Wall and one could see"*: Interview with Lord Archie Hamilton.

280   *"At about midnight"*: Interview with Corporal Richard Ornsby, Royal Military Police.

281   *"There was nothing but this sort of chipping"*: Interview with Lord Archie Hamilton.

Chapter Twenty-Three: Goodbye Checkpoint Charlie

Parts of this chapter are based on home footage taken by Sergeant Michael Rafferty, US 287th Military Police, of the closure of Checkpoint Charlie: https://www.youtube.com/watch?v=2sSgG9sgcSA

283   *Article 23:* The other option available was initiating Article 146, a mechanism to create a permanent constitution for a reunified Germany; however, this route was more protracted and would have had to create a new constitution for the newly established country. In contrast, reunification under Article 23 could be implemented in as little as six months, which was an easy decision to make, considering East Germany's imminent economic and perhaps social collapse.

284   *"The 'Two Plus Four' talks"*: Interview with Lieutenant-Colonel Ron Tilston, Royal Military Police.

285   *"It was kind of neat to see"*: Interview with Sergeant Michael Rafferty, 287th US Military Police.

285 *"Charlie's removal was highly symbolic"*: Ken Clauson, "Checkpoint Charlie's last hours let MPs share historic moment," *Stars and Stripes*, June 22, 1990.

286 *"I was fortunate"*: Interview with Corporal Mark Horton, Royal Military Police.

287 *"Before the official ceremony began"*: Interview with Major General Sir Robert Corbett, British Army.

289 *"Once the Wall came down"*: Interview with Secretary of State James A. Baker III.

Epilogue: Four Memories

295 Interview with Hans-Ulrich Jörges.
296 Interview with Timothy Garton Ash.
297 Interview with Secretary of State James A. Baker III.
298 Interview with Major General Sir Robert Corbett, British Army.

Bibliography

Articles

East Berlin and Its Buildings 1945–1990: Photographs 1945–1990. Ernst Wasmuth Verlag GmbH, Tubingen, Germany, 2010.

Grieshaber, Kirsten. "Secret tunnels that brought freedom from Berlin's Wall," *Independent*. October 18, 2009.

Books

Antill, Peter. *Berlin 1945: End of the Thousand Year Reich*. Osprey Publishing, Oxford, 2005.

Applebaum, Anne. *Iron Curtain: The Crushing of Eastern Europe 1944–56*. Allen Lane, London, 2012.

Baker, James A., III, and Thomas M. DeFrank. *The Politics of Diplomacy: Revolution, War & Peace, 1989–1992*. Putnam, New York, 1995.

Bayer, Marlon, Arno Helwig, and Bernd von Kostka. *100 Object: Berlin During the Cold War*. Allied Museum e.V and Berlin Story Verlag GmbH, Berlin, 2016.

The Berlin Wall: The History and Legacy of the World's Most Notorious Wall. Charles River Editors, 2015.

Boyd, Douglas. *The Solitary Spy: A Political Prisoner in Cold War Berlin*. The History Press, Stroud, England, 2017.

Chappell, Mike. *The British Army in the 1980s*. Osprey Publishing, Oxford, 1987.

Corbett, Major General R. S. J. *Berlin and the British Ally 1945–1990*. Self published, 1991.

Crick, Michael. *The Search for Michael Howard*. Simon & Schuster UK Ltd., London, 2005.

Dallek, Robert. *John F. Kennedy: An Unfinished Life 1917–1963*. Penguin Books Ltd., London, 2003.

Delius, Friedrich Christian, and Peter Joachim Lapp. *Transit Westberlin. Erlebnisse im Zwischenraum*. Ch. Links Verlag, Berlin, 2000.

Dobbs, Michael. *One Minute to Midnight: Kennedy, Khrushchev and Castro on the Brink of Nuclear War.* Knopf, New York, 2008.

Downing, Taylor. *1983: The World at the Brink.* Little, Brown, London, 2018.

Durie, William. *The British Garrison Berlin 1945–1994.* Vergangenheitsverlag, Berlin, 2012.

Flemming, Thomas. *The Berlin Wall: Division of a City.* Be.bra verlag GmbH, Berlin, 2009.

Funder, Anna. *Stasiland: Stories from Behind the Berlin Wall.* Granta, London, 2003.

Garton Ash, Timothy. *The File: A Personal History.* HarperCollins Publishers Ltd., London, 1997.

Gelb, Norman. *The Berlin Wall: Kennedy, Khrushchev, and a Showdown in the Heart of Europe.* Touchstone, Simon & Schuster Inc., New York, 1988.

Geraghty, Tony. *BRIXMIS: The Untold Exploits of Britain's Most Daring Cold War Spy Mission.* HarperCollins Publishers Ltd., London, 1997.

Gibson, Steve. *BRIXMIS: The Last Cold War Mission.* The History Press, Stroud, Gloucestershire, 2018.

Glees, Anthony. *The Stasi Files: East Germany's Secret Operations Against Britain.* The Free Press, New York, 2003.

Griffin, Robert E. and D. M. Giangreco. *Airbridge to Berlin.* Presidio Press, Novato, California, 1988.

Gunnarsson, Robert L., Jr. *American Military Police in Europe, 1945–1991. Unit Histories.* McFarland & Company, Inc., Publishers, Jefferson, NC, 2011.

Hailstone, Allan. *Berlin in the Cold War 1959 to 1966.* Amberley Publishing, Stroud, Gloucestershire, England, 2017.

Hamilton, Keith, Patrick Salmon, and Stephen Twigge (eds.). *Berlin in the Cold War 1948–1990: Documents on British Policy Overseas, Series III, Volume VI.* Routledge, London, 2015.

Hertle, Hans-Hermann. *The Berlin Wall Story: Biography of a Monument.* Christoph Links Verlag, Berlin, 2011.

Hurd, Douglas. *Memoirs.* Abacus, London, 2003.

Isaacs, Jeremy. *The Cold War: For Forty-five Years the World Held Its Breadth.* Abacus, London, 2008.

Jampol, Justin. *The East German Handbook.* Taschen GmbH, Berlin, 2017.

Kellerhof, Sven Felix, and Bernd von Kostka. *Haupstadt Der Spione: Geheimienste In Berlin Im Kalten Krieg.* Berlin Story Verlag GmbH, Berlin, 2017.

Kempe, Frederick. *Berlin 1961: Kennedy, Khrushchev and the Most Dangerous Place on Earth.* Berkley Books, The Penguin Group, New York, 2011.

Kendall, Bridget. *The Cold War: A New Oral History of Life Between East and West.* BBC Books, London, 2017.

Kirschbaum, Erik. *Rocking the Wall, Bruce Springsteen: The Berlin Concert That Changed the World.* Berlinica Publishing LLC, New York, 2013.

Koehler, John O. *Stasi: The Untold Story of the East German Secret Police.* Westview Press, New York, 1999.

Leffler, Melvyn P. *For the Soul of Mankind: The United States, the Soviet Union, and the Cold War.* Hill & Wang, New York, 2007.

Maclean, Rory. *Berlin, Imagine a City.* Weidenfeld & Nicolson, London, 2014.

Mallaby, Christopher. *Living the Cold War. Memoirs of a British Diplomat.* Amberley Publishing, Stroud, Gloucestershire, England, 2017.

McElvoy, Anne. *The Saddle Cow: East Germany's Life and Legacy.* Faber & Faber, London, 1992.

Millar, Peter. *1989: The Berlin Wall, My Part in Its Downfall.* Arcadia Books Limited, London, 2014.

Mitchell, Greg. *The Tunnels: The Untold Story of the Escapes Under the Berlin Wall.* Transworld Publishers, London, 2017.

Molloy, Peter. *The Lost World of Communism: An Oral History of Daily Life Behind the Iron Curtain.* BBC Books, Random House Group, London, 2009.

Rottman, Gordon L. *The Berlin Wall and the Intra-German Border 1961–89.* Osprey Publishing, Oxford, 2008.

———. US *Army Special Forces, 1952–84.* Osprey Publishing, Oxford, 1985.

———. *Warsaw Pact Ground Forces.* Osprey Publishing, Oxford, 1987.

Sarotte, Mary Elise. *The Collapse: The Accidental Opening of the Berlin Wall.* Basic Books, New York, 2014.

Schneider, Peter. *Berlin Now: The Rise of the City and the Fall of the Wall.* Penguin Books, London, 2014.

Service, Robert. *Comrades: Communism, A World History.* Macmillan, London, 2007.

Service, Robert. *The End of the Cold War: 1985–1991.* Macmillan, London, 2015.

Spitz, Bob. *Reagan: An American Journey.* Penguin Press, New York, 2018.

Springsteen, Bruce. *Born to Run.* Simon & Schuster Inc., New York, 2016.

Steil, Benn. *The Marshall Plan: Dawn of the Cold War.* Simon & Schuster Inc., New York, 2018.

Stejskal, James. *Special Forces Berlin: Clandestine Cold War Operations of the US Army's Elite, 1956–1990.* Casemate Publishers, Oxford, 2017.

Taylor, Frederick. *The Berlin Wall: 13 August 1961–9 November 1989.* Bloomsbury Publishing Plc., London, 2006.

Taubman, William. *Gorbachev: His Life and Times.* W. W. Norton & Co., New York, 2017.

———. *Khruschev: The Man, His Era.* W. W. Norton & Co., New York, 2003.

Vazey, Hester. *Born in the GDR: Living in the Shadow of the Wall.* Oxford University Press, Oxford, 2014.

Wapshott, Nicholas. *Ronald Reagan and Margaret Thatcher, A Political Marriage.* The Penguin Group, New York, 2008.

Westad, Odd Arne. *The Cold War: A World History.* Hachette Book Group, New York, 2017.

Zaloga, Steven, J. *Inside the Soviet Army Today.* Osprey Publishing, Oxford, 1987.

———. *The M47 and M48 Patton Tanks.* Osprey Publishing, Oxford, 1999.

———. *T-54 and T-55 Main Battle Tanks 1944–2004.* Osprey Publishing, Oxford, 2004.

———. *Tank War: Central Front NATO vs. Warsaw Pact.* Osprey Publishing, Oxford, 1989.

Photography Credits

Insert

1 Collection of Sir Robert Corbett
2 Collection of Sir Robert Corbett
3 © Getty Images
4 Collection of Adolf Knackstedt
5 © The Royal Military Police Museum
6 © Getty Images
7 © Getty Images
8 © Getty Images
9 © Kansas Eagle
10 © Getty Images
11 © Getty Images
12 © Bob Charetz
13 © Mark Wood
14 Collection of Peter Williams
15 © Getty Images
16 © Getty Images
17 Collection of Peter Spitzner
18 © Getty Images
19 © Getty Images
20 © Getty Images
21 Collection of Sir Robert Corbett
22 Collection of Torsten Belger
23 © Associated Press
24 © Getty Images

Interior

Frontispiece: © Copyright the author
p. 7 © Georg/ullstein bild via Getty images
p. 49 © Leon Herschtritt, courtesy of the Royal Military Police Museum
p. 105 © Royal Military Police Museum
p. 165 © Getty Images
p. 223 © Getty Images

Index

About the Author

IAIN MacGREGOR is an editor and publisher of nonfiction in the UK. As a student he visited the Baltic and the Soviet Union; avidly followed events that unfolded in Berlin on the night of November 9, 1989, when the Wall fell; and then later traveled through the former Warsaw Pact territories and Berlin, visiting Checkpoint Charlie, which was still untouched. He lives with his wife and two children in London. *Checkpoint Charlie* is his first book to be published in the US.